THE
SMALL
BUSINESS
OWNER'S MANUAL

Everything You Need to Know to Start Up and Run Your Business

By

JOE KENNEDY

CAREER
PRESS
Franklin Lakes, NJ

THE SMALL BUSINESS OWNER'S MANUAL
EDITED BY LOIS GOLDRICH
TYPESET BY EILEEN DOW MUNSON
Cover design by Cheryl Cohan Finbow
Printed in the U.S.A. by Book-mart Press

To order this title, please call toll-free 1-800-CAREER-1 (NJ and Canada: 201-848-0310) to order using VISA or MasterCard, or for further information on books from Career Press.

The Career Press, Inc., 3 Tice Road, PO Box 687,
Franklin Lakes, NJ 07417

www.careerpress.com

Library of Congress Cataloging-in-Publication Data

Kennedy, Joe, 1954-

The small business owner's manual : everything you need to know to start up and run your business / by Joe Kennedy.

p. cm.

Includes index.

ISBN 1-56414-813-0 (paper)

1. New business enterprises—Management—Handbooks, manuals, etc. 2. Small business—Management—Handbooks, manuals, etc. I. Title.

HD62.5.K454 2005

658.02'2--dc22

2005046952

Pour ma femme,

Sean et Sophie.

Acknowledgments

This book has actually been underway, at least in my head, for more than 10 years and so many thanks are in order to clients that turned into friends, friends that turned into clients, and a few special people who helped me get thousands of words out of my head and onto paper.

First, thanks to my long time friend and attorney in California and beyond, Bernard J. Cartoon. Thanks for getting me out of so many jams over the last 10 years, and there's more to come.

A great acknowledgement also to my old friend Bill Berteaux, whose keen insight into business development and fun, yet effective, sales management has provided me with much inspiration and insight for over two decades. (Excluding the time when we were young salesmen together at an aerospace company, and he put empty wine bottles in my desk before the boss arrived and he did some other questionable things as well.)

I also greatly appreciate the efforts of Mike Solomon, who is at the cutting edge of understanding how to build and promote e-commerce stores and transition them into big numbers. In addition, Mike has also provided me with valuable counsel on local sports teams.

I would like to extend a sincere thank you to Janet Petroff of Petroff Consulting Group for her generous help with all of the human resources and employment aspects of this book. I thank her as well for her continued guidance on the many challenges in this complex area for almost 20 years. Janet is also a great editor who finally helped me to understand-the correct use-of-hyphens.

And a special thanks to my great agent Jeff Herman, who knows good stuff when he sees it.

Contents

Chapter 1

Introduction

Who would buy a complicated machine without an owner's manual? And who would push buttons and pull levers on a sophisticated new instrument until something good happened? An owner's manual saves time—and lots of money—by describing how to operate a machine and get the best results. Your small business is like a very complex machine. Accordingly, in the following pages we discuss how to quickly and effectively push buttons and pull levers so that this machine will make a lot of money and save a good deal of time.

You've heard the saying, "Success is 90 percent perspiration and 10 percent inspiration." These days we might say, "Success is 90 percent information and 10 percent perspiration." This book will save lots of perspiration, and the time and money gained may well take care of the inspiration part, too. Becoming an expert in running a small business takes a substantial amount of time and perspiration. The objective here is to cut through the chaff and deliver information to small business owners in the most meaningful way, so that they may quickly choose the right direction and get back to business.

The book may be read from cover to cover, or those facing a big decision can rip it open and read any chapter or section.

This book doesn't puff out to over 125,000 words by offering lame advice such as "Liability insurance is complex, so ask your agent." It goes far beyond such platitudes to offer important information specifically for small business owners. In many cases, the counsel given here will help the small business owner make a decision without going any further; in other cases, entrepreneurs will be able to select one or two options from among many choices. For example, there are many forms of business ownership, and attorneys will gladly discuss the characteristics of each for about $150 per hour. Reading this book will permit the small business owner to narrow the conversation. If this book saves only eight minutes of discussion time with an attorney, it has already paid for itself.

The book indicates when material is available for review or can be downloaded from www.TheSmallBusinessOwnersManual.com and other sites, but it does not tell readers to go to other books or simply to look on the Internet. The essentials are right here.

This is a serious book, because running your small business is serious. Still, readers should try to have fun with it. Do the best you can; but whatever the outcome, you'll live longer and enjoy it more by looking at the lighter side of even the most serious problems. This can be seen in many of the "Learn With Joe" stories sprinkled throughout the book. Most of these offer a lesson or reinforce the text, but they are related in an interesting and entertaining way.

Speaking of Joe—that's me, the author. I am not a spectator but have learned most of this through 20 years of opening, owning, and operating small businesses. Along the way, I've worked for and against some of the biggest, and smallest, companies around, including businesses specializing in everything from e-commerce to aircraft leasing to mining equipment. I also earned a B.S. in finance and an M.B.A. in marketing from a great university. I've had some big successes and some tragic failures, and I know what small business owners want. They need to make quick and informed decisions, they don't have time to read a textbook or a dumbed-down version of anything, and they don't want to read material that can be picked up just as quickly on the Internet. In most situations, entrepreneurs want to cut to the chase and move on. *The Small Business Owner's Manual* is designed with all this in mind.

The book assumes that:

- Readers already operate a small business or are planning to start one. There is no need to waste time by asking readers to search their souls and discern what they want.

- Small business is nice, but big business is better. I assume you're aiming for the big leagues and not content to stay small.

- Readers know how to use the Internet.

- I'm in business to make lots of money, and I assume the same for you; so this book is about selling as much as possible, controlling expenses, and minimizing both personal and business taxes.

Reviewing the chapter titles provides a quick summary of the book. Of course, there are entire books written on many of the topics listed. It doesn't make sense for most small business owners to develop "paralysis of analysis" and read that much detail, so here you get the condensed version.

I know you're in a hurry. This is not a textbook, and there are no wasted words that patronize the reader. If you're looking at this book, chances are the information is needed right now, so we get right to it on every subject.

At first I thought it might be hard to write a book that could be relevant to so many different kinds of businesses. As it happened, it was not that difficult. The common denominator is that all small business owners encounter the same issues, need information on the same subject areas, and want to know quickly which path to take. After that, it's up to them. This book gets things moving in the right direction and saves both time and money—and if there are any resources that will solve just about any small business challenge, they are more time and money. So let's get going.

Chapter 2

Beginnings of Your Small Business

If You Need an Idea, You're in Trouble!

This chapter is about developing a unique selling proposal and business plan for managing your new or existing small business and deciding upon the best form of business ownership. The book assumes that you, the small business owner or aspiring entrepreneur, are already passionately excited about a particular business venture and have an extraordinary amount of energy. If your situation falls short of this, then trouble lies ahead, and it's best to get this resolved before proceeding.

Starting or expanding a small business takes an immense amount of energy, passion, and savvy—all centered on a specific idea that gets you excited. It's unlikely you'll find this in a book. The first order of business is to think hard about an idea that can bring the wealth and fulfillment that you desire. Then we'll see if this can be turned into a successful small business.

Your small business needs to completely understand its Unique Selling Proposition (USP). If the USP is unknown, there is no reason for anyone to buy your products and services, and sales and marketing efforts cannot be focused.

Rosser Reeves (1910–1984), who remains an icon in the advertising industry, laid out his ideas about USPs in the seminal 1961 book, *The Reality of Advertising*.

The USP is the package of features and benefits that distinguishes your products and services from those of the rest of the world: your raison d'etre. A well-defined USP sets your small business apart from the rest of the crowd. Customers need to know that when they have a particular set of needs, your small business is the best choice.

The USP is the nothing less than the epicenter of your small business. Once this is agreed upon, every sales, marketing, and communications effort of your company should flow from this. Employees should be informed and reinforced of your USP, and they in turn should communicate this to customers, potential customers, vendors, agents, contractors, and everyone else in the world. Of course, if a USP is chosen that is not accurate ("We can repair any computer in the city within 60 minutes of your call"), marketing and sales efforts are misdirected, customers are unhappy, and your small business is likely to get even smaller.

As a small business, it is especially important to focus on the special niche where you have the assets and capabilities to succeed.

Most business owners have never developed a USP. They turn out their products and sell them because that's what they do. This is dangerous. Such businesses are implicitly communicating that there is nothing unique or special about their product or service—it's just there in case you want it. If competition arises, complacent companies will respond in an unfocused manner.

But some companies do get it right.

Domino's Pizza, for example, uses this frequently cited USP:

Fresh hot pizza delivered to your door in 30 minutes or less, guaranteed.

Notice that Domino's does not mention the words *cheap, good, nutritious, quality cheeses*, or *secret recipes.* Domino's understands it cannot be all things to all people all of the time, and it understands its USP.

The following are also good examples.

Notice that the lighting-fixture manufacturing company whose USP appears below is offering the assurance of a deep inventory (no drop-ship model here) of residential lighting fixtures for consumers (as opposed to commercial products). They are not focusing on price, and efforts are directed at distributors and retailers.

Every season, we will provide the widest selection and inventory of residential lighting fixtures, custom designed, satisfying current trends, and available for shipment within 24 hours, to our customer base of distributors and retailers.

This importer does not fool itself about providing quality products or selection. There is a large market for cheap, common tools that are used in homes and apartments for light projects such as hanging pictures or fixing bicycles. This company sells to anyone—hardware stores, retailers, and direct to consumers through its Website. Their proposition is simple.

We are the low cost leader in tools for the home.

And finally, in the ultracompetitive market for printer and copier toner products, one firm understands that its customers, mostly businesses, do not want to shop around and take chances when a printer is off-line and workflow is slowed due to a faulty toner cartridge.

Any cartridge, anywhere, within 24 hours, or your money back.

A USP is not the same as an advertising slogan. Company insiders understand this best, so first develop your USP and then let your marketing people translate this into advertisements.

Characteristics of Unique Selling Propositions

Great Unique Selling Propositions have the following characteristics:

- They contain one crisp, clear, sentence.

- They are credible.

- They describe the unique benefit associated with your products or services, focusing on your market niche.

- They state in measurable terms how your small business satisfies a customer's needs.

Developing a Winning USP

Are you ready to get started? Here is a great way to develop a winning USP.

- Gather the right people together in a comfortable meeting room.

- Make sure that everyone has a paper and pencil (not computers).

- Explain the purpose of your meeting.

- Brainstorm.

- List the unique benefits your small business offers to customers.

- Eliminate the entire list except for the three most important items.

- Write one creative, concise statement that best communicates each USP.

- Meet again the next day to choose a single winner from among the three, and fine-tune the wording.

Joe's Message to Modem Company: "You've Got Mail— The 90s Are Over"

The CEO of a company that was a huge success in the mid-1990s was talking about his USP, which needed some focus. This small business designed and produced modems at a time when everyone needed one to go on-line for the first time. But the firm never developed a USP. It seemed like a waste of time. Orders and money were pouring in. The industry was constantly moving the product lines upwards, from 2,400 baud modems, to 9,600, 14,400, 28,800, and 56k, and customers traded up accordingly. This firm rode on the crest of the wave, and it seemed like it would never end.

Then the world changed. Customers no longer needed modems, because high-speed DSL and cable connections became available. In addition, PC manufacturers stopped including modems as a standard component, and modem chip manufacturers began sharing designs with anyone that could print a circuit board, including low-cost producers in China.

Revenues dropped like a rock, the production floor closed, layoffs emptied half the building, and it was clear that modems were not coming back. But the firm could not respond. They had no Unique Selling Proposition, no means of looking at their own strengths and resources, and no ability to see their way into the future.

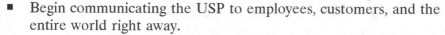

- Begin communicating the USP to employees, customers, and the entire world right away.

- Completely integrate the USP into all marketing and sales efforts, and include it in every communication emanating from your small business.

A Business Plan for You Only

Let's get this resolved right away: Business plans are tedious and take a lot of time. Nevertheless, regardless of whether your small business is new or established, a business plan is needed. This book assumes that you are the captain of your own ship, and the objectives are growth and prosperity (as opposed, for example, to selling your small business or grooming it to attract venture capital). Given these objectives, what's next? The successful entrepreneur must have a plan to get from here to there.

A small business, like a ship, needs a detailed map of its destination and route. Ships don't just head out to sea and churn around. They plan their travels and navigate efficiently to their destination, taking aboard sufficient fuel and provisions, mindful of the known perils along the route. A small business without a plan is like the captain of a ship without a destination. Things may be okay for awhile, but it's only a matter of time before something bad and unexpected happens.

Many books devoted entirely to this subject describe in great detail how to construct an M.B.A.-style business plan with the intent of attracting venture capital or similar major-league financing—and many entrepreneurs have invested huge amounts of time and money in researching and preparing business plans. This may be the best move for your company. In that case, professional assistance from marketing and financial experts may be needed. You may want to consult a book specifically devoted to this subject or obtain software designed to assist in building a business plan. In contrast to a formal business plan designed for investors, however, this book describes how to build a business plan just for you, the small business owner. It will serve as your navigation chart for the next year or so, when it should be revised. If a more formidable plan is needed at a later time, it can be built on top of the business plan described in this chapter.

In building the plan, be sure to talk to as many people as possible to get their ideas, viewpoints, and buy-in. In that way, you are both developing the plan and selling it to important others at the same time.

This business plan is for you and, perhaps, partners or family, so it's okay to be informal and use lots of bullet points instead of writing out everything. If a more formal plan is needed later, it will be easy to do, because all of the research and big thinking is already finished. You will just need to shine and polish.

Elements of a Business Plan

Business plans vary in structure, but most are organized as follows:

- Executive Summary
- Description of Your Company and the Market
- Competitive Analysis
- Marketing and Pricing Plan
- Management
- Operations and Development Plans
- Milestones and Financial Estimates
- Appendices

Executive Summary

The Executive Summary brings together the entire plan, so it is necessary to write it last. This section briefly describes your business, its history, management, and method of ownership; but most important, it talks about the company's products and services and their place in the market. Also, it should state business objectives over the short and long term.

This may seem obvious at first, and you may be tempted to write something such as:

> Our company desires to dominate the local market and then expand around the world, eventually eliminating competitors and then ruling the market as our unassailable wealth allows us to continually release better products.

But a more realistic objective is better:

> Generate net income before taxes of $1 million per year, increasing at 10 percent per year thereafter for five years. This will allow officers and owners of the company to earn income 50 percent greater than could be obtained through employment with competitors, provide the company with adequate working capital, and allow sufficient funds to expand into the new markets described in this plan.

Description of Your Company and the Market

This section defines exactly what markets your small business intends to serve, including market size, growth rates, and trends. Because this plan is for the management of your small business, focus on the specific geographic or niche market targeted, and concentrate only on statistics that will be meaningful to company insiders. You should also provide a little background information on the company. After describing the general market, get specific: Exactly which market segment is the focus of your small business, and what is the strategy for attaining this? Moreover, what are the marketing, sales, fulfillment, and distribution plans?

Does your product or service have any unique features? Remember, it may be acceptable to be terse and brief here, because the objective is for internal management (and not outsiders) to agree on the way to proceed.

Most importantly, indicate the products and services your small business depends on now and which ones hold the most promise for the future.

You are already focusing.

Competitive Analysis

Now that you've established where your small business fits into the market, it's time to get very specific about the competition. You will use and refer to this work for many years to come, and it should be updated at least yearly. Now is a good time to do intensive research and make sure you really understand what's going on in the market and how your company fits in.

To begin, make a chart and list competitors as well as their products, services, and pricing. You may also note the size and market position of other firms and how their strategies differ from yours. Consider further if your small business or the competition can release a new product or service that could significantly change the market.

The Local Market for Philly Cheese Steak Sandwiches

Company	Product Niche	Pricing
Us	Most authentic ingredients	$8.95
Eagle Sub Shop	Football lover's hangout	$8.95
Philly West	Largest (16")	$7.95
Liberty Belle's	Students; near university	$6.95

If there are too many competitors and it doesn't make sense to analyze each of them, pick the ones "in your face" the most often and think especially hard about what they are doing right. You might just figure out how to trump them, because the answers often lie close to the most successful competitors. Speak to mutual customers and vendors and see what you can learn.

Also, answer this question: Why are your competitors successful? More specifically:

- How and where do they advertise?
- How do they sell their products(sales force, telemarketing force, catalogs, Website)?
- What conventions and trade shows do they attend?

This is discussed further in Chapter 3, which deals with selling. Your business plan should map out a strategy that follows this model.

Information is easy to gather if you put in the effort. If an inside or outside sales force is already in place, be sure to ask them about the latest trends and what they hear when speaking to potential clients. It's important to learn about the deals they've lost as well as the ones they've landed. What would have made the difference? Clients may also appreciate being asked.

Many industry trade magazines may have done much of the competitive analysis already, so visit their Internet sites and review a few issues to see what's available. Also, check with industry associations and, perhaps, the local chamber of commerce. Of course, typing a few keywords into an Internet search engine will likely lead to fast and rich returns on the competitive information you need—and your competitors will not mind if you read their Websites and advertisements carefully to learn even more.

Finally, when important questions come into focus, consider conducting a simple, anonymous poll in which potential customers are asked what is good and bad about your company and the competition. Ask for suggestions! A professional market survey firm might be better, depending on the size of your business. This exercise will be very informative to the small business owner.

Marketing and Pricing Plan

Once the market is described, together with the position of the products and services offered by your small business, you are ready to determine the best marketing and pricing plans to obtain your objectives. Of course, this must all be consistent. If, for example, the marketing objective is high-volume/low-cost/big market share, then the advertising plan would likely stress price rather than quality or premium features. If widespread awareness of your company name is an objective, a big advertising budget is in order.

As we discussed previously, the Unique Selling Proposition of your small business is the foundation of the business plan. If this has not yet been developed, do it now.

Management

Management may, in fact, be the most important section of the business plan. Many managers agree with the old saying, "I would rather work with good management and a bad product than with a good product and bad management." List each major partner, employee, or agent for your company, and then do the following:

- List the skill sets needed to accomplish the business plan.
- List each key employee and his or her skills (derived from discussions and long-forgotten resumes).
- Identify areas where extra help is needed, and describe in the business plan how to find the right people.

Operations and Development Plans

In this section, list the assets used by your small business to generate key products and services. Also, consider what is needed to create the products and services needed to meet your objectives. Include current "cash cows" as well as promising new revenue generators.

Next, determine how much extra capacity your small business will need. Will you need to replace any equipment? Is there a plan to improve the efficiency of operations (for example, redesigning work flow)?

Milestones and Financial Estimates

Now that you have done such a good job of presenting your objectives, market, competition, Unique Selling Proposition, and future plans, you need to get a little more specific about when each objective must be reached and who is responsible. Breaking big objectives into smaller tactical goals and milestones is a key part in building your bridge from here to there.

When this is accomplished, your small business is in a position to quantify all this data and create projected financial statements—an Income Statement, Balance Sheet, and Statement of Cash Flow.

- **Income Statement** (also known as Profit and Loss, or "P and L"). Calculates how much the business has earned (or lost) over a specific period of time by adding revenues and subtracting expenses. The presentation varies depending upon the type of business.

- **Balance Sheet.** Provides a "snapshot" of where the business stands at a particular point in time, usually at year-end. In other words, at this particular point in time, projections are made for all important accounts, including cash, receivables, inventory, fixed assets, other assets, and total assets. The balance sheet also tells how the assets are financed—trade credit, payables, loans, or equity (your initial investment in the business plus accumulated earnings after taxes).

- **Cash Flow Statement.** Tells how much cash flowed through your small business over a specific period of time, normally one year. Cash flow includes sales receipts, receivables actually collected, new investments in the business, new loan proceeds, and increases in trade credit—countered by cash paid out for bills and expenses, investments in new equipment, loan paydowns, capital paid out to investors, and some other items. Cash flow is also affected by depreciation and amortization charges that hit your income statement, because these are "expenses" not requiring cash outlays. These non-cash items are added to net income to help figure cash flow.

For most small businesses, it makes sense to build monthly estimated financial statements for the first year, and then yearly statements for the next four years.

I've found that the best way to do this is by building a model with a spreadsheet program such as Microsoft Excel. If the spreadsheet is designed flexibly, different assumptions can be entered, and the effects recalculated in nanoseconds though the financial statements, charts, and graphs. This is of critical importance, allowing management to see how the results may vary.

The structure of these statements will differ significantly depending upon your business model and the level of complexity needed by management. For this reason, the *Small Business Owner's Manual* advises that an experienced financial pro be considered for this part of the project. You can also go on-line and visit www.TheSmall BusinessOwnersManual.com.

Appendices

Here is where the business plan retains all of the backup information gathered to compile the plan. Interested parties will need to refer to this when additional detail is needed. Again, this can be informal because the business plan described here is intended for use by company insiders.

Useful appendices might include financial projections under different "best case" and "worst case" assumptions, competitor catalogs and advertisements, management resumes, income tax returns of your small business for previous years, articles from trade magazines, and sales spreadsheets broken down by product and salesperson.

Business Plans—A Final Note

More than anything, a well-developed business plan will reveal if your small business is headed in the right direction and if it can realistically attain your objectives. The word *realistic* is important here. Many business plans slip into a fantasy as overly optimistic assumptions are made about pricing, revenues, and expenses. It is possible that the final plan will end up much different than what you expected. Just remember that the objective is a realistic plan to help you move forward into the future.

Joe's Big Business Idea Is Not

I once rolled up my sleeves and began zealously working on a business plan that I was sure would quickly put me in league with Bill Gates. I invested a great deal of time doing all of the right things—I saw what the competitors were doing, figured our place in the market, and calculated projected revenues, costs, and income. The final numbers didn't look very good.

I worked the numbers again, stretching the truth just a bit. Still, the returns were not very good no matter how much money I invested. I did my research again and ran the numbers again—and again.

Finally, I realized that if I worked 24 hours a day, seven days a week, cut expenses to the bone, was fantastically successful in selling, and everything worked out as planned with no unexpected problems or delays, I would eke out a miserable existence and barely be able to pay my bills.

Thanks to the business plan, I decided to trash that idea and move on to more profitable endeavors.

Legal Forms of Business Ownership

Most small businesses are structured in only five forms: sole proprietorship, partnership, corporation, Limited Liability Company, or Subchapter S Corporation. The proper form is critical, determining whether owners may protect their personal assets, have the ability to buy or sell portions of the business, minimize taxes, and fully enjoy the benefits of being an entrepreneur. The decision as to which form to choose is important when starting a business, but it should be revisited every few years. The purpose here is to provide an overview of each business form so that small business owners may evaluate their own situation and better assess their strengths and weaknesses in dealing with vendors, competitors, and customers.

Sole Proprietorships

Description

Also known as proprietorships or DBAs ("Doing Business As..."), sole proprietorships are the simplest business structure. In fact, if you make no effort at all to formalize your business (not a good idea), then you are a DBA.

As the name implies, a sole proprietorship can be owned by only one person; if others are involved, another business structure must be chosen. Unlike corporations and L.L.C.'s, a sole proprietorship is not a separate legal entity. The small business owner remains personally accountable for the liabilities, debts, covenants, contractual commitments, and taxes of the business. This includes claims made against employees acting within the course and scope of their employment. If, for example, one employee accuses another of sexual harassment and wins, your sole proprietorship must pay the judgment and everyone's attorney fees.

A sole proprietorship does not have "perpetual life." When the small business owner dies, the business simply ends. The assets are normally distributed under the terms of the deceased owner's will; however, the probate process may last 12 months or more, and this may cause difficulties if the heirs desire to operate or sell the business or its assets.

If a small business needs new financing, the sole proprietorship structure may not be right. Banks and related lending institutions, and investors, are uncomfortable working with individuals; most of their agreements are structured as corp.-to-corp. and desire to eschew the many special laws protecting consumers.

To formalize a DBA, you simply need to register the name at the county or local level. In most places, this involves only a small fee.

In general, a "fictitious business name statement" must be registered and published (printed as an announcement a few times in a local newspaper) if the business name is different from the name of the proprietor, partnership or corporation doing business with that name. For example, Amy Apple needs to register the name "Mediocre Advertising." However, she need not register the name "Amy Apple Advertising." Additionally, if the business name suggests additional owners, you are also required to file for the use of the name ("Amy Apple & Partners Advertising").

Registering a name will also prevent others from using it, at least locally. In most cases, registration is all that is needed. Nevertheless, this is not a "bullet-proof" way to protect a business name, and others may later contest your right to use it.

Another advantage of registering a business name is that the courts can then be used to file legal proceedings, and the legal system will generally support enforcement of a signed contract under a registered name. Finally, and perhaps most important, banks allow small businesses to open accounts in the name of the business only when proof of business name registration is provided.

Tax Treatment

The federal and state tax treatment of DBAs is also straightforward (which is not the same as reasonable). At the federal level, the small business owner completes a Schedule C (Net Profit from Business), which summarizes the revenues and expenses of the business, and then enters the proverbial bottom line onto Form 1040 (Individual Income Tax Return), which everyone must file personally. If the small business made a profit, that is added to other income, and taxes are due at the normal personal rates. Federal and possibly state and local payroll taxes are also due. Note that income derived in this manner is taxed only once (in contrast to corporations, where income is taxed twice). However, use of the sole proprietorship form of ownership generally results in a reduced ability to minimize and defer taxes.

Partnership

Description

Unlike other business forms, a partnership must be owned by two or more people. There are two kinds of partnerships: general partnerships and limited partnerships, both of which are reviewed in the following sections. Every partnership must have at least one general partner who is personally responsible for the firm's debts and liabilities.

General Partnership

In this arrangement, two or more partners enter into an agreement to operate a business. Any general partner may act on behalf of the business unless the partnership agreement says otherwise. It follows that—unless the partnership agreement says otherwise—any of the general partners may, on behalf of the partnership, borrow money, enter into agreements, hire and fire, and execute any other act for the business. So if one general partner grabs the money, maxes out the business line of credit, and then heads to Rio, the other general partners must still pay all outstanding obligations of the partnership, even if it is bankrupt. If protection from personal liability is required, then another structure should be considered.

Limited Partnership

A limited partnership is a general partnership with the addition of outside investors who have limited powers. Not surprisingly, these are the "limited partners." Unlike a general partnership, a limited partnership cannot be established with a verbal agreement. There must be a written document. For all practical purposes, this should be done by an experienced attorney. The limited partners invest (and often loan) funds to the business, but they are "passive investors" who have no further powers beyond the rights granted in the investment agreements. Limited partners cannot assist in management of the firm nor participate in decision-making. However, they also do not need to worry about unlimited liability. When big problems occur, limited partners are only liable to the extent of their capital contributions to the business (original investment plus accumulated profits).

Limited partnerships are often seen in real-estate and many other investment opportunities, where there is a desire to invest or loan funds for the purpose of realizing income or tax advantages. Limited partners usually have little interest in actually rolling up their sleeves to make the business work better; this is the job of the general partners, who desire to operate without the counsel of meddling outsiders. In fact, limited partners must be careful not to become involved in the business, or the law may consider that the hapless limited partner is actually a general partner and is therefore responsible for all obligations of the company.

The Partnership Agreement

Partnership agreements are not required. Oral agreements may actually be binding for general partners, but not with limited partners. However, for all practical purposes, it is necessary to construct an agreement describing the obligations, responsibilities, income, and ownership for each general partner (and perhaps limited partner). The partnership agreement often further describes business operations, goals, and background information for the limited partner investors. An attorney may draft these for $1,000 to $5,000, depending upon the "special twists" needed in comparison with standard boiler-plate partnership agreements. Although this start-up expense is pricier than what one would pay for sole proprietorships or most corporations, cost should certainly not be a significant factor in determining which business ownership form to use.

Unless the partnership agreement says otherwise, a partnership terminates upon the death, disability, or withdrawal of any partner. When this is not desirable, partners may agree (in the partnership agreement) to permit the remaining partners to purchase the interest of the deceased partner. Other associated problems can be solved through the use of specially constructed partnership agreements and careful tax planning.

To register a new small business partnership, most states require filing a certificate with the secretary of state. This also secures the name (although use of the name may well be contested without a trademark; see more in Chapter 4), indicates how meetings will be called and held, and describes legal and statutory requirements.

Tax Treatment

Partnerships must file income tax returns at the federal level and—if your state collects income taxes—at the state level as well. Form 1065 (U.S. Return of Partnership Income) is basically an income statement and is filed with the IRS. Actually, the partnership pays no taxes. Instead, the IRS is informed of the name and taxpayer identification number of each partner, and partners are given the same information on IRS Schedule K-1. Amounts from the K-1 are then transferred to Form 1040 (Individual Income Tax Return), the personal returns of partners.

General partners' income and losses are considered to be "at-risk." This means that their personal assets are available to creditors if problems occur. Therefore, the IRS allows these monies to be classified as active income or loss. This may be netted against other forms of active income such as normal employment wages and salaries from the partnership itself. This is useful in minimizing taxes.

Conversely, limited partners' income and losses are not at-risk, so the IRS classifies this as passive income or loss. Passive amounts cannot be used to shelter (offset) active income but must be netted against other forms of passive income and loss (for example, investment gains and losses, interest income, and interest expense). Passive losses are often less useful in sidestepping federal and state income taxes.

The Corporation (C-Corp.)

Description

The ultimate goal of many small businesses is to operate under the corporate form of ownership. We will discuss the reasons for this, but first let's understand exactly what a corporation is.

Unlike most other forms of business ownership, a corporation is a separate legal entity, chartered under state (not federal) laws, with a perpetual existence independent of its owners, directors, and managers. Among other activities, a corporation can incur debts, enter into agreements with vendors and customers, employ people, and pay taxes. A corporation is owned by shareholders, controlled by directors, and operated by officers. Normally, small business owner(s) hold all these positions. They are at the same time shareholders, directors, and officers. Another important characteristic of corporations is that they are taxed as separate entities. This allows corporate owners (the stockholders) a good deal of flexibility in minimizing or deferring taxes (more on this later).

Included under the "corporate umbrella" form of business ownership are C-Corps., S-Corps., and Personal Service Corporations. All have many similarities, but a few important differences will be discussed shortly.

With this in mind, here are the main characteristics—good and bad—of incorporating a small business:

Limited Liability

Perhaps the most important reason for incorporating is to shield owners from problems that may occur in the business. Specifically, if a small business runs into troubled waters and cannot pay its debts or other liabilities, the assets of the business may be lost, but personal assets are not in peril. Owners, directors, and officers stand to lose any investment (including retained earnings) they may have in the small business. But homes, bank and investment accounts, retirement savings, automobiles, etc., not held in the name of the small business are difficult to seize.

There are at least three possible exceptions to this rule:

1. **Piercing the Corporate Veil**

    When troubles arise and your small business runs into legal trouble, plaintiffs will routinely charge that

    > ...if the small business is, in fact, a corporation, such a corporation is in mere form only, having no existence, and that there existed a unity of interest and ownership between the small business and its owners (the Defendants), such that any individuality and separateness between the small business and its owners (the Defendants) have ceased, and the small business owners are the alter ego of the small business.

    The plaintiff here is charging that your corporation is a sham—which will happen any time troubles arise—and you had better be ready to defend yourself and win on this issue. This is where entrepreneurs need to prove that the small business is indeed a separate entity, demonstrated by the bookkeeping system, the shareholders and directors' meeting minutes, and other evidence. It is possible to lose on this issue if there is too much hanky-panky between the small business owners and the business, or if poor records are kept. In this case, plaintiffs can indeed seize the personal assets of the small business owner.

2. **Personal Guarantee**

    In many cases, lenders or vendors will request the personal guarantee of small business owners before advancing funds or credit. Others understand that it is easy for small business owners to "sell" or otherwise transfer assets out of the corporation and into the names of the owners. They also understand that small business owners sometimes retain little value in the business, but transfer assets out of the company. The intent of a personal guarantee is for the lender to have access to personal assets, which transcends the benefits of limited liability.

3. The Feds

Limited liability is not recognized by taxing authorities when a small business has failed to pay income, payroll, or other taxes. Further, these obligations survive bankruptcy, and both federal authorities and their state-government colleagues will pursue "responsible employees" for amounts due plus interest and penalties.

Tax Planning

Another important benefit of organizing the small business as a corporation is reaping the rewards of tax planning, also known as tax minimization and/or tax deferral. A corporation is an independent and separate tax-paying entity from its owners, so significant tax-minimization and tax-deferral opportunities may be available. This is discussed further in Chapter 7.

For now, let's just say that incorporated small business owners, unlike sole proprietorships or partnerships, may distribute income earned by the small business between their corporate and individual income tax returns, rather than report all business income in the year in which it is earned. Further, small business owners may deduct some expenses unavailable to non-corporate business owners, such as certain types of insurance, vacation, and sick pay.

Charitable and Political Contributions

In addition, the IRS allows corporations to make tax-deductible charitable contributions. Other forms of business ownership are not allowed this deduction. Small business owners, of course, may take income from the corporation and donate it personally to a charity, but note that although payroll taxes must be paid on any amounts transferred from business to owner, these amounts also reduce corporate income taxes, since taxable income is reduced. Since the small business is owned by the same person making the tax contribution, he or she can devise the best overall plan. Other businesses do not have this flexibility and cannot deduct such contributions as a business expense.

Year-End

An incorporated small business may keep an accounting system and report taxes based upon dates that make sense to that business rather than follow the traditional January 1 – December 31 tax year or the owner's personal tax year. For example, a ski resort may find that it makes sense to close the year when winter is over, say on April 30. Things are not so busy then, and interested parties will find the financial statements and tax returns more meaningful. If the year closed in the middle of winter (December 31), purveyors of financial statements would not know how the season really turned out.

Double Taxation

A drawback to the corporate form of ownership is the widely debated anomaly known as double taxation. Here, the federal government (and most states) charge corporations a portion of their earnings for income taxes. After the income taxes are paid, the business may declare that some of the remaining after-tax earnings are payable to owners as dividends. Unfortunately, dividends may not be deducted by the corporation as a business expense, so corporate taxable income is higher by this amount and corporate taxes do not benefit from the dividend declaration. However, after the dividends are paid, the government steps in again and asks you (as an individual) to report those dividends as income on your personal tax return and pay a portion as part of your income taxes.

For this reason, small businesses do not normally declare dividends. However, this declaration may be forced if the IRS accuses a firm of holding excess retained earnings. In that case, the firm is forced to declare dividends, which leads to paying double taxes.

In reality, however, double taxation can be avoided though careful tax planning. Normally, this is accomplished when the small business corporation pays compensation (salaries, bonuses, commissions, fees) to owners before the tax year ends. Thus, the expense is out the door before taxes are calculated. As business expenses go up, taxable income goes down, so fewer taxes are due. On the other hand, payroll taxes are due on the compensation received by the small business owner. In summary, corporate income taxes decrease—and personal income taxes and payroll taxes increase—due to the extra compensation. No general rule governs this particular issue. Small business owners and their CPAs must compute this annually as year-end approaches.

There are, however, limits to this device. The IRS requires that small business owners may not be paid compensation and avoid taxes beyond those amounts normally paid in specific industries and locations.

Perpetual Existence

Unlike sole proprietorships, partnerships or even professional service corporations, C-Corps. live on until the owners decide to terminate or sell off the business, or upon bankruptcy. Despite changes in management or even the death of an owner, corporations enjoy an independent and continuing legal existence. As a result, employees, creditors, vendors, clients and other parties may be impressed by this fact and feel more confident about working with your small business. Outside parties working with fast-growing businesses especially appreciate this corporate characteristic.

Formality

There's no doubt about it: The corporate form of small business ownership commands at least a little more respect from everyone. Incorporating is one of the best ways to tell the world that your business is here, and here to stay. Your company is now ready to enter into agreements and relationships that are normally afforded only to corporations (for example, a service contract with a big company, or a bank loan). This benefit is intangible and impossible to quantify, but it will help distinguish your company from competitors. In the end, many small businesses incorporate for this reason, regardless of the tax consequences.

Access to Capital and Big Deals

The corporate form of business ownership is custom-designed to receive capital through investment and the sale of a wide variety of equity devices; through debt instruments such as unsecured lines of credit, collateralized loans, secured promissory notes, debentures, and the many other options described in Chapter 11; or by landing a big corporate client. When the situation requires special features (such as allowing debt to be converted into shares of stock; conferring voting rights on lenders; providing for preferred stock conversion to common stock, stock options for management, indemnification of large clients, etc.), it is easier to write these into corp.-to-corp. agreements than into any other form of business ownership. In the real world, small businesses requiring access to big-time capital need to be incorporated.

Paperwork and Fees

Some small business owners feel that the corporate form of business ownership requires more administration as well as attention to deadlines and details. For example, California corporations are required each year to announce and hold at least one shareholders' meeting, (re)elect the officers and directors, and convene meetings to discuss special situations, report decisions, or grant special authority (for example, "Owen Owener is hereby granted the authority to open a new business checking account at Corner Bank"). California corporations must also file an annual Statement of Information with the secretary of state ($25 fee); file corporate income tax returns; pay and file documentation for state and federal payroll taxes at least quarterly; pay a minimum annual state income tax of $800, even if the year was a loss; and be aware of many other potential events requiring time, work, and fees. A good accounting system is required to handle these obligations.

The counterargument here is that this is not a great price to pay, considering the benefits of corporate ownership. This is what is required if a small business wants to play in the big leagues—and what kind of business these days cannot afford Quickbooks or similar accounting software?

One disadvantage is the $1,000 to $3,000 fee normally charged by attorneys to set up a new corporation properly. This fee can be avoided, however, if the situation is straightforward (incorporating a new small business with one owner) and the owner has the time and patience to read and follow instructions carefully. Moreover, many of the forms dealing with corporate formalities can be found easily on the Internet and at office supply stores, or may be borrowed from colleagues.

Tax Treatment

In addition to the tax issues described previously, note that the IRS recognizes corporations as entities separate and independent from their owners. Accordingly, corporations must file separate federal and state income tax returns. Federal returns are submitted on IRS Form 1120S (Corporation Income Tax Return). Apart from normal income taxes attributable to dividends received, there are no income tax consequences for corporate shareholders until shares are sold and a gain or loss is recognized. In that case, the gain or loss is treated the same as any other security transaction.

Subchapter S Corporation

Description

A Sub S election is available only to companies that have already incorporated. As described in this chapter, corporations offer small business owners limited liability, which is attained when the small business incorporates. When the owners also make the "Subchapter S election," the company is taxed like a partnership but retains the benefits of limited liability.

The Sub S structure allows investment by a maximum of 75 shareholders, but investors may be offered only regular common stock, thus limiting options such as preferred stock. Further, there are limits on the types of investors allowed to participate. For example, non-resident aliens may not invest. Insurance companies, banks, Domestic International Sales Corporations (DISCs), and certain other businesses are not allowed to seek Subchapter S status. The rules are complex, and a specialist may be needed to determine if they apply to your small business.

All income and losses are reported, but not paid, by the Sub S Corporation. The Sub S lists all owners and their share of the company. Each owner receives a copy of this list from the company via a K-1 statement. Owners then report all of the gains or losses on their Form 1040 (Individual Income Tax Return). Income deferral is not relevant here.

Sub S businesses must comply with most of the same regulatory requirements as corporations, such as filing articles of incorporation, calling and holding meetings of both directors and shareholders, and keeping accurate minutes of meetings. This results in higher set-up and operating costs than some other forms of business ownership.

Tax Treatment

Some small businesses choose the Sub S structure because it allows start-up losses to be passed to investors and deducted against personal income. After this, however, election of S Corporation status makes sense only if taxes at corporate rates are less than those at individual rates. Of course, this varies over time and depends upon income and state taxes. Once a small business elects to be treated as an S-Corp., switching back to a C-Corp. or other form of business ownership may be complex or impossible. Do not assume that it will be simple, easy, or cheap.

As with partnerships, Sub S Corporation income and losses are passed to shareholders and included on their individual tax returns. Corporations elect to be treated as Sub S companies by filing IRS Form 2553 (Election by a Small Business). As always with the IRS, however, there are exceptions (for example, if the LIFO inventory valuation method was used in the year prior to election as an S-Corp.), so it is important to check the regulations.

Normally, then, income is reported (but taxes are not paid) by the S-Corp. on IRS Form 1120S (Income Tax Return of an S Corporation). A Schedule K-1 is generated for each investor in proportion to gains (or losses). K-1's are then provided to each shareholder, and the information ends up on Form 1040, Schedule E, of the Individual Income Tax Return for each shareholder.

Limited Liability Company (L.L.C.)

Description

L.L.C.'s have become an especially popular form of business ownership in recent years, although they first became available in 1977.

An L.L.C. blends some of the features of partnerships and corporations. Perhaps most important, members of an L.L.C. enjoy limited liability, much like shareholders of a C-Corp., but they are not subject to the double-taxation problem faced by corporations. Specifically, the L.L.C. does not pay federal or state income taxes directly but passes gains and losses on to the L.L.C. owners in proportion to their ownership. The gains or losses are then reported on the owners' individual personal income tax returns, as in partnerships.

Beyond this, there is no limit to the number of shareholders L.L.C.'s may engage. Having said this, L.L.C.'s do not actually issue shares, but instead deal with owners in terms of their investment in the small business.

For example, Romeo and Juliet formed an L.L.C. in which Romeo contributed $200,000 and Juliet, $300,000. The R&J L.L.C. earns $100,000 before taxes. Thus, Romeo earns 40 percent of this (40% × $100,000 = $40,000), and Juliet earns $60,000.

Regarding management, L.L.C. owners may participate fully in managing the small business's operations. Unlike limited partners, they face no restrictions.

To set up an L.L.C., the prospective owners establish the entity at the state level by filing articles of organization, entering into an operating agreement that defines their rights and obligations as members (much like a C-Corp. shareholders' agreement). L.L.C.'s do not have a perpetual life, so small business owners must check state laws to learn about limits to the lives of their L.L.C. small businesses, and then plan accordingly.

Tax Treatment

The IRS considers "L.L.C." a state designation and therefore requires taxpayers to file under one of the business ownership forms that it recognizes. The small business L.L.C. will always file at the state level as an L.L.C., but in some cases it will file at the federal level as one of the following:

☐ Sole Proprietorship. The single L.L.C. owner files a Schedule C with a Form 1040.

☐ Partnership. As in a general or limited partnership, the L.L.C. files Form 1065 (Return of Partnership Income); gives K-1's to the investors in proportion to their ownership; and requires that owners enter the K-1 information on their individual income tax returns.

☐ Subchapter S Corp. The Sub S files Form 1120S (basically a corporate tax return), and investors carry this amount onto their personal tax returns via Schedule E, which carries onto individual tax returns. To file as a Sub S with the IRS, the firm must register as a Sub S as described previously.

☐ Corporation. The corporation files Form 1120S and pays the taxes. Individual investors pay taxes only upon receiving gains and dividends. Note that in this case, the L.L.C. may not avoid the problem of double taxation.

Although the L.L.C. is increasingly popular among small businesses, the laws are still new and untested. Accordingly, there is still great uncertainty as to how well the "limited liability" benefit of an L.L.C. will really stand up when attacked by creditors. We can only wait and see how this develops in different states and over time.

Additional protection may be gained by organizing the ownership through an offshore managing company to provide asset protection.

Due to the uncertainties involved in organizing and operating an L.L.C., an experienced attorney or CPA should assist in the structuring if issues such as asset protection and corporate tax treatment are complex.

Professional Corporations

Description

The Professional Corporation form of business ownership provides that certain services may be offered only through persons who are properly licensed to engage in particular professions. The Professional Corporation is recognized only at the state level, not at the federal level. In California, for example, attorneys, chiropractors, clinical social workers, dentists, doctors, and members of several other professions who wish to incorporate must do so as Professional Corporations. Others, such as engineers and financial advisors, may incorporate as a regular "C-Corp." but have many other options as well.

An additional benefit of a Professional Corporation is that persons outside of the chosen profession cannot end up as partners with equal rights. For example, Dr. Sarah Bellum and Dr. Ann Eurism are brain surgeons who are in business together. Sarah dies. Dr. Ann is relieved that Sarah's sit-at-home husband, who aspires to appear on "Celebrity Bowling" will not end up as an equal partner. Of course, this also allows the public to be confident that Professional Corporations are owned and managed only by professionals.

Tax Treatment

"Professional Corporation" is a state designation and has no meaning to the IRS. Small businesses offering professional services must determine whether to file at the federal level as a C-Corp. or as an S-Corp. (both described more fully in this chapter). In either case, the small business files IRS Form 1120 (Corporation Income Tax Return).

Fans of tax minimization may prefer to be treated as a C-Corp., due to the relatively low initial tax rates (currently 15 percent on the first $50,000 in taxable income); however, Form 1120 asks taxpayers to "check [box] if a qualified personal service corporation under section 448(d)(2)." (In case you are not already confused, this will do it: The IRS does not recognize Professional Corporations, but it does recognize "qualified personal service corporations" that perform professional services where substantially all activities involve accounting, actuarial science, architecture, consulting, engineering, health, law, and the performing arts, and where at least 95 percent of the firm's stock is owned by employees performing services for the corporation, retired employees, the estates of deceased employees, or other persons acquiring stock in the corporation by reason of the death of employees.)

When the IRS understands that your small business fits the definition of a qualified personal service corporation, a different—and much higher—tax schedule must be used, in which shareholders pay a flat (not graduated) rate on all income. In fact, the personal service corporation is a penalty situation as far as the IRS is concerned: Corporate taxpayers are slapped on the wrist for even thinking about the 15 percent initial C-Corp. tax rates. The taxable income of qualified personal service corporations is currently subject to a flat tax rate of 35 percent instead of the graduated rates available to most corporations.

The IRS believes that professionals who earn the majority of their income from the performance of services should not be allowed to enjoy the low, graduated tax rates offered to C-Corps. Since the tax-minimization factor is not relevant to professionals, other factors will normally determine the best form of ownership (such as limited liability).

Small business owners must check state laws to determine which professions require registration as Professional Corporations.

Differing Laws and Many Exceptions

It should be clear from our discussion that a general explanation of the different forms of business ownership may be offered, but rules vary from state to state, and there are many exceptions in each state. In simpler situations, this overview may be sufficient for you to understand the alternatives and head in the right direction. Under more complex conditions, however, small businesses may find this overview useful but should seek legal help before proceeding.

Incorporating in Another State

These days it is popular to incorporate a small business in one state and conduct operations in another. As state income tax rates have become more burdensome, some small business owners have reacted by incorporating in states with minimal or no corporate income taxes, such as Delaware and Nevada. This is not a tenable solution.

The essence of the issue is that states want to tax for business activity that occurs within their boundaries. If you drive on their roads, rely on their police, and use their courts, then your small business must pay for this, in part through corporate income taxes.

Small businesses that register in one state and use a sham address for their corporate headquarters may get away with this for a while—maybe even for a few years. But one day, the state really hosting the firm will understand the true situation and the small business will likely need to pay all back taxes, penalties, and interest.

Further, your small business will probably be charged with violating the law. Businesses are normally required to register and qualify to do business in each state in which significant business volume occurs. Registering and qualifying expenses are usually not significantly different from the fees a domestic corporation would pay to register properly, so there is little to be saved in this sense.

When the state finds out that all of this has been going on, there is a chance that your corporate status will be suspended. In this situation, you will likely receive a letter demanding that your company not

> legally transact business, defend or initiate an action in court, protest assessments...[or] use the entity name.

The result of suspension is that the corporation cannot utilize that state's courts to prosecute any claims or initiate other types of actions. Any court proceedings then in process or contemplated where the small business is the plaintiff (for example, trying to collect from a deadbeat customer) would not be allowed. Setting things right again is often very expensive, given the need to pay all back fees, fines, penalties, and interest.

Incorporating out of state does not allow small businesses to avoid payment of state income taxes. In fact, such behavior will lead to big-time trouble when the real situation becomes known.

How to Decide on the Best Form of Ownership

This chapter has provided a good deal of information on the best form of ownership for your small business. You have many options, and each has many implications, including taxes, liability, perpetuity, formality, ease of doing business, filing and regulatory demands, access to capital, year-end, image, and more.

Making a decision is important, and it is not one that is changed frequently. Hopefully, your situation is simple and the various alternatives discussed in this chapter will be enough to enable the right choice. Some small business owners will even be able to set up the business themselves. In many cases, however, it will be necessary to discuss this with an attorney or accountant. For some small businesses, the ability to minimize taxes will be paramount; for others, additional factors will be more important, such as limited liability.

More help and information on this subject is available at www.TheSmall BusinessOwnersManual.com.

Entrepreneurs should revisit this decision every few years, and especially after major events occur (departure of a partner, hiring extra employees), to reassess whether the current form of ownership remains the best for your small business.

Other Start-up Matters

Sales Tax Permit

In addition to other business start-up and registration activities, all small businesses should check with their CPA or call a local sales and use tax office to see if a seller's permit is needed. More than one permit may be needed depending upon the products sold and the location of the business. With this permit, your company is on the state's radar screen and will be able to submit and pay sales taxes. Otherwise, the business may not legally sell products.

See Chapter 7 for a complete discussion on sales and use taxes.

Employer Identification Number (EIN)

The EIN is a special number issued by the IRS upon the request of new small businesses and is used in virtually all communications with the federal government. A similar identification number is probably needed at the state level as well. If the business form of ownership is a sole proprietorship, then an EIN is not needed, because your Social Security number is used instead.

The easiest and fastest way to get an EIN is to call the IRS at 1-800-829-4933. The number is issued immediately. Otherwise, fill out form SS-R (Application for Employee Identification Number) at www.irs.gov. The IRS will send back the EIN in about a month.

Every small business (except sole proprietorships) should get an EIN because it is needed to submit payroll tax returns and pay the associated taxes, even if you are the only employee of your small business.

See Chapter 7 for more information on payroll taxes.

Chapter 3

Sales and Selling:
The Oxygen of Business

The reason that sales and marketing are discussed at the beginning of this book is very simple: Without sales, you won't need any other advice about running a small business. And marketing (the next chapter) is the artillery that helps sales advance more easily.

Many businesspeople do not consider sales to be a real profession—but just ask any seasoned business executive who he or she values the most, and the answer will be the people that bring home the sales. Hunters (people who bring in the deals and make sales happen) and skinners (administrators and those who fulfill sales agreements) are both important in an organization, but sales trumps all.

Some who are starting a small business may believe that a sales force is not needed. After all, family, friends, and business colleagues are impressed by your venture and are promising big deals and sales. It's not a good idea to depend upon this. In today's ultracompetitive environment, serious business volume will only come through serious sales efforts generated in a professional manner.

We begin this chapter with a review of fundamental sales concepts and how they apply to your small business. The discussion includes both sales qualifying and the different stages in the sales process. Every small business should understand how this cycle works for them so that sales resources can be applied to the prospects most likely to buy.

The chapter also discusses various ways in which sales forces are structured and managed, and the pros and cons of each. Here, the small business owner may learn about and consider selling through a direct sales force, an inside sales group, telemarketing efforts, agents, business partners, dealers and distributors, retail (direct), and on-line. The issue of channel conflict is also reviewed, and some advice is provided on selling to government as well as internationally.

There is nothing that can buoy the success of a small business more than an effective sales force, so we provide some tips on how to hire and fire and weed and seed until the best possible group is in place. Managing salespeople is different than managing other employees. They require more maintenance, so we talk about what to expect and how to deal with conflicts over commissions, recognition, and assigning accounts.

Selling your product or service is the most important part of any business; if you find the magic-bullet solution to sales, just about everything else will be easy. Most experienced pros would much rather manage an effective sales force selling a lousy product or service than the reverse. If you still don't believe this, look around at all the mediocre products on the shelves today that were brought to dominance by the right marketing and sales strategies. (I could name more than a few, but then I'd get into trouble!)

Further, there is a common misconception that because entrepreneurs know their products or services intimately, they can sell them easily. Small business owners must face up to the fact that they often are not the best people to generate revenues for the company. This chapter discusses ways of dealing with these issues to get the most productive sales force possible given limited resources.

On the other hand, everyone is a salesperson at least some of the time. You should decide on your role in the sales process and get good at it. Although sales is a skill that is natural to some, it can be learned by others. Most small business owners will not want to be involved in the front end of every deal, but maybe they will participate in the later stages of the sales cycle. Decide where you come in and get good at it. Learn from others the skills you will need, such as how to make a good presentation or how to go for the close. Be honest with yourself if help is needed, and recognize that sales is a complex profession that may be difficult to master right away.

Throughout this chapter, think about how your products or services fit into the market, and when and where it makes sense to buy. As discussed in Chapter 2, this critical determination is your Unique Selling Proposition, or USP. For a small business, a well developed USP is all the more critical because most can offer only a limited range of items. Buyers are smart and will eventually understand where their best value lies, so sales efforts must target market niches where your company is mostly likely to win. Otherwise, large amounts of time and effort will be invested in deals where prospective customers end up saying, "Thanks for the free education, but now that I have studied the market, I can see that your product is good but another is my best value."

Sales Qualifying

Professional salespeople are extremely careful about how they use their time. There are only a few hours during the day to speak with potential new customers, and out of this must flow the sales to support an entire business. It is important to know in advance the characteristics of likely customers and focus on these opportunities. This is called sales qualifying.

Sales pros normally do this by constantly prospecting for new business and immediately qualifying for:

- **Need.** Is the customer buying what I am selling? Ask hard questions to learn what the customer really needs. If he or she requires widgets with blue buttons and yours have green buttons, then quickly move on, no matter how nice they are.

- **Competition.** To further understand need, ask about the competition. Who is in the deal, how far along has the process gone, does the prospect prefer a particular proposal, and why?

- **Decision-Maker.** Are you dealing with someone who can sign an agreement, or a water carrier who only takes information to the boss? Worse yet, has the customer already made a decision but is dancing around with you because the boss upstairs requires at least two bids? (A frequent problem.)

- **Decision Process.** How does the customer make buying decisions? Who is involved, what are the criteria, and should you make additional proposals and presentations to others within this organization?

- **Budget.** Learn what the customer expects to spend, and then make sure he or she understands where your small business fits into the market. If you sense that the customer cannot understand the value of your product or service, then quickly move on.

- **Time Frame.** Is the customer ready to buy soon, or just shopping around? It's usually a bad bet for a small business to romance buyers and spend time educating them on the industry and market. Time is better spent directing efforts toward clients who are ready to buy now.

- **Other Criteria.** Maybe the customer will buy only from local firms, or big companies, or firms that sell widgets and 24/7 widget maintenance plans. Ask a lot of questions to decide quickly if you are wasting time.

In the end, most buyers are smart people and will make rational decisions. Sales professionals who are on top of the qualifying game make the best use of their time by weeding out time-wasting efforts and focusing on real prospects who can actually buy the products and services of your small business.

Stages in the Sales Cycle

Every product or service has a sales cycle, beginning with some form of introduction and ending with money in the bank. To properly allocate time and to structure sales efforts, the sales cycle for each small business must be thoroughly understood.

For some products, such as electronic devices sold on the Internet, the process is rather simple. The consumer "clicks around" with the following thoughts in mind:

- **Research.** I want a Home Theatre System, but I don't know the products; I want information.

- **Shopping.** I know the features I'd like in my Home Theatre system, and now I want to shop around to see who's got the best deal and the best reputation.

- **Buy.** I know just what I want. I'm going back to buy and I hope everything goes smoothly as I choose the products and enter my credit card.

In this sales cycle, sellers do not want to speak directly with buyers because margins are thin and this would not be feasible. Internet-savvy Web-retailers direct potential customers to different pages of the e-store, depending upon the stage of the sales cycle, as indicated by keywords entered during the shopping process. For example, if a buyer uses a search engine to look for "Home Theatre System," a link is returned directing the shopper to a list of the company's products and its place in the market. But if "Bose GS Series II 3·2·1 Home Theater Progressive-Scan DVD/CD/MP3 Player" is entered, the shopper is sent right into the buy-page for this specific product.

For certain B2B (business-to-business) IT services, however, the sales cycle is dramatically different and much time is spent directly with the prospective customer. I once worked with a firm that expected a sales cycle something like this:

- Prospecting (many calls to find the right contacts within the IT groups of potential customers).

- Send letter and information.

- Call for appointment.

- First meeting. Objective: Qualify (as described above) and identify others involved in the decision-making process.

- Meet with internal technical staff to discuss customer needs.

- Schedule a technical call to resolve issues and build the relationship. Objective: Gather enough information to prepare a proposal.

- Meet with marketing and technical staffs and prepare proposal, presentation, and pricing.

- Sales presentation to customer (perhaps several presentations to different groups).

- Meet with customer to learn any objections.

- Request internal legal staff to prepare documents.

- Meet with customer to review documents.

- Arrange for counsel from both companies to resolve legal issues.

- Sign agreements to close the sale.

Not surprisingly, a normal sales cycle here was six to 12 months. And even after the sale, the company had to deliver and install equipment, provide services, get customer acceptance, send an invoice, and wait for payment. This could easily require an additional six months. Fortunately, this firm understood the process and was patient with its sales force.

Small businesses must outline a reasonable sales cycle to estimate the length of time—and the overhead required—to close sales and generate revenues. Small business owners must decide at which stages their involvement is the most productive and stay away from the rest. Be careful, because many firms are overly optimistic when planning sales and revenues.

Structuring Your Sales Force and Channels

With all of this in mind, it's time to figure out the best way to sell your products and services. Consider your ability to reach customers effectively and think about expenses, loyalty, and other issues. Many arrangements are possible, but most small businesses have limited resources and must choose only one or two sales avenues. Perhaps the best hint here will be to take a look at your most successful competitors. Chances are, the solution for your small business will be similar to that adopted by the competition. The most popular arrangements are described in the following section.

Direct Sales Force

Hiring and training an outside sales force is expensive and time-consuming. In addition, managing salespeople is always a little more difficult than managing other employees. They just require more maintenance. A direct sales force is targeted to selling your products and services only. Hopefully, they will not switch to a competitive product when the deal starts slipping away, which can be the case with agents, field reps, business partners, dealers, and distributors. Be prepared to design a commission system that is fair, competitive, clear, and legal in all respects (for example, paying employees "commissions only" is not legal in some states if the amount earned is less than the minimum wage).

A direct sales force is most needed in situations where long sales cycles are the norm, as with rather sophisticated products and services. Of course, the best candidates for this are college-educated, serious, and career-oriented individuals. Be prepared to pay a significant salary, because it never helps if a sales rep resigns when big deals are in the pipeline. On the other hand, good management is required because some direct sales types may become a bit too comfortable with the salary and lose their thirst for commissions. I have said to many salespeople: "Your commissions alone must be at least $50,000 per year; if they are less, that means you are losing money for the company."

Finally, great salespeople are oriented toward the near-term. If your products or services are not yet deliverable or competitive, don't expect customers or salespeople to wait around.

Telemarketing

A telemarketing staff makes outbound sales calls to potential business (not consumer) customers. Telemarketers are a special breed, and I have a lot of respect for them. This is a profession within a profession; not many people can take the rejections resulting from 50 to 100 calls per day. Moreover, telemarketers often work for $8 to $20 per hour, which is relatively low. But, as always, you get what you pay for, so don't expect too much from those at the low end of this range. Plan on paying a lot more in commissions to those who produce.

Telemarketing efforts must be directed toward products and services with a very short sales cycle. Many expect to close sales on the very first call to a potential customer and expect commissions by the end of the week. If your small business deals with longer sales cycles, consider paying a flat commission to a telemarketer for setting up an appointment, and then assign the deal to someone else. The telemarketer gets paid regardless of what happens afterward, since she has done her job and cannot control the situation once the prospect is reassigned.

Recruiting telemarketing people is difficult. My experience is that about 50 percent never show up for the first interview. Others will complete a training program and then quit without notice. Many have alternate lifestyles, and their real life lies outside your small business. As an example, I once worked with a middle-aged man who arrived at my small business and called like a demon, and then went home to write movie scripts. He was polite, but he clearly told me that he had no interest in the products we sold. He was only in this for the money but would work hard on my clock. The situation worked because I respected his position.

For this reason, it is unlikely that your small business will get very far with just one telemarketer. There is too much turnover. Most successful telemarketing operations continually bring in groups of new recruits, train them, get them on the phones, and expect that half will quit within 45 days.

This situation can be mitigated with a pleasant, professional, and modern work environment (no smoke-filled boiler rooms); opportunities to be promoted to other positions; lots of perks and unannounced rewards ("We're giving a $100 bill at the end of the day to whomever sets the most appointments"); a motivated, upbeat, and energetic telemarketing manager; fringe benefits such as medical insurance; and respect from management. Of course, a hot call list resulting in lots of deals and commissions raises the morale for everyone.

Inside Sales

In contrast to a telemarketing staff, an inside sales group handles incoming telephone calls to book sales from both business and consumer-type customers. In smaller firms, they also handle customer service. Of course, incoming calls need to be generated through other marketing efforts, or your small business will be paying a lot of money to salespeople who only sit and wait for the phone to ring. Build into your budget sufficient advertising funds (perhaps through the marketing alternatives discussed in Chapter 4 or through Internet marketing, as discussed in Chapter 5).

Inside sales people are usually paid a higher hourly rate than telemarketers but make less overall because commissions are lower. There is also less turn-over and less maintenance. Most inside sales people want to learn about a particular industry and are more career-oriented than telemarketers. There-fore, it pays to invest more in training. Unlike telemarketers, inside sales people are often encouraged to make their calls as short as possible to book deals and free up lines for the next incoming customer. Also, they must be articulate as well as cool under pressure and in the face of unpleasant customers. Many inside sales people these days are college-educated and at the entry-level stage of their careers—but don't discount moms, seniors, and others who are reenter-ing the workforce.

Unlike telemarketers, inside sales people do not need to be hired in packs but can be recruited as needed, because longevity is preferred. Once again, how-ever, morale, productivity, and longevity are enhanced by a pleasant, profes-sional, and modern work environment.

Finally, when things get slow, don't expect to turn your inside sales force into telemarketers. The personality types are not the same, and turnover will soon result.

Agents and Field Reps

Agents and field representatives (referred to as agent/reps) are not employees of your company but enter into a relationship where they receive the right to sell the products and services of your small business in exchange for commissions.

This is desirable in at least two situations:

1. Your small business cannot yet afford a direct sales force.

2. Your products and services require sophisticated representation in distant geographical areas.

Locating agent/reps may be a bit difficult. This process may be approached through Internet channels (such as Monster.com, CareerPath.com, DICE.com, and HotJobs.com), through contacts developed at trade shows and industry events, and through trade publications. Afterward, the process should be similar to that for recruiting any other employee (discussed in Chapter 6).

The agent/rep agreement normally requires no financial commitment on the part of your small business, but this can be a double-edged sword. On the one hand, these representatives must produce business to earn compensation. But on the other hand, loyalty can be an issue because agent/reps flow in the direction of the easiest money. If a potential customer tilts toward a competitive product after your small business has invested lots of time and resources into a deal, there is often nothing to stop the agent/rep from switching over to the competition.

Another problem is that some agent/reps load themselves up with far more products than they can ever sell. Their thinking may be: "I understand and sell security software for a living, but just in case an important customer requests a relational database product, I will have something to offer." For that reason, many small businesses require that agent/reps complete a training course on the product and then enter into an agreement that can be terminated if sufficient business is not generated. Some even demand fees for the training course to make sure the agent/rep is serious.

Note also that your small business has little control over non-employees. It is possible that agent/reps may make unrealistic promises and commitments and expect the management of your small business to make good on them. Loose-cannon types may also use your company name and logo in ways that bring harm to your small business. That is why many agreements allowing non-employee sales representation require that the agent/rep not represent himself as an employee of your small business. Nor may she make commitments to anyone regarding your company. These must all come from you. Many also require that the agent/rep indemnify the small business against associated problems.

Another issue concerns the legal status of the agreement. Small businesses must take care that the agreement emphatically states that the agent/rep is not an employee. Most agreements are laced with several special paragraphs on this subject, such as the following:

> Since Agent/Rep is an independent agent to Small Business, Inc., and not an employee of Small Business, Inc., Agent/Rep and not Small Business, Inc., will be responsible for paying and withholding all federal, state, local, and FICA withholding and income taxes, including Worker's Compensation insurance that shall become due from Agent/Rep based on payments made by Small Business, Inc., to Agent/Rep under this agreement. Agent/Rep further agrees to provide Small Business, Inc., with proof of insurance if requested by Small Business, Inc., and to cooperate with defending Small Business, Inc., and to indemnify Small Business, Inc., from any claim or assessment made against Small Business, Inc.. by any federal, state, or local taxing authority or Worker's Compensation agency based on payments made by Small Business, Inc., to Agent/Rep under this agreement. Total compensation paid shall be reported via IRS Form 1099.

The Big Business Partner Deal That Wasn't

A friend of mine had a software company, "TDX Optimizer," that specialized in a niche market. He had a great product, a clear-cut Unique Selling Proposition, and the deals were coming in from corporate data centers all over. His only competition was from a multinational computer products and services company, we'll call MultiNationalMegabyte, or MNM, which offered an inferior product.

At an MNM-sponsored trade show, TDX's president excitedly explained to me how he was on the verge of closing a deal through which MNM's sales reps from all over the world would now carry the TDX product. It seemed to make sense because customers were buying it anyway, and everyone felt it was a solid offering.

My friend thought he had MNM by the tail, and explained that he would sign the big deal tomorrow. There was just one catch: TDX could not sell to any current MNM customers (about 50 percent of the TDX market) for two years.

I was at the same trade show a year later and saw the president again. I couldn't wait to ask about the big deal. It didn't work out as he had expected. In fact, almost nothing was sold. As it turned out, MNM's reps already sold over 1,000 different products and services, and TDX was not properly promoted to the hundreds of MNM reps all over the world. It just got lost in the clutter. Besides, with a typical sales price of $50,000 to $100,000, TDX licenses would be an afterthought in the big deals where MNM's systems sold for upwards of $10 million.

But don't worry about the big corporate users that needed an optimizer product—MNM sold plenty of licenses for their own second-rate product to these customers.

I didn't ask my friend but wondered: Was it really an accident that the popular TDX product was put on ice, while MNM's inferior optimizer now ruled the market?

The employee or contractor issue is important these days, and is further discussed in Chapter 6.

On a more positive note, agent/reps may have relationships with contacts that your small business will not get to for years. And if you've got a good product or service, then well-connected, knowledgeable, and respected agent/reps may quickly generate deals that would otherwise be unreachable through other sales means.

Business Partners

The business partner relationship is similar to the agent/reps alternative, but the agreement is business to business. In this section, we are mostly interested in the arrangement whereby a larger firms sells the products and services of your small business.

In this case, the small business usually has less control, in the hopes that the larger player will add its products and services to the Bigger Business catalog of offerings, and direct its much larger sales force to sell in obscene quantities.

This alternative should be played out only when simultaneously attempting to sell through other means. As always, success brings success, and if a potential business partner sees that your small business is already doing just fine, it will make the deal all the better. On the other hand, if your product is still in development or not getting industry visibility, don't expect much excitement from potential business partners.

A business partner relationship normally involves the upper management of both parties, and other parts of the sales organizations are typically involved only after the deal closes. The sales cycle may be very long, but the upside can sometimes bring a small business into the big leagues.

Distributors and Dealers

Depending upon the product, dealers and distributors may be an integral part of your sales model. Distributors and dealers typically carry a wide range of products, including the competition, and have market reach not available to small businesses. Customers depend upon this extension of the sales channel to provide a robust range of products quickly and at low prices. The best way to determine if this alternative should be included in your sales efforts is to look at successful competitors. How do they sell? The answer for you is probably about the same.

The following can be expected when selling through distributors and dealers:

☐ **Loyalty.** Don't be offended, but most distributors and dealers will be happy to add your product to their catalogs: If it sells, it sells; and if it doesn't, it doesn't. Don't expect loyalty or hard selling efforts from distributors and dealers.

☐ **Product Knowledge.** Distributors normally utilize an inside sales force to sell their offerings; dealers may actually have face-to-face contact with customers. In both cases, sales efforts flow to the easiest money. If the distributors and dealers are familiar with competitive products, adding your offerings to their knowledge base may be relatively easy. Expect to do a lot of promotion to gain visibility, or competitive products may be offered instead of yours.

☐ **Promotion.** If your small business expects serious revenues through distributors, expect to spend heavily to push and pull products through these channels, as described below.

☐ **Pulling.** Pulling is when your small business advertises and otherwise promotes products directly to consumers, who then buy through dealers and distributors. Always be on the lookout for opportunities to pull products through these channels, because trading partners expect vendors to make their phones ring.

☐ **Pushing.** In some cases, small businesses should consider hiring distributor reps who push products through D and D channels by visiting new and existing contacts frequently to announce new products and changes, for training, to make sure catalogs and databases are current, to resolve administrative issues, to promote special sales incentive programs, or just to take everyone to lunch. An experienced distributor rep with lots of contacts may quickly generate some big revenues.

☐ **Volume Discounts.** This is easy. Set up a schedule where D and D sellers get discounts as volume increases, such as "If shipments exceed $250,000, Seller shall receive a 1 percent discount on future purchases; if shipments exceed $500,000, then 2 percent..." The program must be promoted, or some sellers will receive discounts without knowing it.

☐ **Co-op Marketing Programs.** Many small businesses offer special programs to dealers and distributors where extra discounts are given to sellers who send approved mailings to customers or place approved print ads. For example, one co-op deal may allow that

> If dealers print their name in the designated area of this four-color brochure and send it to recent customers, our small business will pay up to $2,000 by offering an extra 4 percent discount on all new products purchased for the next 30 days.

When this program is offered, be sure to have lots of marketing materials printed and ready to ship the same day, especially the four-color brochure.

Retail

Many small businesses begin as retail operations, where products are sold out of a storefront location. The pros and cons of such operations are reviewed here as a checklist for new businesses and for small businesses who currently sell through other channels and are contemplating retail:

☐ **Expensive Overhead.** Retail stores are relatively expensive, because small business owners must spend heavily on higher rent, design, furniture and fixtures, computerized point-of-sale systems, back-office computer systems, and a great location. It's often not feasible to keep significant inventory at retail outlets, so extra warehouse space may also be leased. Further, a solid, well-thought-out business plan must be in place because most leases require a three- to five-year commitment.

☐ **Better Prices.** Your products should fetch the highest possible revenues in a retail location. If other channels are currently in use—such as dealers, distributors, agents, or the Internet—check out the local retail competition, note their prices, and then set yours to about the same for walk-in customers. Expect some static when customers realize that the same product is available from your small business at a better price through other channels.

☐ **Recruiting and Compensation.** Cashiers in retail locations often double as sales representatives if they have a good knowledge of your products and perhaps those of the competition. It's relatively inexpensive and easy to hire retail salespeople, and commissions should be considered if they can affect customer purchases. Check-out clerks, for example, don't receive commissions because there is no customer contact during the buying process. However, commissions might be considered for representatives of a light-materials handling operation, because they often advise retail customers on the best configuration of parts for a particular need. As always, make sure that the compensation plan is congruent with the goals and Unique Selling Proposition of the company.

☐ **Advertising.** Depending upon your location and industry, heavy advertising may be needed. See how your competition and nearby retail locations have resolved these issues and consider doing something similar.

☐ **Speaking of location,** this and *location* and also *location* are critical in the success of small businesses engaged in retail sales. Sales will be a function of many factors, including population and demographics, local foot and car traffic, visibility, signage rights, competition, parking, location history, image, zoning and local restrictions, competition, interior design, and expansion alternatives. Choosing a location is discussed further in Chapter 10.

The Internet

There is no avoiding the Internet these days, so every small business should have a Website to augment sales efforts, and many should also consider e-catalogs, e-commerce, and keyword ads, as described in the following section:

Website. Every small business must have its own Website. A Website validates your business and provides information critical to new customers, such as your Unique Selling Proposition (Chapter 2), business specialty, location, and hours. It also helps many other new customers find out that your small business simply exists! Setting up a Website is easy and inexpensive (as detailed in Chapter 5). Once the site is up, it becomes the foundation of related initiatives such as on-line catalogs, e-stores, and e-mail accounts. Your domain name should then be added to all marketing materials, such as business cards, brochures, and even the side of delivery trucks. The Website is heavily used by inside and outside sales reps when customers ask common questions or need information.

E-Catalog. A catalog in this sense simply means many Web pages describing the products and services offered by your small business; but customers cannot buy from a catalog—they must buy from an e-store (described in the following section. The e-catalog option is especially relevant to small businesses selling complex, expensive, or regulated products, where on-line sales are not feasible but where customers want detailed product information. A distributor of pharmaceutical products, for example, cannot ship prescription drugs to unknown buyers. The same reasoning applies to products such as guns, industrial chemicals, capital equipment, and many others. In each case, it is not realistic to sell the product on-line, but the sales force will greatly appreciate the ease and speed of guiding customers to Web pages where detailed product information and details are immediately available and can be reviewed on the telephone or in person. Perhaps the most important reason for a good e-catalog is that customers can no longer put off the sale by saying "Mail me some brochures, call me in two weeks, and we'll discuss it some more."

E-Commerce. E-commerce, through an e-store, is where products are actually sold on-line with little or no help from your sales force, and customers pay through credit/debit cards, PayPal, or similar electronic means. E-commerce continues to grab an increasingly large share of total retail sales. In 1999, e-commerce sales totaled $5 billion, increased to over $16 billion in 2004, and are expected to reach $316 billion by 2010 (Census Bureau, Forrester Research, ClickZ, as reported in *Processor Magazine*, October 2004, 4.) Many small businesses are finding the setup and operation of an e-store increasingly easy and affordable. The e-commerce alternative should be seriously considered because customers from all over the world may shop 24/7; the growth numbers cited above are compelling; and many small businesses believe this is the future. On the other hand, e-Commerce requires new methods of doing business and may affect existing sales channels. Many small businesses find that an e-store is a handy augmentation tool to supplement the inside sales force. The e-store attracts buyers, but many want to speak with a real person for a few minutes before entering a credit card and committing to the sale. The inside sales force or call-center can then fully explain products, convince customers to purchase more, suggest high-margin accessories, or work out expedited shipping arrangements. In any case, an inbound call-center and customer service desk is needed to augment the benefits of an e-store.

Search Engine Marketing and Keyword Ads. The rage in Internet marketing these days is keyword ads, having supplanted alternatives such as e-mail, banner ads, and others approaches. Keyword ads (also known as Adwords on Google and called various other terms elsewhere) appear when an Internet browser searches certain keywords. The search results include sites and articles of interest, as well as small advertisements. When browsers click the keyword ad, they link to the seller's Website and hopefully then call or buy something on-line. Some firms have reported huge increases in business from keyword ad campaigns. Still, keyword ads can be expensive, and much time is required to maintain these programs.

Much more information on Websites and Internet marketing is provided in Chapter 5, which is dedicated solely to these subjects.

Channel Conflict

Be aware that success in selling through new channels may not please other parts of the sales and distribution network. For example, when small businesses open Internet stores and sell directly to the public, dealers and retailers are often unhappy because products may now be purchased on-line at lower prices.

This conflict exists on two levels: legal and marketing. On the legal level, there may be agreements in place between parts of the distribution channel that prohibit your small business or others from selling directly in certain areas, and this could kill plans to open new channels. Review existing agreements with your legal counsel to see if vendors or various resellers have a legal basis for objecting to the new plans.

On the marketing level, perhaps no legal agreement is in place but valued distributors simply object to being cut out of the deal. They may threaten to stop buying or selling products that are sold through other means.

In both cases, the management of your small business must weigh the risks and rewards to make a strategic decision and either terminate existing agreements and move into new channels, or hold off on opening new channels. Obviously, it may be difficult to cut off existing revenue-producing relationships in favor of promising but untested new sales channels. The decision may be complex and will vary with each small business, but a decision must be made.

The "Retail Store" That Doesn't Want Customers

I recently helped a new small business set up operations and sell a popular electronics product. Sales mushroomed from zero to over $1 million per month in only 18 months. The company sold exclusively through three on-line stores and was set up as a call-center and shipping operation.

One day I noticed that overnight, the firm installed a cheap and badly designed retail showroom. A few products were on display among dozens of empty boxes, tape, and computer cables. It wasn't pretty.

Did the company have aspirations of becoming a big retailer? Not exactly. A major vendor had apparently received a complaint from aa local retailer, who said that my client was selling products exclusively on-line (which was true), in violation of the distribution agreement that allowed for on-line sales only to supplement sales through a retail location.

Fortunately, there have been no visitors to the "retail location" so far: neither customers nor auditors from the distributor.

Selling to Government

Small businesses looking to sell to the government should consider separately efforts directed to the federal government and the state/county/city/local levels.

Selling to the Federal Government

The U.S. Government purchases products and services through the General Services Administration (www.gsa.gov). The GSA is thus the one-stop purchasing agent and business manager for the world's largest buyer. Just in case you're not sure if that's big enough, note that the GSA acquires equipment, office space, supplies, and services for more than one million federal workers in more than 8,000 buildings in 2,000 U.S. communities.

The good news is that instead of contacting every U.S. government office that could possibly need the paper clips manufactured by your small business, just pursue the GSA. The federal government consumes incredible quantities of just about every possible good and service—and the GSA is mandated to spread the business around by purchasing from many vendors rather than just a few heavy hitters, which works in the favor of small businesses. That's the good news.

The bad news is that even though the GSA has attempted to simplify its procurement processes for years, selling to the U.S. Government remains a special undertaking. Dealing with the GSA requires a significant amount of time and attention, probably unlike any other initiative ever attempted by your small business.

Also, pricing is cutthroat, so before commencing these efforts, small business owners must ask themselves, "Can we afford to offer these products to the federal government at the most competitive prices in our industry?" If your firm is not geared toward low pricing, then save yourself the time and stop now.

Notwithstanding these concerns, the GSA is seeking small businesses able to provide services and products anywhere in the U.S. and worldwide. All GSA contracting opportunities over $25,000 are advertised on FedBizOpps at www.fedbizopps.gov/. This Website allows vendors to register to receive e-mail notification of opportunities in specific business areas. FedBizOpps is somewhat similar to Monster.com or other job sites, in that buyers post their needs and requirements and sellers may respond with offers.

GSA contracts are managed by GSA headquarters and regional offices, while managers of federal buildings also purchase products and services.

Most small businesses, and even the largest of large businesses, employ special sales groups to deal with the federal government. That is because of the regulations, processes, procedures, systems, etc., put in place to consider everything from good pricing, to the "Reduced Greenhouse Gas Intensity of Electric Power," to Section 508 of the Rehabilitation Act of 1973, to Amendments of 1998 [29 U.S.C. § 794(d)] requiring that the federal government acquire only electronic and information technology goods and services that provide for access by persons with disabilities. It takes a great deal of time to get familiar with all of these requirements, to remain in compliance, and to keep abreast of the constant changes.

If there is a strong desire to sell to the federal government, it's best to seek outside help, probably by employing or contracting experts who are knowledgeable about dealing with the federal government, and, more specifically, with the products and services sold by your small business.

Another approach is to establish a close relationship with the "big fish" that can afford the long and tedious selling processes required to gain larger contracts from the federal government. Here, the strategy is to appear after the deal has been awarded, and the larger contractor needs products and services offered by your small business. Becoming a subcontractor to larger private businesses is usually an easier and more familiar process for small businesses.

Small business owners must consider if it is realistic to sell to the federal government. Access to the very best pricing and the ability and staying power to deal with the GSA bureaucracy are the minimum prerequisites. Otherwise, attempting to sell to the feds can be a time-consuming foray that ultimately does not bear fruit.

Selling to the State and Local Government

Selling to government at the state, county, city, and other local levels may be a bit less intimidating to small businesses. These situations vary widely from hopeless bureaucracies to informal deals that any newcomer can quickly win if the price is right.

The best approach here is to call government entities that use the products or services sold by your small business and learn if there is a current need. If the answer is positive, learn about the processes needed to sell.

In many cases, this will first require becoming an approved vendor. Approved vendor status usually means that your small business is properly registered and in good standing, financially sound, in compliance with local laws and regulations, and has signed a thick contract concerning everything from kickbacks to subcontracting to indemnification.

The advantage here is that approved vendor status normally allows small businesses access to databases or printed notifications of all upcoming business opportunities. This makes finding new business opportunities much easier.

Most purchases by government are managed through a formal Request for Proposal process, in which small businesses prepare a written response or price quotation and submit this for consideration. Selling (in the traditional sense) and presentations are less relevant, which may require a change in thinking at many companies.

Selling Internationally

Many small businesses suspect that their products would sell successfully outside the U.S. but feel that they should first exploit fully the huge domestic market before venturing outside American borders. Besides, selling overseas may seem intimidating because of unknown regulations, taxes, customs, competition, and pricing. And there are so many countries. Where to begin?

International selling may be easier than many small business owners believe, and there are ways of testing the market without opening offices in the major capitals of the world. Here are some alternatives:

- **Trade Magazine or Internet Site Ad.** Buy a continuing ad in a trade publication or Internet site visited frequently throughout your industry. In the ad, offer to ship your product anywhere in the world, but require that the buyer pay for shipping, taxes, customs, and import fees. This is common. Expect to make a few telephone calls overseas in the middle of the night. You will need a customs broker to deal with the foreign buyer and help figure out the fees and compute the total costs paid by the buyer, such as local transportation. Just handle the deals as they appear, and later see where the sales are coming from. You may be pleasantly surprised when contacted by a foreign distributor seeking a reselling relationship.

- **Foreign Distributor.** Contact companies that are already selling related products overseas, and discuss whether it makes economic sense to import and resell your product through their channels. (Regarding the language issue, it's not much to worry about these days: Just about everyone in business speaks English.)

- **E-Store and eBay.** This is the easiest alternative and requires simply that products sold through your e-store allow for international shipping. Again, add language stating that buyers pay shipping and all other fees once the product leaves your location. If your small business does not yet have an e-store, try a few listings on eBay (selling a single product is acceptable on eBay, but an e-store must have many products). Once again, see where the business is coming from, and expand efforts accordingly.

The overall strategy here is to test the market and let buyers do the footwork in the various countries where your products may sell. As business develops, consider reducing costs and expanding volume by contracting a sales representative or opening a sales office in the most productive overseas locations.

80/20 Rule

The 80/20 rule is one of those mysterious phenomena which seem to occur all the time in sales. It is worth mentioning here. Many small businesses notice something like this:

- 80 percent of sales are generated by 20 percent of the sales force.
- 20 percent of products generate 80 percent of sales.
- 20 percent of customers account for 80 percent of revenues.
- 80 percent of sales and marketing efforts are directed at 20 percent of the product line.
- 80 percent of problems come from 20 percent of customers.
- 80 percent of profits come from 20 percent of the product line.
- 20 percent of your competitors are seen in 80 percent of deals.

Don't be surprised to notice the 80/20 rule hard at work in your small business.

Tips on Hiring and Managing Salespeople

Salespeople require a little extra care and attention. Here are some tips on how to find the best people, build morale, point everyone toward the same objectives, and get better results:

☐ **Measure Sales Objectives Against the USP.** To meet business objectives, make sure that salespeople are measured by goals that tie in with the Unique Selling Proposition (Chapter 2) of the small business. Everything must be consistent. For example, if growth in revenues is the most important objective, tie compensation to sales volume and discount the importance of customer satisfaction surveys or units shipped. Of course, all this is important, but clarity in tying compensation to the USP will yield best results. Sales objectives must be congruent with the USP and overall business objectives.

☐ **Manage Consistently.** "Plan your work and work your plan" is an old adage that works well in managing salespeople. Once a plan is in place, be consistent about applying it to everyone all the time, under both positive and negative circumstances. This sends the message that personalities and politics do not rule in your small business, but results do. Everyone must see that the only thing that matters is results, and they must know for sure that certain results yield certain actions. Consistency also suggests confidence, and helps salespeople manage their efforts and set expectations.

☐ **Recruiting Salespeople.** Where is the best place to recruit established salespeople? Why not poach from competitors? It's an ancient trick to quickly pump up business. But be up-front about your expectations, and watch out for "non-compete" agreements, where your new sales star may have signed an employment contract with a competitor stating, in part, that the departing employee may not call on certain clients for a period of time (usually one to five years) after leaving. Such agreements are difficult to enforce but may still get in the way.

☐ **Hire 5; Get 1.** The 80/20 rule at work again. Sorry, but that's about the ratio of successful hires to duds. Both employer and employee may try as hard as possible to make the relationship work, but most of the time only one in five salespeople really produce. (Of the other four, one or two will barely meet expectations, and the others will be on a downhill slide from day one.)

☐ **You Get What You Pay For.** Expect to pay serious money for good salespeople. Remember that more than anyone, salespeople are money-motivated.

☐ **Meet Frequently and Manage Consistently and Closely.** It's a good idea to hold weekly meetings with all salespeople to learn what they are selling, to whom they are selling, and how they are spending their time. If things are going in the wrong direction, sales management must act quickly and decisively to fix the problem. Otherwise, no one will be happy when sales efforts are terminated after much time and expense.

☐ **Big Commissions for Bad Business.** Related to the aforementioned topic, creative salespeople may be leading the company into the wrong kind of business, when loopholes are found in commission agreements. Sales managers must be prepared to referee situations where, for example, two people are chasing the same deal, or where a new salesperson calls on a forgotten account of a more senior rep.

☐ **Compensation Agreements.** Be prepared to spend considerable time designing and writing the sales compensation plan, and especially details on salary, commissions, and bonuses. If a mistake occurs and an eager salesperson wants commissions for something that wasn't really considered, it's okay to change the agreement but only after the commissions are paid in full. One way to limit this problem is by placing caps on commissions. Good salespeople are difficult to find, and a good way to lose them is through unclear and frequently changing commission agreements.

☐ **Perks are 'Preciated.** Salespeople these days are motivated by commissions, but other perks are appreciated as well, and money spent in this direction may buy a lot of goodwill and loyalty. Consider the personalities of your team members and the importance of building a collegial environment where everyone enjoys coming to work. Here are some ideas to reward top performers and motivate everyone:

- Entertainment event attended by everyone making quota (sports event, monthly awards dinner).

- Primo parking space

- Dinner with the boss

- "Salesperson of the month" plaque and photo mounted in a prominent place

- Article and photo in company newsletter and Website

- Newer offices and computers go first to top performers

- Company pays for an educational course

☐ **Some of this may seem cheesy at first, but look around at all the other businesses successfully employing these motivational tools.** Build fun and recognition into the lives of your salespeople: It's often cheap and easy. A couple of final notes however: Perk plans must have minimums. The deal is off if the company normally sells 100 units per month and then sells 50 units in the first month of the new "basketball game with the boss and top five producers perk plan." Also, make sure that these programs serve to bring the group together and are not divisive. This will depend upon your small business and the personalities involved.

☐ **Having said all this, be prepared to "weed and seed" your sales staff quickly.** Tell recruits before hiring that they have a certain amount of time to achieve predefined results; if the numbers don't come in, it's over (for example, "I need to see you working on three good deals in the first 30 days, and close one sale in 60 days."). Sales managers must then stick to the plan to maintain credibility, and because it's the right thing to do.

Just Don't Ever Stop Selling

Success in sales is an ephemeral victory. For the moment, everything seems easy. One deal follows another, and the successes become bigger and bigger. But small business owners can never relax. Other entrepreneurs see your success and are tempted to enter the same market. Success attracts larger companies, too, who could not be bothered when the numbers were smaller. Competitors are not standing still either. The market continues to change, and customers have new alternatives. It's only a matter of time until change hits home, affecting your small business.

For this reason, it is imperative that sales efforts never cease. Small business owners should always examine their products and services; keep track of the competition, selling channels, and methods; and watch the markets to learn the best way to keep reinventing the small business and remain competitive as the world moves on.

Chapter 4

Marketing: Artillery for Sales

A small business has many ways to generate awareness of its products and services, and all are expensive! It is therefore critical that small business owners devise a marketing mix that best reaches likely purchasers. This can hopefully be thought out in great detail and then modified over time, but the initial plan is especially important: Its success could bring abundance to the small business, but failure could result in wasted money when the firm is most vulnerable.

There are four parts to this effort:

1. Determine the Unique Selling Proposition of your small business (as described in Chapter 1).

2. Define your target market.

3. Decide upon the message to these customers.

4. Choose the best media to deliver the message.

Determine Your Unique Selling Proposition

How to determine the USP of your small business was discussed in Chapter 1. The USP is the nexus of your business. This must be resolved before proceeding.

Define Your Target Market

This should be easy. Simply write down the characteristics of your most likely customers.

Choose the most important metrics and forget the others. Your target customer base may include age, gender, profession, income level, residence, reading interests, hobbies, university, etc. Or, if you are selling business-to-business, you might consider company size (revenues, number of employees), type of company, number of workstations, etc.

A few examples:

- A pizza restaurant in a small town targets hungry people within delivery distance of the shop.

- A titanium-dioxide distributor targets companies within 500 miles that produce white products—anything from paper to paint to cast-polymer products such as white countertops (titanium dioxide is a chemical whitening agent).

- A company producing small motors targets model-airplane enthusiasts around the world.

- A computer services firm offering backup services targets small businesses in the $500,000 to $50 million revenue range, within a 50-mile radius.

- An aircraft valuation expert targets banks, lessors, and insurance companies involved in commercial aviation, as well as aircraft operators and owners worldwide.

- A sporting equipment retailer targets families with children of school age and the directors of sports leagues (Little League Baseball, AYSO, etc.) within the county.

It's not complicated to define your market. If this part of the effort gets bogged down, then you're probably going in the wrong direction. Defining the market is actually the easy part. Reaching the market, which we discuss later, is more difficult.

Decide Upon the Message to These Customers

Now that the Unique Selling Proposition and target market have been considered, it's time to decide upon the message itself. It will then be easier to decide how to deliver the message. We assume here that your small business is interested in a direct-response advertisement (that is, the prospect will buy something now) rather than image or branding ads, which create or reinforce awareness.

During this time, you will decide how much to say about your product and services, and this will help determine the best advertising media. If the message is very short and simple, a billboard, yellow-pages ad, or post card may work. If much needs to be said, a complete mailer, brochure, or television ad may be the best delivery medium.

In all cases, the use of images such as photos, drawings, charts, maps, etc., should be included whenever possible. Images attract attention in ways that words cannot. Notice, for example, that newspaper ads for grocery stores present dozens of common items such as batteries, trash bags, and paper towels, and include color photos. Why is the photo necessary? Everyone knows what batteries look like. Technically, the image is not needed—but well-placed images attract attention and increase sales.

We will review two types of ads: AIDA and Announcements.

AIDA

Many ad agencies use a simple but effective method for producing advertisements: AIDA. This technique is a great tool for bringing attention to ads and converting lookers into buyers, regardless of the media used.

Small differences in ad content can make a huge difference in pull rates. AIDA provides a structure for constructing the ad to draw a direct response.

AIDA is an acronym for Attention, Interest, Desire, and Action.

Attention

Ads must begin with an attention-getter, directed at your target market. Fear is always popular; so is appeal to an interest (for example, vacation spots or antique autos) or a surprising statement. Drag prospective customers into the ad by hooking them on your attention-getting device. This is a good time to be loud and abrasive—but keep it short.

Here are a few examples:

Cool your computer to ensure peak performance and stable operation.
(Plays on fear; we will develop this ad later.)

Mortgage rates at five-month lows!

You deserve the smell of new car leather!

Lose 6 pounds per week without dieting!

Less Money—More Options on our newest models!

These headlines catch your attention. Make a list of some other headlines that will catch the attention of your target audience, then ask around to gain a consensus on which is the best.

Interest

Interest is created by describing one or more benefits your product or service offers that will improve the life of the buyer. Remember, customers buy on benefits not on features, so stress the benefits.

When a CPU overheats as your old fan fails, your computer will experience problems right away. Much slower performance, malfunction, noises, and even fire can spell the end quickly. Beat the heat with the AsterTech.FX-D2000A CPU Cooler. Running with an ultrapremium Xidec permanently lubricated dual ball-bearing fan makes for trouble-free operation and twice the life of other ball-bearing fans.

Here, we again stress the problem to generate attention but then build interest in a credible solution. Note that no one cares about "ultrapremium Xidec permanently lubricated ball-bearing fans"—that is merely an impressive sounding feature. The benefit is "trouble-free operation and twice the life..." and that solves the problem.

Desire

Build desire by making your offer compelling. This is the time to describe free shipping, bonuses (for example, "free adapter included—normal retail price, $4.95"), guarantees, endorsements, etc., to seal the buying decision.

Continuing our example from the previous section:

> Since 1999, over 825 Value-Added Resellers nationwide have insisted on using the FX-D2000A in every machine they install.
>
> Comes with industry-best two-year warranty.
>
> From Palm Chemical—the leader in quality industrial resins.

Note that these statements are not time-related; they build interest and a desire to own the product, but do not compel the buyer to do anything now. But the call to action is coming.

Action

The purpose of the ad is to convert the ad-recipient into a customer right away. It's futile to hope that the prospective customer will remember your ad and come back later. Great ads close with a call to action—immediate action. Without a call to action, shoppers will keep on shopping and the next competitor will close the deal instead.

Examples:

> Order by (week + 1) and get free shipping!
>
> Buy now and get a $25-off upgrade coupon for our next model (which buyers may fear is coming soon).
>
> Sign up by January 31 and receive 256MB of extra memory—for free!
>
> Limited quantities, so act now!

The call to action is the most important part of your ad.

Announcement Ads

Announcement ads are easy, compared to AIDA-structured messages. Announcements assume the audience is already shopping for your product or service, so the message gets right to the point. In other words, attention and interest are not so important here. The purpose is to inform and call for action.

A good example is shown on page 59.

A 2" × 3.5" ad like this was seen in a trade magazine for computer resellers. The seller ran similar ads for four products side by side. Computer resellers have a continuing need for this type of product, which is resold to their customers. Thus, there is little need to convince resellers of the need to purchase tape storage devices—this is assumed. Announcement ads get right to the point and assume the buyer is already looking for this type of product.

Advertising people are not usually enthusiastic about announcement ads because they don't require as much creativity, but they can be very effective when used in the right places and repeated frequently. They are normally short, simple, and in a specific format. Announcement ads are used most often in trade publications or professional situations where other formats would not be appropriate.

A few final tips on writing an advertisement:

Consider the appropriateness of the AIDA and announcement formulas for every piece of sales collateral now in use at your small business. In addition, use these techniques to develop all new ads. This may take some time, but the difference in response rates generated by great ads as opposed to mediocre ads can be dramatic.

Finally, look at the ads produced by your best competitors—yours should probably not deviate too far from them.

Choose the Best Media to Deliver This Message

Once the ad content is determined, picking the vehicle to deliver your message to a particular market becomes much easier. If the message is complex, a letter with a brochure or catalog might be required. "Sam's—the largest selection of commercial electrical supplies in Kern County" (announcement ad) is complete in itself, so a billboard, yellow-pages ad, or post card mailed to a carefully selected mailing list could yield great results.

Of course, we determined our target market earlier, so this makes media selection that much easier. Once again, an overall theme here is that the plan should probably not differ greatly from what your most successful competitors are doing.

The advertising world has been kind in offering us limitless opportunities to spend money and reach various target markets. This includes everything from bus-bench ads to T-shirts to browser pop-ups to Google AdWords (Google is a registered trademark of Google, Inc.). They show a lot of variety but have one thing in common: All are expensive.

We review a few of the most popular ads here:

Direct Mail

The science of mailings includes four key variables: what to say, what to send, whom to send it to (mailing list), and when to send it. Many great books have been written on this subject, but the topic is reviewed here in enough detail that small business owners may construct a good program.

Advertising people say that mailers have a success rate of around 2 percent to 5 percent, but the real low-end answer is 0 percent. That's right: It's actually possible to spend a lot of money designing and mailing thousands of mailers and end up with zero extra revenues.

The easy solution is offered first, for those who have a little more money and a little less time: Find a mailing house and outsource the whole job. Companies that specialize in this area will advise your small business on how similar projects have worked for related companies, and thereby determine whether a simple post card will work or whether a large envelope with a four-color letter, glossy brochure, postage-prepaid reply card, and other enclosures are necessary. These companies can also acquire mailing lists and perform labor-intensive tasks such as adding mailing labels, folding, stuffing, sealing, stamping, and sorting (sorting by zip codes is required to get better postal rates). These tasks may seem simple, but they can cause huge headaches for small business owners who are accustomed to other types of work.

To find a local company that specializes in turnkey mailing projects, ask around among printers, designers, and list brokers. These people all seem to know each other, and many have worked together before. A printer, for example, will refer you happily to a mailing house with the expectation of getting the print job.

If outsourcing the job is not an option, here is some more information on doing the direct mailer internally:

What to Say

Fortunately, you've already accomplished this part, as described earlier in this chapter.

What to Send

Most small business owners should concentrate on simple mailings, such as large post cards (my favorite), form letters produced in Microsoft Word or a similar program, or a mass-mailed brochure. If the sales situation is simple, the piece will call upon the recipient to buy. In more complex situations, recipients can be encouraged to call a sales rep rather than read a large and complex assemblage of printed items.

The Mailer Is Sent on November 63

This story is short, but the stress caused by a simple newsletter mailing will be easy to understand.

I worked with a small business that published a newsletter every two months for a group of database users. We wanted the December issue to be mailed in late November, in advance of the holiday crunch.

The project got off to a rather slow start, and the text was not approved until November 20. But the printer needed five days to produce the piece, which, of course, was really 10. The printer claimed that this was because he had to wait for us three times as we approved the design copy, which was partially correct. Unfortunately, "November issue" was still printed on the newsletter.

Blinded by wishful thinking, the management expected that the printed newsletter would be in the mail within a day after printing was finished, but clerical people needed to be found who could add labels, stamp, seal, and sort into postal containers. Everyone was busy on another big project, so the newsletter was temporarily shelved.

On December 11, everyone was assembled to begin again, but then someone asked, "Where are the mailing labels?" The newsletter was mailed to an internally developed mailing list that resided on a computer somewhere in the company, but only the systems administrator knew exactly which mailing list file to use, and he was out of town until December 16.

On December 16, the list was printed, but the folding, stuffing, labeling, sealing, and stamping operations took longer than expected. Clearly, the mailing could not reach the post office before December 21, and that was too close to the holidays.

Management was then faced with two bad choices: (1) mail on December 21 and expect that most newsletters would be trashed by readers who were on holiday until January, or (2) mail on January 2 for receipt around January 9, and hope readers would not notice the November date printed on the newsletters.

The "November 63" option was finally selected, and the mailing finally went out in early January, despite additional delays in coordinating the tasks required to organize the work among vacationing employees.

Note that when form letters are produced, an additional complication arises where the letter to Mr. Gray must be placed in the envelope addressed to Mr. Gray, and not in the envelope for Mr. Blue. This may seem simple, but when thousands of envelopes and letters are lying around in boxes at your small business—and some letters did not print correctly and some envelopes were ruined—headaches will result and the project can stall.

Since the message is known, the issue here is reduced to finding a designer who can create a piece that will attract the target market. After you approve the piece, the designer turns over the computer files to the printer. Printers often work with designers, so ask for a referral.

Who Gets It?

There are basically two sources of mailing lists: internal and purchased. The best results will be obtained from internally developed lists, where previous customers and contacts are culled from one or more databases. However, these lists are often not large enough. If that is the case, supplement the internal list with one from an outside source.

Utilizing mailing lists purchased or rented (good for one mailing only), direct or from a list broker, are quick ways to get your mailing to thousands of new customers. Databases (lists) may be purchased or rented directly from sources such as InfoUSA, the Harris Directory, Dunn & Bradstreet, and other companies. Many trade magazines also sell or rent their subscriber lists to vendors with relevant products and services, so this may be the best source for specialized small businesses.

InfoUSA (www.infousa.com) allows customers to select and sort lists in various ways (for example, health services companies in the 312 area code, with 10 to 999 employees, sales from $1 million to $500 million, and an A or A+ credit rating). The list can then be purchased with a credit card and downloaded immediately.

Finally, most lists these days are delivered in the form of a spreadsheet or similar (for example, tab-delimited) computer file, so someone at your small business must be familiar with this format and understand how to use it to produce mailing labels, print form letters, and load the data into related programs such as ACT (contact management programs, described in Chapter 14).

Pricing will vary greatly, depending upon the list quality, quantity, and extra information required (such as telephone number, fax number, title, department, SIC code, etc.) and many other factors, but as an order of magnitude, expect to pay about $0.10 to $1.50 per name. Don't acquire the list until it is needed, because a portion (maybe 2 percent to 10 percent) of the names will already be outdated, and as the list sits on your computer, unused, the situation will only grow worse.

A firm able to help in acquiring, importing, and producing mailing lists and mailers is described at http://www.ant91.com/InfoUSA.htm.

When to Send It

Most small business owners will be able to determine for themselves the best times to send various mailing pieces. Sporting goods companies, for example, know the seasons in which their products are purchased, and plan accordingly. Allow large amounts of slack time because mailing projects always seem to take longer than expected, and a late mailing can be a complete waste of money (for example, a ski equipment mailer sent in April; yes, it can happen).

Budget for repetition, because almost all experts agree that response rates increase after recipients see a similar ad several times. Once again, watch what your successful competitors are doing: If they send out a large format card every quarter, consider sending a larger format post card every quarter, too.

Publicity and Public Relations

Good PR is often the least expensive and most effective means of generating greater awareness of your product or service—and getting lots of new business.

Publicity (free publicity is what we really mean here) in this context means getting print or broadcast coverage of your small business as a news item, not as an advertisement. Good publicity is better received by prospective customers than advertising because the seeming objective of the story is to inform or interest and not to sell, and because information disseminated by the media as news is perceived as more credible than advertising.

Editors of trade magazines, newspapers, and local radio and television newsrooms have a ravenous and continuing need for stories that will be of interest to their audience. Therefore, they will be receptive to your suggestions. On the other hand, most are sensitive about being duped by businesses into releasing stories that are thinly veiled advertisements. If your small business can properly disseminate news of interest and cooperate with the media, the benefits to your bottom line may be huge.

Many small businesses prefer to retain a publicity agent, who should constantly inform relevant media outlets about new developments at your company. PR agents normally know exactly who to call, what to say, and how to spin mundane events into something exciting. This can mean quick, effective results for you.

Otherwise, always be on the lookout for any kind of information that could be of interest to the media, even if you have to dress it up a little. Then, write a press release. A press release is a short (one- to five-paragraph) article describing what is going on and utilizing the standard who-what-when-where-why format. Popular themes are: how the world will be a little bit better because of this development, fear (always popular), or how a local company is making a splash elsewhere. Creative PR releases may yield important results.

Here are a few other points to keep in mind:

☐ If the press release is event-related, be sure to send it out at least two weeks before the big day to get maximum exposure.

☐ Be sure the press release includes contact information such as the name, telephone number, and e-mail address of your PR person. This makes it easy for the media to call for more information.

☐ Most press releases quote the president or a top officer of the company.

☐ Most press releases offer a short company description at the end.

Sample Press Release

The following press release may not be entirely serious, but note that it does have all the elements needed to interest editors and producers. This item would be released to industry sources, such as trade magazines.

* * * PRESS RELEASE * * *

<u>SkoolTel Announces New Telephone for In-Class Use</u>

Educators Expo, Washington D.C., August 30

SkoolTel® today unveiled its newest product, an apple-shaped cell-telephone for the desktop with a small but high-resolution graphics screen, aimed at the high-school student market. The new SkoolTel Rotten A+® model boasts a 2-inch active matrix LCD monitor, understands Morse code (entered when students tap pencils), and operates in "dead mode" - meaning it dumps all memory and appears to turn off in less than 10 milliseconds after students tap a small, playful-looking worm on the top of the unit.

The Rotten A+ model will be especially popular with students who rely upon cheating to improve their grades.

Pricing & Availability
The new Rotten A+ will begin shipping worldwide in mid-August—just in time for the new school year—and will retail for $199.99 in leading consumer electronics outlets. See www.skooltel.com to find an authorized SkoolTel retailer nearby.

The new Rotten A+ also ships with:

2-inch LCD with 1680-by-1050 pixels

1.8 GHz 64-bit PowerXX5 processor

iCheat AV, an easy-to-use desktop video-conferencing solution customized for in-classroom usage

128-bit encryption technology to keep test administrators at bay

AutoClass Networking, which automatically and silently connects all students in the classroom using high speed CheaterNet, 802.12 wireless connection protocol

The entire GlobalBook Encyclopedia, current year edition, so that students may look up just about anything in seconds

Invisible, wireless earpiece and microphone

AC Adapter and batteries

Everything needed for the modern high-school test-taker is included right out of the box.

"The Rotten A+ will raise the bar for all students, because test scores will improve dramatically," said David Reebar, SkoolTels's senior vice president of worldwide product marketing. "With the entire system, including a gorgeous 2-inch display, all shaped like an apple sitting on the student's desk, even teachers will love it."

Formed in 1999, SkoolTel ignited the multi-use cellular-telephone market for students with the Crabby II. Today, SkoolTel continues to lead the industry in innovation with its award-winning products. SkoolTel is also spearheading the digital music revolution with free music downloads of major artists to cell telephones with its "Crabster" music download service.

Press Contacts:

Derick Sheeter

SkoolTel

(800) 555-5555

dericksheeter@skooltel.com

NOTE TO EDITORS: For additional information, visit Skootel's, www.skooltel.com, or call our Media Helpline at (408) 974-9288 x101.

SkoolTel, the SkoolTel logo, Rotten A+, iCheat AV, Crabby II, AutoClass Networking, and CheaterNet are either registered trademarks or trademarks of SkoolTel. Other company and product names may be trademarks of their respective owners.

■

The press release can be fine-tuned a bit for local media by using the same text as above but adding the following paragraph:

Skooltel, an area firm employing 55 technology workers, is making a mark on the national scene. SkoolTel is improving the educational system by helping high-school students all over the U.S. improve their test scores.

The first press release should be sent to a well-researched list of industry experts. It's worth a few phone calls to find the appropriate contact person at major trade publications, research firms, Internet sites, etc.—and keep this list updated.

The second press release is sent to the local media, including television, radio, and newspapers. Again, keep the list current and send the press release directly to the appropriate contact, not simply to the newsroom.

Press releases will eventually generate great publicity, goodwill, and increased revenues for your small business.

Promotional Items

The use of free promotional items such as pens, mouse pads, kitchen magnets, yo-yos, stress balls, T-shirts, and zillions of other devices can be effective if the message is extremely short, or if the objective is to reinforce a message that is developed in detail elsewhere.

Promotional items may travel far and wide, and you never know where they will end up. Many also have very long lives and can bring new customers to your small business years after distribution.

Some items are more effective for a particular demographic group, such as golfers or office workers. However, many end up with the children of the intended recipients, which may be of limited value to your business.

If you are considering promotional items for your marketing mix, contact a company that offers these products. Most will ask about your intent (for example, "We are giving these away with brochures at a trade show," or "We put these in the bag of every customer at checkout"), give you a catalog offering hundreds of different items in various colors, sizes, etc., and then advise on what may work best in your particular situation. A graphics person will advise you on what message can be effectively applied.

Customizing the design and producing and shipping these items will take at least three weeks, so plan for a month. Although these giveaways are free to your customers, they are hardly free to you: Expect to pay from $0.25 for a cheap pen to maybe $10 for a good coffee cup or calculator. In most cases, printing, setup, and design charges are additional.

Most small businesses do not have widespread name recognition, so the short messages imprinted on promotional items should be used in conjunction with other devices if the products and services offered are not apparent. For example, hand out a brochure with the promotional item, or make the items available to customers only: They already know your business but may need a reminder when it comes time to purchase in the future. On the other hand, "Tommy's Tire Shops" need not be concerned with developing the message since the company name says it all.

Monopolizing the Show

I once exhibited at a trade show where vendors competed furiously for attention from attendees. The most successful gave away increasingly expensive promotional items, and the most popular of all was a well-known board game that had been customized from its original 1930s format to a modern, industry-specific theme.

The game was a big hit, but the savvy exhibitor did not just hand it out. Interested attendees had to sit and listen to a well-produced 15-minute demonstration of the company's services and pass a simple test before they were handed the coveted box.

The exhibitor had no trouble filling seats for each presentation, and making attendees "earn" the game increased the perceived value of both the prize and the company's services.

Print Advertising

Print ads are the basis of all other forms of advertising.

Print ads, in this sense, mean newspaper, magazine, or trade-journal placements, in contrast to brochures (described later). Although newspaper advertising is not a great growth area, an increasing number of specialty trade magazines serve just about every possible niche and interest of every possible industry in every geographical region. As a result, the number of print advertising choices available to small business owners continues to increase. Since print ads can be expensive to produce and run continually, the big question is: Are they effective?

It takes a lot of time and money to get the answer to this question. Many companies have experimented with many publications over long periods of time (repetition is important). Further, many potential buyers have become accustomed to looking in specific publications when certain products and services are needed. For many small businesses, the answer is simply to see where your most successful competitors are advertising and then do the same.

Note also that there is a big difference in expected results from newspapers as opposed to magazines or trade journals. Newspaper ads enjoy a shelf life of only one day. Results can be expected almost immediately: If the phone does not start to ring within 24 hours after release, it's not going to happen. Magazines or trade journals, in contrast, may have a shelf life of several months, as they sit around in waiting rooms, on conference room tables, and in the briefcases of interested but busy executives.

In addition, newspaper ads are normally black and white, while print ads in trade journals and magazines are usually in high-resolution full color. This results in better quality and impact, but higher design and production costs.

Timing of your ads is also of critical importance. In advertising, timing is everything. A newspaper ad run by a toy store in January will probably not do well. In contrast, an ad for an industrial products distributor describing the availability of the new HotHead welding gun in the very issue that names HotHead as the most advanced gooseneck-design 400 amp welding gun on the market, should draw a much better response.

Timing requires advance planning. The time required to design and approve a printed ad and send it in an acceptable form to the publisher may vary from an absolute minimum of two weeks to three months.

Speak with your advertising rep to learn more about this. While some reps will say just about anything to get the business, others will suggest upcoming special issues or insert sections designed to attract special groups. Also, learn about production schedules, printing deadlines, and discounts for a long-term commitment. Repetition pays. And repetition pays.

And also, repetition pays.

Brochures

Company brochures may be the best overall way of describing to prospective customers the Unique Selling Proposition (USP) of your small business, although the usefulness of this marketing device is sometimes questioned. The purpose of brochures is to give the prospective customer the warm, fuzzy feeling that your small business is for real and can be trusted to deliver, whereas most other media focus more on messages that issue an immediate call to action ("Buy Now"). Consequently, brochures may be most needed in more complex situations, where the products and services offered require real trust from the new customer before a sale can be contemplated. Or, the prospect may need to know more about the exact USP of the seller.

A distributor of mail-order point-of-sale (POS) devices, for example, may need a brochure to communicate to prospective customers across the country that the seller is a large, established firm. Seller credibility is needed here, since POS orders may be large, and if problems occur, an entire store may need to halt business until the right equipment arrives. Here, a brochure with a picture of the huge warehouse, a company history, a 1945 black-and-white photo of the founder (the current president's grandfather), and the normal feel-good statements ("The customer is our number one priority") would accomplish this purpose. Note that the brochure does not contain an immediate call to action.

On the other hand, a company selling similar devices primarily from a retail storefront most likely does not need a brochure. The living brochure is the store, its employees, and its inventory. Printed hyperbole will not work as well here because customers easily can see the real situation.

A brochure is normally a four-color production on high-quality paper stock (read: the most expensive type of printed collateral) and requires a significant amount of time to develop and print (read: design expenses not cheap). Because of this, most companies design brochures to last a long time, even though specific products may change much more frequently. For this reason, most brochures focus on the company and its USP, values, history, founders, and clients—and not on specific products, services, and pricing. When prospective customers need more specific information, then catalogs, spec sheets, line cards, customized proposals, or other marketing materials are used.

For small business owners in some industries, a well-designed, high-quality brochure is mandatory. In other cases, the usefulness of brochures is sometimes questioned because few prospective customers actually read them. As with Websites, it's too easy to end up with "company propaganda," overstating the firm's credentials. Many readers become bored when every brochure they read describes how every business is the best at everything.

Also, many adept sales reps sense that they are being turned away politely by prospective customers who say "Send me a brochure and I will call you back later."

Look around. Most doctors, attorneys, CPAs and other professionals do not use brochures, even though the business relationship requires great trust from clients. In most cases, theses professionals prefer to sit with new clients for a while and sell themselves.

Small business owners should think carefully about the value of brochures before investing in this potentially important, but potentially useless, marketing device.

Newsletters

A newsletter can be an inexpensive and effective way of reaching your target audience, but when should it be used, and what can you say so that readers don't think it's just another advertisement?

The purpose of newsletters is to generate goodwill and serve as soft reminders that your small business offers certain products and services. The goodwill part is accomplished by including articles and information of genuine interest to prospective customers. These articles should answer questions and address concerns picked up by your sales force or customer service reps. The newsletter may also include direct ads.

For example, I once worked with a small business that offered a popular disk storage subsystem to its medium-sized-business customer base. Many current and prospective customers were asking if this device could be connected to more than one server. The small business wrote an article in its newsletter laying out customer options in a straightforward manner, including the pros and cons of each choice, without any sales hype. The newsletter was well received and generated a number of calls.

Newsletters don't need to be long and complex. My favorite format is a folded 11" × 17" sheet, resulting in a four-page newsletter where each page is a standard 8.5" × 11". This can be folded in half again, and half of one page can be used for the mailing area (postage, return address, and mailing label).

As the name implies, newsletters should be sent regularly (for example, every two months). If the newsletter conveys information of real value to your target market, it may be read and passed around to others for some time. Otherwise, it will be treated as just another advertisement. Useful newsletters are often valued by readers, so to gain new contacts, be sure to include text such as the following:

Address Additions, Changes, and Corrections

Want to receive Teramarkets? Just send us your name, title, business address, and telephone number, as shown below. Already receiving Teramarkets? Make sure we have the correct name and address information for you and your associates. Please check the mailing label (below), write in the corrected information (or additional names to add), and fax back the entire page to (555) 820-6361. Or e-mail xx@xxx.com.

Double-Oh Joe (or Bond, Joe Bond)

I once worked with a small business that sold a product used by large corporations and certain parts of the government. This product was manufactured and sold by a Fortune 500 company directly to large users, and to resellers such as our small business.

We knew the CIA used this product, and our sales force had tried for some time to contact the right group. We wanted to sell directly to the CIA and displace the Fortune 500 company, but we had no success at all. In fact, it became a bit of a company joke—just try calling the CIA and asking, "Can I have the name and telephone number of the people who use this product?" It's not going to happen.

We sent out a company newsletter, but the CIA was not on our mailing list because we had no contacts there.

Then one day, out of nowhere, the CIA called us and inquired about buying from our firm.

Someone had seen our newsletter and passed it to the appropriate people. Flattered and full of curiosity upon learning this, I said, "I'm glad to hear someone gave you our newsletter. Tell me who it was and I would like to call and thank them." My question was met with silence, and then the caller flatly replied, "I'm not allowed to tell you that."

I quickly moved on to the business at hand. We finally did connect with the right contacts at the CIA, and I never did learn how they acquired our newsletter.

Once a newsletter is printed, it's a great idea to post it on your Website. It will need to be translated into a format understood by Web browsers, however, which involves a little more time and money.

The cost of printing a well-designed color newsletter may range from $1,000 to $3,000 per issue, plus maybe 10 to 20 cents per copy, plus mailing costs. It may be tempting to save on these expenses and produce just e-mail version of your newsletter; however, a large portion of the recipients will hit the delete key before reading it. Although it is easy for readers to forward a good newsletter to others, most are too sensitive to the spam issue these days to do that, so it is increasingly unlikely.

Spam, er...E-Mail Marketing

E-mail marketing was once seen as the great new frontier in advertising. Brilliantly designed pieces can be produced easily and cheaply and sent to millions for about the same expense as e-mailing to just one person. In addition, buyers can click a link and be directed straight into e-stores to complete a sale. It's all true. Many legitimate companies have set up carefully designed databases where potential buyers see only the information relevant to their interests, and others may easily opt out. Theoretically, e-mail advertising should rule the world.

Unfortunately, e-mail ads are also a cheap and easy way for spammers to produce and send millions of e-mails to disinterested parties. As a result, recipients trust neither the seller, the product, nor the opt-out provisions. It is increasingly difficult for busy e-mail users to distinguish spam from legitimate e-mail marketing, and as the level of spam increases to over 80 percent of all e-mail sent, most recipients simply hit the delete key before reading all unfamiliar e-mails. Worse, legitimate e-mail offers sent by your small business to carefully selected recipients will be regarded by some as spam, and the effort may do more harm than good. Or, your small business may be labeled as a spammer by Internet deities, and all e-mails sent from your company could be stopped.

The industry has discussed and tried all possible ways to stop spam, including legal efforts, technical means, and other strategies, but none have seen significant success. Spam continues to plague and dominate e-mail marketing.

The new world of e-mail marketing has been challenged by spammers, and the battle is over: The spammers have won.

For that reason, e-mail marketing is an unlikely source of new customers for your small business and is therefore not recommended.

Internet Marketing

Promoting your products and services through the Internet is the rage these days. Visitors to major search engines such as Google, Yahoo, Lycos, MSN, and Netscape learn of your small business, click through to your Website, and then either spend lots of money on-line or call directly to spend even more.

This subject is so important that an entire chapter of this book is devoted exclusively to designing, building, promoting, and operating your Website and e-store. Please see Chapter 5 for more information.

Yellow Pages

Yellow Pages advertising is essential to certain types of small businesses, such as plumbers, electricians, and insurance brokers. Just about every home and business keeps a copy of the Yellow Pages around, and when they open the book to your section, they are looking to buy.

As always, check the competition: Do similar companies advertise here? If yes, it's a sure bet that you should piggyback on their success and do the same. Customers are in the habit of looking here.

An interesting characteristic of Yellow Pages advertising is that an ad may be effective for years, because many consumers keep copies around for a long time. This is quite unlike other media, such as newspaper advertising.

Yellow Pages advertising is expensive, though, so think this through before giving approval. Ad reps will increase the tab by suggesting listings in several sections of the same book, and, of course, a larger ad, in color, attracts more attention. In larger metropolitan areas, ads also must be purchased in several books to reach different geographical locales. Still, none of this may be necessary. If your small business seeks a niche market on a national scale, for example, the Yellow Pages will do little good.

Also, be aware of the many scams out there, where Yellow Pages look-alikes attempt to trick busy small business owners into buying an ad in the wrong book. The Yellow Pages offered through local telephone companies is really "the" Yellow Pages. Similar offerings like "Local Metro Yellow Pages" or "Horizon Yellow Pages" may actually contain a directory with yellow-colored pages, but distribution and usage may be smaller because many consumers throw away all but one book. Before buying, know what you are paying for.

Radio, Television, and CATV (Cable Television) Ads

Broadcast advertising has a place in many small business situations. Through this technique, a great deal of information may be conveyed quickly to a large number of potential customers. Nevertheless, broadcast ads are expensive and ephemeral.

For these reasons, small business owners should approach this form of advertising by asking the following questions:

- Who exactly are my potential customers? (This may seem obvious, but think about it, because the cost of reaching unlikely customers may dramatically increase the price of your campaign but lessen its effectiveness.)

- Are my competitors using radio, TV, or CATV advertising? Have these ads run for a long period of time?

- Will the products and services offered by my small business be complimented by the imagery (for example, shots of your beautiful premises, large inventory, special equipment, or a map of your great location) available from broadcast advertising?

After obtaining rates, decide how this form of advertising compares with alternatives (for example, newspaper ads).

There are, of course, major differences between radio, television, and CATV advertising. Here are some to consider:

- Radio is more of a background medium than TV, which dominates the attention of the viewer.

- Radio may reach working people during the day and during drive-times, whereas television generally does not.

- Television is watched by just about everyone at night.

- The format of television allows advertisers to take advantage of the creative qualities of sight, sound, color, and motion. This is a powerful way to convey information and elicit emotion.

- CATV can provide extremely detailed information on the demographics of viewers, and small businesses can reach almost surgically defined geographical areas. In contrast, the reception and reach of broadcast television, and especially AM radio, may vary between day and night and depend upon the weather.

To move forward, speak with account executives from local stations as well as with local colleagues and customers. Learn whether companies like yours have advertised, and for how long? Was it a one-shot experiment, or a longer-term affair?

In all cases, account executives from the various broadcasters will provide detailed demographic information on the reach and impressions of each spot, using industry jargon such as AQH Persons (average number of persons estimated to have listened to a station for a minimum of five minutes during any 15-minute period, and AQH Ratings (the estimated number of listeners (AQH Persons) as a percentage of the survey area population). This can get complicated. Be attentive, because most advertising vendors have a way of presenting the numbers to show that they are the best. It's up to you to make the final decision.

This is where brokers come in. Radio and television advertising brokers know the market and can cut through the hype, providing your small business with:

- An overall advertising strategy

- Direction on what to say and help in writing the scripts

- Counsel on how to reach your market, thereby transcending the complex and confusing demographic information provided by advertising account executives

- Advice on an advertising schedule that makes sense (frequency, time slots, duration). This alone is a huge issue. Given a certain budget and objective, should your spots be spread over the day or appear only in the morning? On one station or several? Should your first test campaign last for one week or 10 weeks?

- Here's the big one: Buying through ad brokers will often result in less expense, because they are adept at hammering the local broadcasters for better rates, which they pass on to you.

Unlike the big national players, small businesses normally do not need to spend large amounts of money to produce an ad. For radio, carefully write your 30- or 60-second spot and record it yourself a few times. Then e-mail the script to your grateful radio account executive, who will have a local radio personality record it. This increases the professionalism and credibility of the message. Beware of offers in which the radio or TV executive wants you to be in the ad, unless you're in this for ego-gratification purposes.

Most stations now use digital recording techniques, so MP3 files may be e-mailed back and forth until the message is just right. If you want to pay more and fancy it up a bit, add sounds and music from prerecorded libraries available to the stations.

Producing a local television or CATV advertisement may cost $500 or more, but most can be capped at around $2,000. This is negotiable, however, and advertisers who agree to longer campaigns may get the ad produced for free.

Most small businesses want to test a broadcast advertising campaign before committing to a large expenditure. If you choose to do this, capture the benefits of repetition by selecting a limited time of the day, and just one or two stations. Depending upon the results, adjust accordingly and try again.

Ad brokers are aware of techniques that will measure ad effectiveness, such as using special toll-free ("800") numbers that forward to your office. The statistics are then available through Web-based browsers.

Once the ad is produced, economies are realized only when it is played over and over again. Make sure your budget allows for the production of a good message, and lots of spots. As with all forms of advertising, repetition is critical.

It's often a good idea to piggyback on the success of your competition by mimicking their advertising strategy. Your competition may have spent a great deal of time and money perfecting this strategy, so why reinvent the wheel? If customers accept a competitive ad, it's likely they will accept your ad, too.

Trade Shows and Conventions

If you've ever been to the vendors' exhibition hall at a large trade show or convention, attracting new business seems like a turkey-shoot. Exhibitors just seem to stand there as new business prospects queue up in line. Nevertheless, this form of marketing is more expensive and draining than it looks, and small business owners should analyze carefully the benefits that really accrue.

Standing at a table and signing up new customers may look easy but the reality is different. Let us take, for example, the actual costs paid by a small business that recently attended a computer trade show in a different city. At first, the $6,000 show fee seemed steep, but that was just the beginning as shown in the list on page 75.

The show continued for four days, but that is really six days when you include travel time, or 24 days for four people. The convention hall, however, was open for only 18 hours. Because show attendees were in classes most of the time, there were only about six hours of significant traffic. The rest of the time was spent in special meetings with an occasional customer and throwing toy footballs

The Full Expense of Exhibiting at a Trade Show

Fee for 10' table in the vendors' exhibition hall $6,000

Print new literature * $2,500

Print mousepads (free giveaway) $3,200

Design and construct trade show booth * $2,200

Ship booth and materials to and from trade show $750

Travel, hotel, meals (four people, four days) * $8,200

Clothing (30 blue shirts with logo; eight pairs of khaki pants) * .. $1,100

Entertainment $950

Miscellaneous (union handling fees, tips, etc.) $900

Total $25,800

* Note that some of these items can be spread over more than one trade show.

After determining the total cost, there are two questions that must be answered to determine the viability of attending trade shows and conventions:

1. How much new business can we identify that can be directly attributed to this event?

2. How does this cost for attracting new business compare with other alternatives?

Small business owners must determine the answer to the first question by asking show participants and sales reps several weeks after the event (depending upon the normal sales cycle of the products and services sold by your business). The answer to the second question, of course, must be separately calculated.

In many cases, a large amount of interest can be generated at the show, but harried attendees are bombarded with so much information that little is retained. Some marketing experts claim, for example, that 70 percent of trade-show literature is thrown away before attendees even get on the plane to return home.

Therefore, it is critical to get the identities of visitors and follow up by telephone after the show. Here are some other tips to maximize your investment in these events:

☐ During the year, keep a folder of mailings and e-mail announcements regarding all types of tradeshows, conventions and related industry events. Review all of them once or twice a year to determine which ones to attend.

☐ In some cases, money is not the only factor. Consider that the prestige associated with attending—or not attending—certain important industry shows must be weighed. Further, consider the value of solidifying on-going relationships through face-to-face contact at events.

☐ During the event, the first objective is to get business cards and notes. Expect that once a conversation with a prospect is concluded, there is no chance that he or she will call later for additional information. The obligation to call rests 100 percent with the staff of your small business.

☐ Before investing, ask how many people attended this event last year—100 or 10,000? Many show sponsors have detailed information on the number and types of attendees. Are these the kinds of buyers sought by your small business?

☐ Is attendance free, or must attendees pay a fee or prove industry credentials? (If anyone can attend, then expect to spend a lot of time meeting with bored hotel guests or passersby.)

☐ At some shows, the exhibitor hall is hardly the main event. Attendees come to attend classes, hear important speeches and presentations, or even for social reasons. Can you expect show attendees to spend much time in the exhibitor hall? This may help determine which shows to attend. (See "Joe Loses Out At Trade Show To California Girls.")

☐ Location at a trade show is important in predicting expected traffic. Many well-run events plan carefully so that all exhibitors receive similar exposure, but make sure your booth is in a main corridor, near a major attraction, or otherwise in an area where walk-by traffic is heavy.

☐ A great way to attract attention to your booth is to give a speech, presentation, or class. You cannot directly "plug" your company, but this will still attract positive interest and gain a lot of preshow publicity (in printed programs, Websites, etc.). At some shows, there is a fee for this.

☐ Most trade shows or conventions offer endless opportunities to spend a little extra money and more heavily promote your presence. For example, announcements such as "lunch today is sponsored by Hi-Temp Plastics Co., booth 117" are available at a price. Consider if this may be effective.

☐ Consider that attendance at trade shows or related events is just another part of the marketing mix. Is this where your small business gets the most value for the marketing dollar? Adjust spending up or down accordingly.

Joe Loses Out at Trade-Show to California Girls

Our company once exhibited at an annual trade show for database companies in San Diego. Attendees arrived in February from all over the world for three days of classes and speeches by industry leaders. We hoped that many would visit the exhibitors' hall.

Most of the attendees were young or middle-aged males, and San Diego was a welcome respite from the cold winter. It was not until after we had set up the booth that we realized our problem: After listening to 90-minute presentations about new database software, attendees had the choice of either taking a break by heading into the basement of the building to see the exhibitors' hall, or strolling outside the hotel, inhaling the fresh ocean breeze, feeling the sun, and viewing legendary California girls sunning on the beach.

Attendance in the exhibitors' hall at this event was uncommonly low.

Co-op Advertising

Many small businesses work within a chain of manufacturers, wholesalers, distributors, and retailers, or among a group of interrelated service providers. If this is the case, look into co-op advertising programs.

Co-op programs normally work something like this: "The manufacturer will credit your account for 2 percent of the cost of all approved mailers in the next 90 days."

The process here is first to design or change a mailing piece to the manufacturer's liking. (The manufacturer will like ads that feature only their name and products. Ads prominently promoting the competition will not be approved.)

Keep track of costs and send receipts and sample ads to the program originator. If $10,000 is spent on the mailing program, $200 will be credited to your vendor account, which will reduce the real cost of future purchases.

These programs often do not make sense all by themselves, but they may sweeten and change the shape of advertising campaigns that were planned anyway.

Ask business partners about co-op ad programs, or suggest a similar plan that makes sense for your small business.

Chamber of Commerce and Networking

Many small business owners enjoy networking with other entrepreneurs at chamber of commerce meetings, or those of related organizations. Chambers ostensibly exist to represent the business side of issues to local government, and there are many special committees through which this can be accomplished. Still, the overriding reason to join chambers of commerce is—to make commerce.

Most business meetings and social events are structured to encourage as much networking as possible among members. For example, many events begin by allowing each participant 60 seconds to explain his or her business. To some extent, this is a great way to make new contacts in the business community; but organizations such as this should be viewed in a "what goes around comes around" sense—that is, be prepared to develop real long-term relationships and buy as well as sell to other members. The problem with these organizations is that some meetings turn into selling frenzies, with 40 salespeople presenting and selling to each other. Everyone is there to sell, not to buy.

Organizations such as these are heavily attended by local service providers such as dentists, lawyers, financial planners, insurance agents, bankers, doctors, printers, contractors, marriage counselors, CPAs, computer types, and many others. Most are classic small businesses. Larger firms are normally represented by salespeople (sorry, it's unlikely the director of purchasing will be attending).

Look for chamber of commerce and related organizations such as "Le Tip" in your area. This can be accomplished on-line by searching for "Chamber of Commerce" on Yahoo, and then entering a local zip code into the directory search. Or search for "LeTip" (no space between the words) on any major search engine.

Ask to attend a meeting for free. Then, when the pressure is on to join, learn the total benefits package and don't be shy about asking how the group may benefit your small business. Consider the whole concept, and not just the opportunity to sell to other members. Expect to invest real time in a sincere effort to help the business community and get to know other members. Then decide if the overall commitment has a place in your marketing budget.

Corporate Image and Identity

The image and identity of your small business are augmented by the company name, logo, slogan, colors, and related collateral such as business cards and letterhead. Many firms spend an inordinate amount of time churning over these decisions, so here are a few points to remember to keep all of this in perspective:

> A favorite saying:
> "Advertising hates a void"

Trademarks

Before choosing a company name, slogan, or logo, it's important to do a trademark search. Trademarks can identify and protect company brands and products.

If a name or slogan is already being used by a local business, a great deal of money may be spent advertising someone else's company, and your small business may be sued for doing so. This would not be a good use of marketing funds.

Trademark protection is not exclusive, but depends upon the distinctiveness of the name. Ordinary and common words are difficult to trademark. Imagine, for example, if only one company in the U.S. was allowed to advertise under the name "Tony's Pizza." On the other hand, no one had better mess with the Nike name and swoosh logo.

In some cases, a small business may retain the right to use a name merely by proving it was the first to use it. This could occur if another firm challenged your use of the name long after promotional efforts had begun. Here, proof that it was used (for example, showing old newspaper ads) might hold off others and even trump trademark registration, but this is a cavalier approach to protecting such important properties.

A trademark is the best and most formal way of securing a name or logo for your small business, and a trademark search is the place to begin. It's now easy to search and register names without an attorney, through the U.S. Patent and Trademark Office (www.uspto.gov). The USPTO site answers many questions and allows on-line searches, access to forms, and registrations. If things get complicated, a trademark attorney (sorry, it's not a good idea to use a generalist) must be called in—and they are not cheap. The entire process may take several months, assuming there are no challenges.

The final product here is federal registration of your trademarked names, slogans, or logos. This means that these items are locked-down and seen in searches by others, on a nationwide basis. No other company may say, "I thought no one else was using that name or phrase or logo." TM'ing is also evidence and presumption of ownership.

Company Name

Keep your company name simple and descriptive. "Pittsburgh Plate Glass," "Comfort Inns," and "Burger King" are companies that started out small but are now well-known examples of company names describing their product or service. Of course, the business was successful for reasons well beyond the company name. A good name will make a marginal difference in some situations, but don't spend excessive time and money on this. It's hard to go wrong with a short, simple, descriptive name, even if it doesn't have sizzle.

Many small business owners use their last name in the company name (for example, "Smith Printing"). Some feel, perhaps, that this is a small, but deserved, measure of ego gratification. However, using your last name may actually be counterproductive unless it carries positive associations. When negotiating with new customers, for example, do you want them to know right away that the first person they have met is the owner, founder, and president of the company? An exception may be in situations where the last name is well-known in a positive sense. For example, local boy and ex-professional baseball player Slider Wilson returns home and opens the Wilson Insurance Agency. Even this can be dicey because not everyone may agree that this is a positive association.

> ### Jose Bernstein Does Not Compute
>
> Here is one I can't figure out. This is a Los Angeles restaurant that breaks just about every marketing rule but is successful.
>
> Jose Bernstein's may sound either Mexican or Jewish, but it sells American-style burgers made by a cook from Brazil. Most of its customers are Asian. Right next door is a thriving Persian café (not big fans of Bernstein's). JB's is located in the middle of other businesses that cater to UCLA students, but there is a red-and-yellow neon sign in the window. Red and yellow are the colors of arch-rival USC.
>
> Everything works just fine.
>
> Sorry, but I can't explain this one.

Slogan

A company slogan is often used as a tag line to the company name and should flow right out of the Unique Selling Proposition of your small business. The slogan should be as ubiquitous as the company name, appearing on the Website, business cards, letterhead, brochures, trade-show booth, and even radio and TV ads. A slogan is not essential, however, and small business owners should not dwell on this unless there is a compelling message that needs to be associated with the company name.

Examples of well-known slogans are:

United— "Number One in The Sky Wherever We Fly"

GE— "We Bring Good Things to Life"

Frankie Auto— You've never heard of this one, but where I grew up, an auto dealership continually ran radio and TV ads imploring listeners in a nauseating voice to "Try me first or try me last but just try me. Try me." Eventually, this became a joke as locals repeated the mantra to each other to " just try me." But 40 years later, the message is still repeated.

Large companies periodically refresh slogans as marketing campaigns run their course. Small businesses may do this also, but use caution in this regard because a change may jeopardize goodwill and recognition that has accrued over the years.

Logo

A good logo may be nothing more than your company name in a selected font. To get a little fancier, perhaps underscore the name, in alternating colors, and enclose it in a simple box.

Notice that many successful small—and large—businesses have very simple logos. Don't spend a lot of time and money on this. In fact, simple logos usually scale to small and large sizes (needed for different advertising materials) better than more complex designs.

Colors

There is no chance you will think of a stunning, new, and undiscovered color combination, so it's probably best to stick with tried-and-true combinations such as black, blue, and red on white. Depending upon your business, other colors may be acceptable, but fortunately there is so much color out there today that it's hard to make a mistake.

In more complex situations, where company image and identity may be more important, small business owners are encouraged to work with firms that specialize in this area.

Company image and identity are important, but these decisions will only go a certain distance in growing the business. Despite all the hype, buyers still prefer substance over style. The cleverest materials of this sort may get some initial attention, but this will not be enough to prevail as the products and services offered by your small business are analyzed and compared with those of competitors.

Decisions associated with your company image and identity should be made quickly and without undue time and expense. Stick with your choices, remain consistent, and, most important, offer good products and services. Goodwill will build over time.

Advertising and the Law

Laws concerning advertising are generally administered by the Federal Trade Commission (FTC), but this area is also governed by a number of state and local agencies. Consumers also may sue companies that make false offers, usually to compel performance. For example, if a small business offers "free shipping on all orders placed this month" and buyers later find that this applies only to purchases over $100, a class-action attorney may force your company to pay restitution to every buyer during this period of time, plus damages and legal expenses—yours and theirs.

Beyond this, the FTC is generally on the watch against false and misleading claims. This is a complex legal area, but problems may normally be avoided by making sure all advertising is factually correct. For example, it's acceptable to say, "We are a leading supplier of aerospace fasteners," because "leading" may be interpreted in many ways; but if the ad says "We are the number-one seller of aluminum aerospace fasteners in the U.S.," then this fact had better be correct. If not, expect your competitors to speed-dial the FTC.

Unwanted attention may be received regarding claims about competitive products, such as "twice as effective as the same product from Acme Chemical." In this case, you may receive notice to defend the claim in a libel lawsuit.

Finally, your small business may get sued if your advertising program is too successful. This may occur when consumers line up to buy the products and services offered in an advertising campaign, but they are not available. The thinking here is that you have made an offer, and must therefore perform—or it was a false offer. An example might be, "Close out! Any RCX Color Television for only $100!" What you really mean is that old inventory must be cleared out. The ad should have included three extra words: "Close out! Any RCX Color Television for only $100! While supplies last."

Attention from the FTC usually begins with informal communications to gain voluntary compliance. This may result in an expensive settlement, but it is better than slugging it out in court. In a battle of attrition between a small business and the FTC, the FTC will always win. Other actions available to the FTC include cease-and-desist orders, civil lawsuits, and forcing your small business to run an embarrassing corrective advertising program.

Visit www.TheSmallBusinessOwnersManual.com for additional help with trademarking.

Budget

Advertising is not for the feint-of-heart small business owner. Although spending in most areas of a company is closely regulated and monitored for effectiveness, attitudes towards small business advertising are usually something like, "Let's throw some money into this idea for a while and see if it works." In the beginning, results are usually less than expected, and changes are made until the effort is fine-tuned. Of course, this may take a great deal of time and money, more than some small businesses have.

Consumers are bombarded relentlessly with non-stop advertising in just about every possible media, so even if your small business has the world's best products and highest-quality services, no one will know without advertising. Therefore, some real money must be budgeted for advertising, especially in start-up firms.

Begin by getting statistics on how firms like yours prefer to advertise. The answer for your small business is probably similar. Check trade publications, other industry resources, or the U.S. Small Business Administration for statistics on the percentage of revenues committed to advertising by similar companies in other areas, or across the U.S. If the competition is a publicly traded company, check SEC filings to see what dollar amount and percentage of revenues is spent on advertising and marketing. For example, an insurance broker may learn from his company marketing group that colleagues operating in other cities spend 5 percent of revenues per year on advertising, with a minimum of $5,000. This well-established company statistic may be of immense value to a new agent.

Once your small business is underway, watch carefully where new business comes from. This information is best gained by asking customers directly. Budget accordingly. If you devise a way to predict revenues based upon advertising and your small business cannot afford this expense, perhaps it's best to wait until sufficient funds are available before entering the business.

In any case, be prepared to play around with variations of marketing programs and see what works best. This will cost a lot of money, and some carefully designed programs may yield absolutely nothing. Still, as we said, advertising is not for the feint-of-heart small business owner.

Once the budget is established, small business owners are ready to consider other parts of their marketing and advertising strategy, described in this chapter.

Model for Calculating Return-on-Advertising

Comparing different types of advertising and marketing alternatives can be mind-boggling, so how does the small business owner calculate the best value?

It is best when a small business can reduce marketing costs directly to sales and profits, such as "radio spots cost $1,000 per week but generate $5,500 in increased revenues; $5,000 in extra revenues means $1,800 in additional profits. So $1,000 in advertising yields back my expenses plus $800 in profits."

This model may be extremely effective. Study the structure below, and then add or delete lines, change the percentages and amounts, and otherwise customize to your own situation:

Cost of campaign per week $1,000

Reaches how many new prospects? 50,000

How many prospects will call for information?   1% 500

Of the call-ins, how many will request a price quote?   25% 125

What percentage of price quotes do we normally win?   20% 25

What are the average revenues of a new deal? $220

Multiply by number of deals: 25

= Incremental revenues per week from the advertising campaign $5,500

What is our margin from new deals? $72

Multiply by number of deals: 25

= Incremental margin per week from the advertising campaign $1,800

Therefore, $1000 in advertising yields $5,500 in extra revenues and $800 in additional margin after advertising expenses.

Now look at each number in this model. Is it realistic? If not, change the amounts until each value is believable and yields the margins needed to pay the expenses of your small business. Is this amount affordable?

As your small business considers different forms of marketing and advertising, using this model may be the best way to measure and compare the effectiveness of everything from newspaper ads to trade shows.

Writing and Designing Ads: In-House or Outside?

As noted in the very first sentence of this chapter, all forms of advertising have one thing in common: They are all expensive. Is it a good idea to at least write and design your ads in-house? The answer to this question is no, unless you have significant previous experience in this area.

Small business owners should always be concerned with where they can add the most value, and although it may be tempting to write your own ad copy and use in-house computer skills to lay out the ad, in the end, this may be a tragic waste of money. In a classic case of "win the battle and lose the war," ads designed by amateurs will still cost the same amount to produce and distribute, but may be dramatically less effective.

Advertisers should be intimately involved in all phases of the campaign, beginning with the first copy and design. There is no one who understands your small business better than you. But in general, it's best to let professionals do the creative work and step back into the role of subbing out the project and limiting your involvement to editing, reviewing, and approving. Delegating this task to experienced copywriters and designers offers a certain peace of mind, assuring you that the look and feel of the advertising campaigns is professional.

Whatever Works

American businesses of all sizes are blessed with an extraordinary range of choices in marketing and advertising our products and services. Advertising can be purchased just about anywhere, anytime, and in any format. Do not stray too far from what the competition is doing, but be open-minded about new possibilities.

Chapter 5

Your Incredible Website
and E-Store

This chapter reviews the essentials of setting up and operating a basic Website, one with advanced features such as an e-catalog, and an e-store. We also advise the small business owner when it's okay to "do it yourself, do it for less," and when outside expertise should be considered.

There is just no getting away from the necessity for some level of Internet presence these days, so small business owners should consider what level of involvement is appropriate for now, and also plan for the future. As we proceed, it is important to remember two concepts.

First, think of the key objective of your Website. Is it to create visibility and attract customers? Is it to sell your products? Perhaps call-ins regarding professional services offerings are desired. Is it to provide information to build goodwill and reduce the number of calls to your staff? Keep this in mind as the initial Website is built, and add on additional features later.

Second, remember that a Website is not a project that is started and finished (say, like a brochure), but is a continuing work in progress. Unlike printed materials, a Website should be updated frequently and always reflect the latest news about your small business with an exciting spin, to encourage visitors and customers to return often.

Website

The most basic Internet presence is a one-page Website; because these are so cheap, easy to set up and effective, the smallest of small businesses must have one. Even if the Internet site is a single page and merely gives your name, address, and business hours through a template from Yahoo or a similar operator, it's still a good deal. Something like this will cost about $12 per month, and you won't find a more effective form of advertising, as we shall see.

Small business owners can have a site up and running within a day by investing less than $30 in fixed expenses, and by sailing through two on-line sessions of 30 minutes or less. For example, Yahoo.com, MSN.com, Earthlink.net, and hundreds of other smaller Internet operators offer many attractive "fill-in-the-blanks" Website templates (more on this shortly) and hosting services, and do the job just as well as the bigger companies.

You can set up a Website in three steps:

1. Choose and register a domain name.

2. Select a place to host the domain.

3. Design and publish the Website.

Choose and Register a Domain Name

The first step is to register the desired name, such as www.dwightkennedy.com. This is your domain name and is critical for two reasons: First, once the name is registered, it belongs to your small business and to no one else; and second, an Internet Protocol (IP) address is issued immediately in the format of four numbers separated by periods. Each of the four numbers can be up to three digits in length, for example, 66.218.79.155. Servers on the Internet desperately need IP addresses for just about everything, such as knowing where to go when someone types "www.TheSmallBusinessOwnersManual.com," for delivering e-mail, for routing bits of music, video, or telephone traffic to the right place, and much more. However, people find it much easier to recall words and phrases. Imagine, for example, how Amazon would promote their site with just an IP address of "We are Amazon. See us on the Internet at 207.171.166.102." Not too elegant. So the DNS directories cross-reference IP addresses and domain names so that Internet users do not need to work with geeky IP addresses but only need to remember snappy domain names. (IP, DNS, and other terms are defined further in Chapter 14.)

Pick something that is descriptive, memorable, and as short as possible. The company name is always a good idea but is not required. If your company name doesn't say enough, consider something more descriptive. An increasingly common tactic is to register several names, with each domain either a separate Internet location or redirecting browsers to a single main Website.

For example, the owners of Heckler Accounting Services, LLC, may consider:

- www.HecklerAccountingServices.com—the main site

- www.LosAngelesQuickbooksHelp.com—a one-page Website about the Quickbooks expertise offered by this firm

- www.SouthernCalBusinessAccounting.com—when users click this link, they are directed to www.HecklerAccountingServices.com

- www.BizTaxHelpLosAngeles.com—when users click this link, they are again directed to www.HecklerAccountingServices.com

The name "Heckler's Accounting Services" may not say enough in Internet parlance, but the other names, such as www.LosAngelesQuickbooksHelp.com, do. A good name in itself is an advertisement, leaving no doubt as to what browsers will see at this site.

There are many places where it's fast, easy and inexpensive to find and register a domain name, such as http://smallbusiness.yahoo.com (then click "Domains"), or www.DomainBank.net, www.Register.com and www.GoDaddy.com. Or go to www.Google.com and search for "register a domain name."

Select a Place to Host the Domain

Once the name is registered, the next step is to tell the Internet where the Website will reside. In other words, there are millions of servers out there, but which one hosts the files that make up your site? This information is needed so that traffic will be directed to the correct place.

For most small businesses, selecting the host site is an easy decision that should cause little consternation. For example, if the domain name was registered with one of the big names described above (e.g., Yahoo), then just go with the flow and let it stay there. If you are working with a local Website design company, in most cases it's fine to use their servers. Larger operators must worry about downtime, input/output speeds, and bandwidth. Small businesses normally do not need to be especially concerned about these issues, because technology has improved so much in recent times. After the site is up ("published" or "online"), visit it at least once a week and click a few links to make sure everything is still there and to see if the response times are acceptable (that is, how long does it take after clicking a link until a page is fully visible?).

To select the place to host a domain, enter your IP address and two DNS server names (primary and secondary). For example, if your small business is hosting its Website on Yahoo, the primary DNS server is "yns1.yahoo.com", and if that server runs into trouble, the secondary DNS server is "yns2.yahoo.com". Don't worry about finding this information. Most Internet companies put it in your face as much as possible to make it easy to register the domain on their systems.

A second choice is to host your own Website by purchasing a Web server and attaching it to the Internet (a Web server looks like any other workstation but has a few extra hardware features and is configured to serve up pages to the Internet). A Web server (in contrast to a file server, print server, etc.) attaches to a DSL or T1 line through a modem, switch, and router. All of this—including hardware, software, and installation—will cost from $2,000 to $5,000. The bottom line will be substantially more than the $15 to $60 per month charged by Website hosting firms, especially considering maintenance costs, but some small businesses prefer the security and ease of access of operating their own Internet server. This depends upon many internal factors. In general, however, small business owners should not attempt to get into the Web-hosting business, because other alternatives are so easy and inexpensive.

A middle way between option one (renting space on commercial servers) and option two (buying and operating a Web server) is to purchase a server and have it installed and managed at a "colocation site" through a Dedicated Server Hosting provider. Here, the server is normally installed in a rack-mount cabinet at a professionally managed facility offering many related services, such as tightly controlled access into air-conditioned, secure data centers; modern firewalls; nightly data backups; backup electrical power systems (battery for short-term, falling over to diesel generators); backup cooling systems; lots of extra capacity for peak-use periods in routers, switches, load-balancing equipment, and disk storage space; higher-speed connections to the Internet; and perhaps, most important, capable hands to fix both software and hardware problems immediately. The Dedicated Server Hosting option may be the best for small businesses that need a high-capacity, high-availability server but do not want to purchase the infrastructure needed to keep all of it going.

Many Website design firms can recommend a good Dedicated Server Hosting option, or provide one themselves. Or just search under "Dedicated Server Hosting" on a favorite search engine. Because there is no reason to ever visit your server, the collocation site may be located anywhere, and it is not especially important to work with a local provider.

Design and Publish the Website

Once the name is registered, find a Website hosting company. These companies have hundreds of templates available where small business owners need only enter the name, address, and a few other points of interest about the company. Voila! Your Website is up and running and visible to the world. A more formidable site with additional features can replace this at a later time.

Just about anyone who can get on the Internet with a credit card can register a domain name and set up a simple site. For those who are too busy or not comfortable enough with all of this, pay your nephew or the kid in the shipping room a little extra to do the job. The skills needed at this level are very easy to find, and many aspiring Internet mavens are eager to get some production experience on their resumes. Make sure the information entered is correct, and make sure you have the user names and passwords to get back into the account and later take over or reassign the job.

The simplest Website should explain commonly asked questions about the company, such as location, hours, business specialty, and your Unique Selling Proposition (Chapter 2). In fact, many sites have an FAQ, or Frequently Asked Questions page, to provide the most needed information quickly to visitors.

This, and any text or pictures describing a small business, is called "content." Writing content is normally the job of the small business, not the Website designer. Be prepared to do a lot of writing, or rewrite existing marketing materials for the Internet. Once the Website is up and running, the new domain name should be added to all marketing materials and can be used by inside and outside sales reps to reference when customers need commonly requested information and to establish credibility.

As the Website grows, extra features are commonly considered that require expertise beyond the skills of most small business owners. Applications such as Adobe Photoshop and Macromedia Fireworks are used to create or edit pictures (GIFS or JPEGS); Macromedia Dreamweaver or Microsoft FrontPage and HTML are used to lay out and design Web pages and structure sites; and when "dynamic content" is needed (the Web page changes depending upon what the visitor wants to see), expertise in programs such as Java, Java Script, .NET, ASP, mySQL, osCommerce, php, and Perl may be required.

Remember that in all marketing efforts, form and substance work together to create an overall impression in the minds of visitors. Make sure the people working on the site have a good feel for the latest designs, colors, and structures of other successful locations. This is where great value may be gained from working with the right outside Website design company.

Internet sites are normally built on developmental machines and then sent to the Website server when completed, where they are then "published" or available for the world to see. The files are usually sent via FTP, or File Transport Protocol, with easy-to-use programs such as CuteFTP.

Remember that a Website is never really finished but should be considered a continuing work in progress. After the first few pages are up and running, the next step for many firms is to add extra features, as described in the next section.

Additional Website Features

Once your first Website is set up, it won't be long before extra features seem like a good idea. At this point, the skill sets needed are more formidable, and so a Website design firm should be contracted. The objective here is to gain a modern, appropriate look and feel in the context of the small business, and fast, professional work. Also, the overall structure of the Website is critical in allowing visitors to find what they need quickly, and thereby promote your company.

A local Website design company is not required because the latest changes can be viewed on the Internet quickly and easily, but there are benefits in dealing with a vendor doing business across town rather than across the country. Locating a good Website design firm is not difficult. It can be accomplished in much the same manner as finding computer expertise, discussed in Chapter 8.

Some of the extra features to be considered are:

☐ **E-mail Newsletter.** This could be a great way to continually promote products and services. The newsletter should contain relevant information and articles so that readers don't consider it to be spam, and it should be sent twice a month at most for the same reason. Various Internet services and software

are available that allow small businesses to set up and administer the production and distribution of e-mail newsletters quickly. Professional administration is especially important these days so that your e-mails are not labeled as spam and blocked by big hitters such as AOL and Earthlink. Features such as automatic opt-in (where the newsletter is sent only to those who have requested it) and one-click remove (recipients may immediately stop receiving e-mails by clicking one link without remembering user names and passwords) are essential in this respect.

☐ **Support Center.** Visitors can download installation instructions, technical information, diagrams, and details on how to fix problems. This could be an important selling point to prospective customers.

☐ **Industry Information.** Some Websites seek to draw visitors by becoming a community resource. A doctor specializing in hyperbaric medicine (problems associated with deep-sea diving), for example, might offer information such as diving tables and information about shellfish poisoning. The doctor is providing information needed by this community.

☐ **On-Line Catalog.** A catalog in this sense means lots of Web pages describing the products and services offered by your small business, but customers do not have the option of buying from the Website. This option is especially relevant to small businesses selling complex or regulated products, where on-line sales are not feasible but where customers may need detailed product information. A distributor of pharmaceutical products, for example, cannot ship prescription drugs to unknown buyers. The same reasoning applies to gun dealers, industrial chemical suppliers, and many others. But in each case, the sales force may greatly appreciate the ease and speed of getting customers to Web pages where detailed product information and details are immediately available and can be reviewed on the telephone or in person, rather than spending the time and money and suffering the loss of sales momentum in mailing the same data.

☐ **Lead-Generation Tools.** This addition to the on-line catalog allows viewers to push a button, fill in a form, and request more information or a telephone call from a sales rep. This may be an inexpensive and effective way to increase sales.

☐ **Live Chat.** One way to reduce the number of inbound telephone calls for customer service and support is to set up an Internet chat service (for example, Groopz, at www.groopz.com), where customers are encouraged (usually, by not giving out your telephone number) to communicate via computer with operators in real time rather than call. Website visitors type their concerns into a chat window, where a live operator on your end can manage several calls at once. For special situations, such as an opportunity to sell the customer a better product, promotional Web pages and files can be pushed (sent) to the customer.

☐ **Search.** Many larger sites offer a search feature where visitors can cut through all of the mumbo-jumbo and just see pages with a particular keyword. This is a relatively easy add-on, and is especially relevant for sites with a lot of information. The search capability may be a key feature in enhancing useability and separating your site from others.

☐ **Customized Features.** Special services can be added, such as asking visitors a series of questions to help them select the best product, calculate the financial effects of a purchase over time, or other special needs they may have. Such services are custom-developed by programmers in the various disciplines listed previously.

Considering an E-Store

On-line sales continue to grow at an unbelievable rate. Even when the economy is chugging along at a 2 percent to 3 percent growth rate, sales on the Internet are increasing at a rate of 10 percent to 20 percent per year (depending upon the market segment). In some cases, Internet sales are simply displacing purchases that would have occurred in retail locations, but maybe your small business should take advantage of this sales channel, which now exceeds $1 billion in revenue per week.

E-commerce also continues to grab a larger share of total retail sales. In 1999, e-commerce sales totaled $5 billion, increased to over $16 billion in 2004, and are expected to reach $316 billion by 2010 (Census Bureau, Forrester Research, ClickZ, as reported in *Processor Magazine,* September 2004).

Gaining an additional revenue stream from e-commerce is an alternative that should be carefully thought out. Customers from all over the world may shop all day, the growth numbers cited above are compelling, and many small businesses believe this is the future. On the other hand, e-commerce requires new methods, concerns, and infrastructure and may affect existing sales channels.

Many small businesses are finding the setup and operation of an e-store increasingly easy and affordable. Many find that an e-store is a handy augmentation tool for the inside sales force. In some cases, the entire sales transaction takes place on-line, and buyer and seller have no direct communication. In other cases, the e-store attracts buyers, but many want to speak with a real person for a few minutes before entering their credit card and committing to the sale. Some operations are set up so that the inside sales force or call-center can fully explain products, close the original sale, and then up-sell customers into higher revenues, suggest high-margin accessories, or work out expedited shipping arrangements. In any case, your small business will need to commit resources to a call-in center to fully maximize benefits from the e-store and handle customer service issues.

The theme of this section is how to consider, set up, and launch an e-store. All the major dimensions of running an e-store are discussed, along with the resources that will be needed.

Access to Cheap Prices

The most important factor to on-line sellers these days is access to low prices. Pricing on the Internet is hypercompetitive, and the only way to make a reasonable margin is by purchasing and reselling at discount. If your small business is accustomed to selling at normal retail prices, this will prove untenable on the Internet because it's just too easy for shoppers to check prices and shop elsewhere. Shoppers can check dozens of competitors in a minute or less, and there is little loyalty. Every small business contemplating an e-store must have access to very low prices or everything else is for naught. An important exception is firms who manufacture or have access to difficult-to-find items, such as replacement parts for business equipment.

Estimating product margins through the e-store is easy. Because the costs are known, pretend you are shopping on the Internet and see what these products sell for in other e-stores, then subtract direct expenses. Can you make serious money this way? Don't try to answer before reading the rest of this section.

Will Your Product Sell?

Beyond pricing, determine first if your products can really sell through an e-store. For example, some products cannot legally be shipped (certain chemicals, alcoholic beverages, animals, weapons); others may require government

Joe Turns Trash to Cash on eBay

Our small business had a large number of high-end, esoteric computer products used only by larger businesses, and they weren't selling. This subsystem could be of use only to certain businesses that had already installed similar equipment, and these companies were scattered across the U.S. Potential customers were difficult to find through our conventional methods of smiling and dialing. And as always with technology-related equipment, prices were always headed south.

We decided to try eBay. I worked from my computer at home late into the evening one night to open an account and set up the ad. I though I was wasting my time and money. Selling high-end business equipment through the Internet seemed unlikely.

It actually took a few days to get the first auction up and running, as we edited and posted digital pictures and learned a little more about credit cards, Paypal, html, and other details.

We set the first auction for seven days, but after only three days had our first bid. This was exciting. Although we thought the equipment would sell only to large businesses, a small business owner in Alabama had found the equipment and placed a bid for $2,100. We would not have ever found this buyer otherwise—and the bid was considerably more than the $300 we were getting by selling the same equipment as parts. Things were clicking.

The auction ended and we soon had our equipment on a truck headed to Alabama. The buyer was delighted with the purchase and our business relationship expanded into other areas from this first sale.

approvals to sell (imported toys, cosmetics, vitamins), and still others are too fragile to be shipped (to test, drop-kick a packaged sample item across the room; this is what happens after the delivery truck leaves your loading dock).

Also, most on-line selling these days is centered on keyword searches. For example, from Yahoo! or Google, a shopper types in a keyword (also known as "search term") such as "Seagate," and hyperlinks to dozens of e-stores appear on the screen. If there are great keywords to associate with your ads (for example, Nike, Ralph Lauren, or other household names) and access to great prices, then we're off to a great start. If there are no distinguishing search terms that shoppers frequently use when looking for your product, it will be difficult for anyone to find the e-store through keyword searches. Other promotional means would be needed, which are often prohibitively expensive except when a firm selling business or industrial parts promotes an e-store to other businesses through its sales force.

Fast Shipping

Most Internet shoppers these days expect shipment of their order within 24 hours. If your small business is already shipping products, this may be easy to do. Otherwise, be prepared to hustle furiously to process orders in the morning, pack after lunch, and finish before the UPS pickup in the afternoon. Even though we are talking about the Internet here, many sellers cannot completely automate these processes, and much work and stress is involved in processing credit cards, printing shipping labels, packing boxes, etc. And attention Quickbooks users: Don't expect much integration between the e-store and the accounting system. This is also generally true of other accounting and e-commerce applications, where seamless integration remains a dream.

For some products, it's necessary to offer the full range of shipping alternatives from cheapest-and-slowest to expensive-and-expedited. Since there may be many different products and different weights, and since buyers may purchase several items from an e-store at once, some sellers offer different size-and-weight combinations in addition to different delivery methods. This can get very complex very fast. The easy solution? Find a competitor with a simple shipping deal, then offer the same to your customers. For example, if a competitor offers "Standard Shipping $9.95 anywhere in the continental U.S. in three business days," then a simple plan like this may be the best. In some cases, shipping expenses will actually end up costing more than this, but on balance, the whole store may produce more revenues and profits.

As business grows, there are powerful shipping options that can be connected to the e-store. These allow buyers to punch in their zip code and see many shipping alternatives at once. Once again, this is a great feature, but can be too much to handle in the beginning. Perhaps the best advice is to add full shipping options after the e-store is a success.

Additional information on shipping solutions for e-stores is available from UPS.com, FedEx.com, USPS.gov, and through e-store providers such as Yahoo (http://smallbusiness.yahoo.com).

Credit Card and E-Payment Systems

Accepting, managing, and accounting for credit cards and other forms of e-payment is a major component of running an e-store. Chapter 13 is devoted to this subject.

Ad Copy

Small businesses that already use printed catalogs certainly have an advantage in setting up an e-store, but be prepared to spend time checking each ad in the catalog and review for appropriateness in the new Internet store. For example, an inside sales force may know how to look up in a printed catalog and describe K5E-1KSTP-YL, CAT-5E Cable, 24AWG, STP, 4 Pairs, Solid, 1000', Yellow, $57.30. But this description will need to be prettied up and expanded to please new Internet customers. Also, remember that buyers love photographs, even if they know exactly what they are buying. So you'll need digital photographs of each item, cut to a white or neutral background. Be sure to budget enough time and money for all of this.

If your small business distributes a large number of products, consider offering only the hot sellers initially in the e-store. Allow a few weeks to resolve any problems, and then expand to include the entire product line.

Call-Center

Many Internet shoppers prefer to conduct research on the Web but then call a toll-free number to ask a few final questions and place the order. A call-center is also needed for customer service. For a small business, this can be as simple as adding one PC to the network, installing an extra phone line, and assigning a cheery, sharp person to handle calls. But call-centers add to the cost of doing business and must be carefully factored in to business plans because margins will already be thin. And what kind of sales volume is needed to support all this? If the business plan shows that 100 shipments per day are needed to break even, and expects that this will require 50 inbound telephone calls, is it feasible that your small staff can do this without extra help?

Interestingly, many successful e-stores strive to create a well-designed e-store that attempts to answer all frequently asked customer questions and that does not promote a toll-free telephone number. At some sites, there is much information and guidance allowing customers to research, compare, and purchase on-line—but many sellers don't necessarily want to speak with customers, because each call is extra time and expense. These vendors are striking the balance between converting e-store shoppers into buyers and striving to minimize costs.

Despite this, a call-center with toll-free lines is essential and can distinguish your store from others, give comfort to customers, even if they never call, react quickly to customer service situations, and perhaps most important, take orders from the many customers who want to give their credit card information to a real person rather than an Internet site.

Vermont Company Gets Its Bear-ings On-Line

Here's a great story about a successful small business that was around for a long time but really came into its own by selling its products on-line.

Vermont Teddy Bear sold the majority of its products through a telephone call-center for more than 20 years. Most of its customers are men, and the biggest holiday season at this company is Valentine's Day. The problem with telephone call-centers, however, is that customers often have trouble visualizing what they are buying. Catalogs help, but printing and mailing costs are expensive, and the time frame is slow.

Then, in 1997, Vermont Teddy Bear (www.VermontTeddyBear.com) opened an e-store. Once grizzly customers could now browse through the Website and see different products before ordering, and compare clothing and accessories, too. The amount of time needed to complete sales through more expensive telephone sales reps decreased, and the company could now pander (they say "panda") to customers by shipping most orders the same day.

Of course, this small business uses on-line marketing techniques to promote its products, but good old radio spots directed to male audiences are also heavily used. The company has found that sometimes, men and women have un-bearable problems, but just about everyone melts when a nice teddy bear appears.

Bearing witness to the effects of a solid Unique Selling Proposition, a well run e-store, and both on-line and traditional marketing efforts, Vermont Teddy Bear has seen sales through its e-store increase to $28 million per year, accounting for around half of total revenues, while the remainder of the industry has been in a state of hibernation.

Fulfillment Companies

When sales volume approaches 100 units per day, its often time to consider outsourcing e-store and call-center activities to a fulfillment company. Fulfillment firms are happy to take over just about any ordering and shipping activity, and are frequently a good option for small businesses that don't want to get overly involved in e-store operations. Most of these companies got their start in the mail-order business as infomercial-related commerce gained steam in the 1980s, and now happily serve e-store operators. Utilizing these firms allows small business owners to focus on sales, marketing, and cost controls, while outsourcing functions such as call-centers, warehousing, shipping, inventory control, accounting, order processing, returns, and exchanges.

There are many fulfillment companies across the U.S. The easiest way to find a local firm is to search for "Fulfillment Company" on your favorite search engine.

Recruiting

Your small business will need lots of grunts to build the store, upload the catalog, process, ship orders, and make the accounting entries. The good news is that it's now easy to recruit great people at low prices for this type of work. Many job searchers, especially towards the entry level, are looking for an opportunity to break into e-commerce and develop their skills. Place a well-written ad (see Chapter 6) and ask for responses by e-mail. The recruiting in-box will soon be bulging.

The skill sets needed will vary depending upon the type of e-store you envision. At a minimum, anyone building the store or catalog will need to know HTML and associated products such as Macromedia's Dreamweaver, Fireworks, and Coldfusion; Microsoft's FrontPage and Excel; as well as Adobe PhotoShop. If additional functionalities are needed (such as dynamic pages), other skills may be necessary, including Java, Java Script, .NET, ASP, mySQL, php, osCommerce, Perl, Microsoft VBA (Visual Basic for Applications), and Microsoft Access. If these skills are well-known within your small business, consider managing the project internally. However, if the programs listed above sound like a bunch of mumbo-jumbo, start off by contracting an e-store development vendor since all of this is a bit much to learn quickly. A checklist and sample e-store development proposal and agreement may be seen at www.TheSmallBusinessOwnersManual.com.

Extra marketing help may also be desirable. A marketing analyst is often needed to tweak pricing and specials continually relative to competitive sites, watch the success of keyword ads, and drive marketing campaigns such as cross-sells, up-sells, holiday specials, express-shipping options, etc. In this case, the new hire already should be familiar with dozens of Websites frequented by shoppers and Internet-selling mavens, and know how e-stores are affected by variations in keyword ads.

For other recruits, however, fewer technical skills are needed. Administrators who process credit card orders and handle e-mails, packing and shipping types, and customer service reps may only need basic PC and Internet skills. Entry-level types do need tight and effective management, however, to schedule staff around the various tasks and to optimize efforts on a continual basis.

Hopefully, in-house staff can be used for some of this, but beware if the project is off to a slow start. The best argument for using an outside contractor is that things get done quickly and with fewer headaches, and the cash begins rolling in sooner. Although e-stores are easier to set up and operate than before, much has not been automated and never will (for example, taping boxes), so as business volume grows, expect to work with lots of new staff to keep things moving.

Channel Conflict

Small business owners should be aware that others may not be wild about your new on-line store. Consider how distributors, dealers, retailers, VARs, or other parts of the sales channel feel about getting cut out. Many retailers, for example, become angry at vendors when a customer walks in the store, examines a product, asks lots of time-consuming questions, and then leaves to buy the exact same item for a cheaper price on the Internet. Antagonizing established and lucrative parts of the sales channel is risking a revenue stream that is here-and-now, versus the promise of perhaps selling more at some later time on the Internet. This is the dilemma faced by many small business owners.

Some traditional sellers have found a way around this by setting up a separate company to handle all e-commerce sales.

In some cases, setting up an e-store may displease the channels, and in other cases selling outside of channels may not be allowed at all, according to agreements signed with customers. But the small business owner may still decide that the future is coming and that ultimately an e-store will be the best means of growing revenues.

eBay

Ebay is an alternative to an on-line store, where specific items are "launched" and then either auctioned or sold in a limited period of time (for example, 10 days). Entire books are available on the eBay experience, but a few words are offered here to help you consider the overall situation.

Ebay is sometimes used by small businesses as a separate selling channel, and, just as important, as a means of pulling shoppers into the e-store. The biggest issue among on-line sellers remains how to drive traffic to their sites. For example, if your small business sells bicycles, a few hot-selling, low-priced models can be offered on eBay. But in one subtle way or another, the eBay browser is encouraged to visit your on-line store directly and shop for more expensive models and lots of high-margin accessories. In this way, eBay can be the most effective means of driving traffic to an e-store. Many sellers even set up a store on eBay for this purpose only. Not surprisingly, eBay is happy to accommodate vendors in this way through its "eBay Store" program, since transactions are still settled on their site and eBay earns handsome fees. Ebay is less happy when sellers lure buyers away and onto other sites, and they thereby miss out on the fees.

Don't expect high prices on eBay. It is true that most items sell at heavy discounts off normal end-user prices to buyers who can wait a few days for the transaction and shipping to conclude. The competition on eBay is extreme, and there are many sellers with "high-feedback ratings" (meaning that buyers know they are legitimate and reliable). It is interesting that a seller such as "aaaaronsairplanes," selling model airplane motors from an apartment in the middle of nowhere, can be a serious competitor to an established small business with a leased warehouse and business office, lots of employees, design know-how, computers, taxes, and overhead.

Fraud, Scams, and Viruses

Credit card fraud and related scams are an unfortunate part of the Internet landscape. Small businesses that do not worry about this much now will need extra vigilance as e-mail and credit card systems are put into place.

To begin, insides sales and administrative people working the e-mails must constantly be on the lookout for new viruses, phishers, worms, scams, hackers, and frauds (see Chapter 14). Extra vigilance is required, and small businesses must set up systems and shift gears in thinking, so that all are aware that these systems are constantly under attack. An e-store is only as strong as its weakest link.

A related problem for the small business owner is that all new employees must be informed of these threats quickly, because just about everyone needs access to one important on-line account or another. In the rush to keep things going, it's easy to forget.

For example, anyone working the e-mails should expect several official-looking "urgent notices" every week describing the importance of pressing a link right away and reentering user names and passwords of the most important on-line banking and related accounts. Virtually all of these are scams. It takes just one hapless error for an important account to be lost to bad people across the country or on another continent.

If an account is compromised and something terrible happens, law-enforcement agencies will barely lift a finger to help. The problem is too small, spread among too many jurisdictions, too complicated, and too intangible for busy and disin-terested law-enforcement authorities. Scammers know that the chances of get-ting caught are extremely slim, so if your small business loses money in this manner, it's probably not worth the time even to file a police report.

Finally, expect that at least one virus-laden e-mail per day will test your sys-tems. Know how to deal with this by making sure that antivirus definitions are updated daily and that employees know how to minimize the risk of computer virus infections.

Sales Taxes

Sellers must generally collect, report, and pay sales taxes on shipments within their state, and various counties and other taxing jurisdictions may also want a piece of the action. This can be a real headache, especially in the beginning. There are three ways to approach this problem.

First, learn what must be done to comply with sales tax laws, and do it. Most small business owners must learn something about sales taxes anyway, so conduct a little more research and learn your responsibilities and liabilities when orders are shipped from specific locations to customers in diverse areas. Although compliance with sales taxes are complicated, most states offer taxpayers supporting seminars, informative Websites, call-centers, and printed materials.

Normally, a seller is responsible for collecting and paying sales taxes on transactions shipped to states where they have a physical (for example, office) presence. (Theoretically, customers in other states are supposed to report their purchase to local taxing authorities and pay the corollary of the sales tax, which is the use tax. This is undoubtedly a rare occurrence.) Learn if the order-processing system collects this information and if appropriate sales tax reports can be generated. And, by the way—is the system charging sales tax to customers? Don't assume that your e-commerce system knows what to do regarding sales taxes, because the seller is liable to pay the state regardless.

The second solution: Ignore sales taxes for a few months. After things have settled down from opening the e-store, time will be available to run the reports, fill out the forms, and pay sales taxes due. Also, taxes due will most likely be a very small amount because buyers often jump to a competitor anyway when they realize that the total price, including sales taxes, is no longer the best deal.

Finally, the entire matter may be turned over to a CPA. Professional accountants are very familiar with sales taxes, but many are not familiar with e-stores. The CPA will probably be able to prepare sales taxes only after special reports are run from the e-store. Be prepared either to run these reports or to give the CPA access to the on-line store.

Much more is said about sales and use taxes in Chapter 7.

There is much to be considered when setting up an e-store, and it takes a large amount of work and time to set up the required systems. Nevertheless, on-line sales continue to soar, and an e-store may become an essential part of your revenue mix. Small business owners should consider this selling option carefully and be prepared to bring in the help that is needed to study, design, set up, and operate a successful Internet shopping site.

Setting up an E-Store

Considering all of this, how do you set up an on-line store? There are too many alternatives to review here comprehensively, but a few are outlined. Our purpose is to give small business owners enough information to decide which options to fully investigate.

Rather than buy workstations, servers, special software, extra Internet services, and lots of people to make all of this work, the easiest place to begin might be to use the programs already available at locations such as Yahoo, Amazon, MSN (Microsoft Network), and many others. In simple situations, there is no need to reinvent the wheel.

At Yahoo, for example, new sellers may go to http://smallbusiness.yahoo.com/ (note no "www" in this address) and sign up for a low-end package such as "Merchant Starter," where $40 per month buys a catalog, shopping cart checkout system, software tools, a domain name, e-mail accounts, and more. After this is set up, sellers jump back on their local machine to make a product spreadsheet, including prices, descriptions, photos, and other information. This is then pumped (in technical terms, FTP'd) from a local workstation into the new e-store.

Running Faster but Losing Ground

Selling many items on the Internet these days is easy, but sometimes it's difficult to actually make a buck, especially on electronics products. Often, the decision comes down to who has the lowest price on certain model numbers. When buyers search and see pricing from many vendors at once, they inevitably pick the lowest number.

I once helped a small business move large quantities of disk drives on both eBay and an e-store, and everyone was delighted—we were selling for around $60 each and the disks were flying off the shelves. Lots of sellers had the same model, SZ118202LX, but our prices were the best by about $2—and it made a difference.

Then suddenly it slowed. Our volume declined by about 50 percent in just a couple of days. We checked and found that major competitors had lowered their prices to the $55 – $58 range. We sweat megabytes. Our company had huge quantities of the disks, and we could not afford to sit on them. It was only a matter of time until prices fell further, so the only way to keep them moving through the Internet was to lower our prices.

We did. The disks started flying off the shelves again. The competitors did the same. Their sales went up and ours went down. This went on and on.

It was a race to the bottom. In the disk-drive world especially, prices either fall fast or they fall slow. But they are always falling. No one wants to get caught with inventory. We had huge quantities on our shelves, however, and great determination not to get caught holding the bag.

We finally came across a marketing trick that paid off royally. Rather than sell the disk as a single model number, we turned our SZ118202LX into many different products. Suddenly, we were selling larger quantities by calling our product "SZ118202LX for IBM", "SZ118202LX for Compaq", "SZ118202LX for Dell", and so on. Buyers paid a bit more because they had an extra assurance that this disk would work on their specific computer.

Finally, the last SZ118202LX was gone from our shelves, but we learned that the secret to Internet sales is not in inventory, but in marketing.

Once the e-store is established, credit card authorization and acceptance systems must be set up. Fortunately, this is much easier these days, as many card merchants are familiar with Internet stores and almost everything can be done on-line. Be prepared to pay slightly higher rates than brick-and-mortar retail stores to make up for the extra potential fraud. Overall discount rates are now about 2 percent to 3 percent off the gross amount of the sale, plus 20 cents to 30 cents per transaction, plus a flat fee of about $20 to $30 per month.

For more information on credit and electronic payments systems, see Chapter 13.

Promoting Your Products and Services on the Internet

The best Website is of little use if no one knows it's there. That is why small business owners must strive constantly to ensure that their Website is promoted to both old and new visitors. Much of this depends on having a good listing with the search engines. It is well-known, for example, that when most Internet browsers conduct a new search, they carefully read the listings on the first page, sometimes get to the second page, and rarely go further. Several means of promoting your Website are described below.

Search Engine Marketing and Keyword Ads

The rage in Internet marketing these days is keyword ads and Search Engine Marketing (SEM), which have supplanted alternatives such as e-mail (heavily used but not effective), banner ads, and other techniques. There are a few steps in this process.

First, sellers of products or services set up accounts at Google (to advertise on Google, of course), or Overture.com (for advertising on parent company Yahoo.com as well as AltaVista.com, CNN.com, Excite.com, Go2Net.com, InfoSpace.com, MSN.com, Sympactico.ca, and others).

Sellers then enter their Website domain name, brief informative ads (perhaps 150 characters and no superlatives), and keywords relevant to the specific product or service. These are called "keyword ads" (also known as "Adwords" on Google.com, "Precision Match" on Overture.com, and other terms elsewhere). Sellers also enter the price they are willing to pay for the ad. Top bidders get top placement, which is the first listing on the first search results page; lower bids appear later.

Keyword ads then appear to browsers who conduct keyword searches from sites such as Google.com, Yahoo.com, and many others. These are also known as "sponsored" or "featured" listings. Sellers pay only when an ad is clicked, which then sends the browser to the seller's Website or e-store.

Once you attract browsers to the seller's site, your objective is to turn the browsers into buyers. At this point, small businesses offering relatively inexpensive and commodity-type products should direct the shopper right to the e-store to purchase and continue shopping. It is a "best practice" always to send the browser to the exact product page they searched for or a "jump" page that contains a number of products that fall under a more general search term. Overture.com has an Advertiser Center with a number of tutorials that provide great reference tools for newer on-line advertisers.

For firms offering more complex and expensive products, or for service-oriented businesses, viewers are directed to relevant pages at the company's Website, where the objective is to generate interest and telephone queries.

As an example, go to Google.com and search for "Garmin Streetpilot." Or for services, search for "Los Angeles Quickbooks Help." Virtually every site shown on the results pages is generated from keyword ads.

As noted previously, an interesting facet of keyword advertising is that the seller pays only when someone clicks the link from the search engine. This allows for carefully tuned marketing programs. Depending upon the search term used, prices can vary from 5 cents to more than $70 per click. Depending on the business model, some firms can afford a high cost per acquisition (that is, determining an affordable price for one new customer). *The Wall Street Journal* reported that "Mesothelioma Lawyer" is the most expensive keyword, and law firms have paid over $70 per click for the highest possible listing. Most clicks cost from 10 cents to $2.

Many new advertisers are quick to think, "What if my competitor just sits at the computer and clicks my links all day—I'll pay a fortune for that!" But keyword ad vendors are quick to point out that they have the means of detecting fraudulent clicks and will not charge advertisers when they occur.

For many small businesses, keyword ads are now *the* way to promote products and services on the Internet. Still, as with the e-commerce selling alternative already described, Search Engine Marketing programs can augment but not replace an inside or outside sales force. Keyword ads can be used to generate visitors to your e-store or Website, or calls to the call-center. Some firms have reported huge increases in business from well-thought-out SEM campaigns, and many newer small businesses rely almost exclusively on keyword ads to generate their revenues.

Here is a summary of the pros and cons of keyword ads.

Pros:

- Sellers advertise only to customers interested in very specific products or services.

- Advertising budgets can be set with great precision per day, week, or month by using built-in budgeting features.

- You get great marketing statistics on program effectiveness.

- Advertisers can set a maximum price per ad (click-through).

Cons:

- Much time is required to monitor, administer, and track the performance of these programs.

- Some buyers distinguish between these "featured results," which they correctly consider to be an advertisement, and natural results (to be discussed), which often are considered to be more credible.

- Ads on the Internet, of course, lead to sales on the Internet—which often means reduced prices and increased exposure to credit card fraud.

Many small businesses will find it difficult to mount an effective paid keyword search marketing program continually. A great deal of time is required to keep up-to-date on the industry and to monitor SEM programs. Here, better results may be obtained through working with a Search Engine Marketing firm. How do you find one? Why not try an Internet keyword search? It seems these firms might know something about this. Just type "Search Engine Marketing" into your favorite browser and see over 10 million links.

As long as we're looking at these links, notice the difference between paid and natural results (the other links). The importance of this is discussed in the next section. In Yahoo, for example, the paid links (labeled "Sponsor Results") are at the top of the search results in the left-hand column, and comprise all of the listings in the narrower right hand column. The other links are natural results.

Natural Search Results, Spiders, Robots and Crawlers

In the previous section, we described paid search results. But even more powerful results may come from "natural" or "organic" searches. There is nothing complicated about natural search results; they are simply the natural—or unpaid for—links that appear in just about any Internet search. Since the links do not have the look and appearance of a paid result or advertisement, they are ostensibly non-biased, meaning that the search engine did not accept money to influence the rankings. Thus, many Internet users consider natural search results to be more credible.

Understanding this is important, because savvy searchers who know the difference are more likely to hold natural search engine results in higher regard, just as television viewers may watch a local news story about a new restaurant more carefully than a paid advertisement from the same firm.

Even in this time of mushrooming popularity of paid searches, about 70 percent of user click-throughs are to natural search results. And the legitimacy of natural versus paid searches is likely to increase in the future, as more Internet users become aware of the differences. On the other hand, there may well be more than enough for all, as many Internet shoppers will be happy to click through known paid search ads to find the prices and selection they desire.

The next question is: How can your Website gain a high ranking in a natural keyword Internet search?

One way is by feeding the spiders, robots, and crawlers who come to visit your Website. These are programs run by the search engines that automatically follow links from one page to another as they crawl around the Internet. When a new site is discovered, it is examined for keywords, and these are then sent back to the search engine, analyzed, and indexed. Because Websites change frequently, these creatures return often to look for new updates so that search engines can quickly pick up changes. Google, Inktomia, and AltaVista are examples of crawler-based search engines.

Search engines known as "directories" use actual humans to analyze Websites. Editors who visit Internet locations categorize them, and write the titles then assemble directories and descriptions that form the basis of what appears in searches. LookSmart is an example of a human-powered directory.

MSN and Yahoo are hybrids in that both Crawlers and human-powered directories are used to analyze Websites.

The good news here for small business owners is that no extra work at all is required for the Website to be visited and reranked. The results may not be to your liking (your Website appears low in the rankings), so many firms take steps to insert certain words and links into areas of their Internet sites and adjust the architecture to improve natural search rankings.

Some Websites try to trick search engines by exaggerating their offerings. As a result, a kind of cat-and-mouse game takes place where search engines constantly change the algorithms used to evaluate Websites, Website owners then tune their sites to tilt the results of the search engines, the search engines change their algorithms again, and the game goes on.

It is impractical for a small business owner to get ahead of this game, so the solution is to work with firms specializing in Search Engine Optimization (SEO). These small businesses keep up-to-date on the latest techniques used by the various search engines and perform the following tasks to increase the visibility of their Website:

- Keyword selection.
- Competitive analysis.
- Optimize Web pages to get the best search results.
- Build links to related sites.
- Submit the newly tuned site to search engines for analysis.
- Continually test search results, report, and modify as needed.

There are thousands of SEO firms all over the U.S. Everyone approaches this continually changing area differently, but if Internet marketing is important to your small business, it is important to work with professionals to achieve the best results. To find a firm that can increase the natural search engine rankings for your Website, type "Search Engine Optimization" into a favorite search engine. Note also that many firms offer both SEO and SEM (described previously) services.

From a marketing perspective, many firms need to complement their paid marketing leads (see previous discussion) with free marketing leads (this section) in order to achieve a cost per acquisition that falls within the target range. While SEOs are expensive at first glance, think of this as a one-time expense that can be amortized over several hundred conversions.

Website Architecture

The design and content of your Website, especially the home page, greatly affect the listing position with search engines. The architecture also significantly affects the user's experience when visiting the site. A well-designed site is easy to navigate, and information can be located quickly. Visitors will not hang around for long at a badly designed site, which means low conversion rates and reduced sales.

The design, architecture, and overall look and feel of a good Website for your small business remains an art, not a science or something amenable to straightforward rules. That is why a Website designed by professionals will make a huge difference in the marketing results realized by your small business. Beyond Website design, Website promotion is developing into a separate art form, and there are many SEM and SEO firms that specialize in just this area. For all but the simplest of sites, the small business owner is encouraged to play a different role and contract experts to make all of this look good, produce results, and fully exploit the vast potential of Internet marketing.

The small business owner should walk through the store as a customer and note awkward, unclear, or problematic areas, as well as needed extra content and features. If something does not make sense to the seller, it definitely will not make sense to the buyer. Simple things such as a search box for the site can make a huge difference in customer satisfaction. Test every button and small feature, because this is often where the problems lie. Go through the entire buying process, including ordering by credit card and entering real shipping instructions. Then make sure the order is processed correctly. Problems may then be reported to the Website designers, who will fix them.

This process is not a one-time audit but should be a continuing effort, because things break down even in e-commerce.

Link Exchanges

Another popular and inexpensive feature used to increase Website traffic is to exchange links with other sites. Visitors to these other sites then see links to your Website, and search engine spiders see the links and increase the site's ranking in keyword searches. The hyperbaric doctor (problems associated with deep-sea diving, described earlier in this chapter), for example, might exchange links with hyperbaric chambers in the area, equipment rental locations, diving instructors, and doctors in related specialties.

Conventional Advertising

Finally, we sometimes forget that Websites can and should be promoted through conventional forms of promotion. These might include printing the name of your Website on letterhead, business cards, envelopes, packaging materials, bus benches, giveaways such as pens and T-shirts, printed advertisements, and just about any other form of communication used by your small business.

The "Vermont Company Gets Its Bear-ings On-Line" story presented previously is a great example of how a successful e-store does much of its advertising off-line.

Many good articles have been written and there are Websites concerned with building and promoting effective Websites. Stick to the recent ones, because things are changing all the time. Two sites worth investigating are www.bruceclay.com, with information and advice on search engine optimization and search engine ranking, and http://www.monash.com/spidap.html, which is about understanding and using search engines. There is also a great deal of additional information on these subjects at http://SmallBusiness.Yahoo.com/marketing (no "www"), www.TheSmallBusinessOwnersManual.com, Google.com, and Overture.com.

Finally, look into www.InternetRetailer.com. Here, small business owners may learn a great deal about e-commerce from the Website, and then keep up-to-date with an e-mail newsletter and a subscription to a hard-copy magazine.

Chapter 6

Hiring and Firing: Weeding and Seeding

Hiring the First Employees

Your small business is expanding and it's time to hire your first employee—and *double* the workforce. Or maybe a full staff is already in place but it's time to become more formal. If you've never hired anyone before, then this is one of the biggest decisions so far. After all, the company's payroll is about to explode. Hiring the wrong person will result in months of wasted time, thousands of dollars lost through investment in the wrong person, and bad feelings for all. On the other hand, recruiting the right person can make life easier, customers happier, and keep the business growing.

Chances are, money is tight and things are tenuous, so the quality of the new hire is critical. There are many things to consider when hiring the first employee and then recruiting and managing correctly as the company continues to grow. Inevitably, employees will move on, and so it is equally important that the small business owner understands about resignations and terminations and their legal implications.

The big word to remember for the moment is "recruiting," because even after the right person is found, your company and the opportunity you are offering must be presented as a worthwhile investment of some part of someone's life. Good employees do not take this decision lightly. Beyond getting paid well, they want a pleasant place to work, like-minded co-workers, benefits, and the prospect of growth. That's often not an easy sell for a small business. Many potential employees may be wary of getting trapped in a difficult job with an amateur entrepreneur. Keep in mind that throughout the hiring process, and especially after employment commences, you may be buying the services of employees; but the benefits of working for your small business must be sold at the same time. Further, all of this takes longer than you may expect.

Time Frame for Hiring

Many small businesses get blind-sided by not realizing that it takes a long time to find, recruit, and hire a new employee. Here are the steps, taking from 51 to 103 days—if nothing goes wrong:

- **Decide it's Time to Hire a New Employee.** It often takes 10 to 30 days from that feeling of "Gee, things are getting too busy around here" until "Okay, I guess I'd better hire a new employee."

- **Write the Job Description.** Allow one to three days to think, decide, and write—especially if the input of others is needed.

- **Inform the World.** Getting the word out can take just a few hours with a little luck and by asking the right person, or by calling a temp agency (to be discussed later). On the other hand, it may easily take 30 days before certain printed publications go to press, get distributed, and the details are communicated to the right recruiter—let's say 10 to 20 days, on average.

- **Call Candidates, Screen, and Set Up Interviews.** Allow five to 15 days, because some great candidates may apply late, and there may be difficulties scheduling interviews on short notice. (I always like it when candidates push me a bit for an interview right away.)

- **Check References; Credit and Criminal Background Check.** You'll need five to 10 days, including telephone-tag time, to catch up with references; time for the candidate to review, sign, and return the credit and criminal background check release; and for the background check to be completed. Let's hope that the promising new recruit doesn't flame out at this stage, because you've already invested a lot of time.

- **Make and Negotiate an Offer of Employment.** Each offer is unique, depending upon the recruit's situation (flexibility is one of the advantages of a small business, so take advantage of this). It's always complicated when there are two great candidates and one job. If you dance around with the first candidate too long, the second one may be lost. And then we're back to square one in the search. But let's assume it takes five to 10 days to make and present an employment offer and get back a "Yes!"

- **Resignation Period.** Most employees will need to give their current employers two weeks' notice. If they don't, is this a concern? In the meantime, it's a good idea to worry and lose sleep wondering if the current employer will offer more money.

- **Day One.** Hope the employee shows up fully dressed and completes the first day without doing something weird.

That's 51 to 103 days until help arrives—if everything goes well. So when it's time to hire someone, do yourself a favor and begin looking now.

Joe Hires Ms. Dependable

Hiring is a time-consuming and stressful process for the small business owner, and sometimes it can all fall apart despite hard work and the best intentions.

Our business had a surge in orders, and I urgently needed someone to help out. I went through the steps described above and realized that we wanted an entry-level university student. I asked around, advertised on the Internet, and then called several applicants without success, until speaking with a young lady who went to school close by. We met at a local coffee shop for an interview and she seemed perfect for the job. She had recent and similar part-time experience, she was graduating and not yet employed, and she was presentable and well-spoken. I figured that in a short period of time, I could have her working directly with clients.

Everything else checked out just fine, and we mutually agreed upon a starting date. I accommodated her desire for a little vacation before she began work and explained that I would be flexible about her hours, because she would be commuting sometimes from a long distance. I offered her an hourly compensation rate and she wanted a little more, so I agreed. After all, time was short and she was a capable candidate. And I had no one else. She agreed to everything. In fact she agreed so readily, I felt that something was not quite right.

As the starting date approached, I grew a little uncomfortable. It was too quiet. We exchanged a couple of e-mails where I welcomed her and "confirmed" some small details, but I was really trying to see if she was still committed. She acknowledged the e-mails without incident. Meanwhile, our workload increased even more, and I feared we would soon fall behind schedule.

Finally, her starting date arrived. As I walked in, I noticed that she had not yet arrived—not a good sign for the first day of work. I checked my e-mails. Sure enough, there was a polite note from the new recruit thanking me for the opportunity but informing me that "something else has come up" that would preclude her from accepting my opportunity.

If she had been an employee, I would have asked why she waited so long to tell me this, but I had no control over the situation. In retrospect, I believe she had an offer from another company, and I was the backup deal in case Job #1 fell through. There was little I could do, and it would be futile to ask her to change her mind. In addition, it would set a bad precedent for any future relations. Despite the increasing workload, I began pounding the phones again in search of a replacement for Ms. Dependable.

Exempt vs. Non-Exempt Employees

What are exempt employees, and how are they treated differently? Exempt employees are those who are not subject to the overtime pay requirements mandated by state and federal laws.

Federal Fair Labor Standards Act ("FLSA") rules require that an exempt employee be paid a full salary for any week in which work is performed, even if some days are not worked. For example, exempt employees must normally be paid the full weekly salary even if work is missed due to a temporary business closure, for arriving later and leaving early, and for medical problems lasting less than a week. Compensation also may not be reduced for civic duties such as jury duty and military service lasting less than a week. Employers may make deductions from exempt employee pay for taking full workdays off for personal reasons. In contrast, non-exempt employees are paid at an hourly rate and must be paid overtime when applicable, per state laws.

Many small businesses believe that giving an employee the title of "executive," or "manager," or "professional," or "administrative" something makes them exempt from overtime pay. Nevertheless, federal and state laws look at the substance and not the form of the relationship. Very specific criteria must be met to satisfy these requirements, and the employer's interpretation of the situation means little. These issues may surface years after an employee is improperly classified as "exempt," subjecting the employer to back pay at overtime rates, penalties, and interest.

For example, to be exempt in California, truly exempt employees need to spend at least 50 percent of their time performing duties that meet the state's definition of exempt work, such as administrative or managerial tasks. Additionally, the exempt employee must receive a salary of no less than two times the state minimum wage for full-time (40 hours per week) employment.

Before classifying employees as exempt, small business owners must review the FLSA and state laws to make sure that this treatment is correct.

At-Will Employment

Most small business owners will prefer to hire employees at-will. What does this mean?

Simply put, an at-will employee works at the will of you, the employer, and there are no promises regarding the future. At-will employees can be terminated at any time, and a reason is not needed, except that employees may not be terminated:

- Because they are of a different race, religion, ethic background, gender, sexual orientation, age, or because of disabilities.

- In retaliation for filing complaints against their employer, such as those related to OSHA, workers' compensation, whistle-blower situations, and others.

- For jury duty or military service.

Beyond this, you may simply decide that someone else is better in this position, and that is good enough to fire an at-will employee. But even this thinking does not need to be disclosed.

The good news is that the default situation is at-will employment, so small business owners do not need to craft agreements in special ways to gain this status. It is prudent, however, to mention this explicitly in a memo signed by the employee (sample at www.TheSmallBusinessOwnersManual.com).

Care should be taken that at-will does not accidentally morph into something else over time. The employment status may change unintentionally if the employer makes express assurances (in writing), or even implied assurances, such as saying, "If we get this deal, you'll have enough work for years." It may take just one careless slip for this to occur, such as referring to a position as "permanent," rather than "full-time."

In situations where employment is not at-will, the relationship is more onerous on the employer, because terminations are allowable only "with cause." With cause occurs when the employee has breached or defaulted on the conditions of employment as expressed in an employment agreement, the employee handbook, or perhaps has broken a law (for example, stolen company funds).

Employee vs. Contractor

In today's musical-chairs job market, many potential employees will ask to be contractors, or "1099s" rather than employees. This is especially common in certain industries. This important decision—employee or independent contractor—must be determined in advance before proceeding further in the hiring process.

Benefits of an Independent Contractor vs. Employee

There are many reasons small businesses prefer adding new personnel as independent contractors rather than as employees:

- Specific skill sets may be required only for a limited duration, such as for a special project.

- Extra help may be needed during a particularly busy period.

- The small business may not able to attract highly skilled professionals as employees because it is still too small or financially fragile.

- Small businesses must generally withhold the proper amount of taxes from employee checks, pay much larger amounts to local, state, and federal taxing authorities, and submit timely returns accounting for federal, state, and local taxes, FICA taxes, FUTA, unemployment taxes, and more. Yes, this is all a major headache. The government is more than happy when small businesses screw up, because crushing penalties and interest are immediately assessed. (See Chapter 7 for more information on payroll and withholding taxes.)

- Employers must make sure that employees are paid the minimum wage, whereas this is not a concern with contractors.

- Employees generally receive benefits paid for by employers, including medical insurance, vacations, paid holidays, retirement and profit-sharing plans, and more; contractors do not.

Of course, all of this depends upon the price. Most contractors must charge much higher rates to make up for all these factors. That may explain, for example, why a computer maintenance contractor charges $75 per hour for on-site fixes, whereas an employee performing the same work would be paid less than half of this hourly rate.

Still, the use of contractors vs. employees is growing. Great caution must be used in this area because it is the true substance of the relationship that determines whether the new hire is an employee or a contractor. Even after both parties sign an agreement that says "independent contractor" on every page, a small business may still lose on this issue if challenged by the employee/contractor, the IRS, other federal government agencies, or state authorities. This often surfaces when "contractors" do not pay required taxes or become upset about not receiving benefits, and then later claim that they were employees all along. The IRS and other interested parties will listen carefully and may easily reach the same conclusion. The small business owner must then pay back taxes, penalties, interest, and lost benefits that would have accrued to an employee (such as vacation time, paid holidays, etc.).

IRS/FICA/FUTA Treatments

The determination of employee vs. contractor status is complex, and just to keep it that way, different federal government agencies may classify the same person in different ways. In certain cases, the following agencies apply their rules first. Common-law tests (next section) are invoked after consideration of these agency requirements:

- **Internal Revenue Service - Federal Income Tax (FIT) Treatment.** "Licensed, qualified real estate agents" and "Direct Sellers" are normally classified by the IRS as independent contractors. That means IRS rules apply, but not necessarily FICA or FUTA rules. In all other cases, common-law tests are applied.

- **Federal Insurance Contributions Act (FICA) Treatment.** FICA requires that, in addition to regular employees, five types of workers must be treated as employees: (1) corporate officers; (2) drivers (agent or commission) delivering food, beverages, laundry, or dry cleaning; (3) industrial home workers paid $100 or more per calendar year; (4) full-time life insurance sales representatives; and (5) full-time salespeople soliciting orders from retailers for later delivery. This means that FICA rules apply, but not necessarily IRS or FUTA rules. In all other cases, common-law tests are applied.

- **Federal Unemployment Tax Act (FUTA) Treatment.** FUTA requires that three types of workers must be treated as employees and not as contractors: (1) corporate officers; (2) drivers (agent or commission); and (3) traveling or city salespeople. This means that FUTA rules apply, but not necessarily IRS or FICA rules. In all other cases, common-law tests are applied.

In these cases, workers may be classified by the IRS as either "statutory employees" or "statutory non-employees."

Now let's move on to the common-law tests that are applied after the FIT/FICA/FUTA treatments.

Common-law Tests

The following common-law tests determine whether a worker is an independent contractor or an employee. These amount to an overall analysis of the level of control that the small business exerts over the worker.

As more and more of the tests below are answered affirmatively (meaning that the employer is in control), the likelihood increases that the relationship is employer-employee, regardless of whether the person has signed an independent contractor agreement:

☐ Must the worker follow your instructions in accomplishing objectives?

☐ Are the specific personal services of the worker required to fulfill job objectives satisfactorily?

☐ Is the success of your small business dependent upon the specific worker's services?

☐ Are work hours mandated by you?

☐ Is the overall working relationship continuing or temporal (continuing suggests employee; temporal suggests contractor)?

☐ Do you have the right to hire, fire, manage, determine compensation, or pay others controlled by a specific worker?

☐ Is the worker discouraged from advertising and actively seeking assignments with other customers?

- ☐ Do you require that work be performed at a specific location, such as your office?

- ☐ Have you invested in the facilities used to perform the services?

- ☐ Do you direct the exact manner and schedule in which tasks are performed?

- ☐ Are progress reports required? How often and in how much detail?

- ☐ Is compensation determined by hours worked, or by deliverables, progress, or percentage of job completion (hours worked suggests employee; deliverables et al. suggests contractor)?

- ☐ Does the worker work only for your company?

- ☐ Do you provide and pay for items such as meals, travel expenses, and other business expenses?

- ☐ Do you provide training?

- ☐ Do you pay for the worker's tools and equipment?

- ☐ Do you pay for indirect expenses incurred by the worker, such as telephone, insurance, and other overhead?

- ☐ Do you provide a compensation plan such that the worker's gain or loss from the work is minimal?

- ☐ Are you the only revenue source of the worker?

- ☐ When the job is completed, is it expected that the working relationship will continue?

There is no hard rule allowing an employer to answer these questions, make an independent contractor-employee determination, and know for sure that the IRS will agree. It depends upon the entire context of the situation, including the "Safe Harbor" and "Special Rules" described below. It is important to think these tests through carefully because the decision often turns on these common-law tests.

Safe Harbor Rules

In some cases, however, Safe Harbor rules apply. If the relationship fits the tests indicated, the worker is considered an independent contractor, even if the common-law rules already discussed suggest otherwise. Safe Harbor exceptions may apply if your small business:

- Never treated similar workers as employees for employment tax purposes but as independent contractors

- Always treated this worker and similar workers as contractors by complying with tax reporting requirements (for example, the worker did not start out as an employee and later switch to contractor)

- Can show the IRS that previous rulings, technical advice, and precedent have consistently considered this situation as an independent contractor relationship

- Can cite previous IRS audits at your firm and others in the same industry finding that the worker's situation was that of an independent contractor

- Can point to longstanding industry practices as treating this type of worker as a contractor

Special Rules

In addition, the IRS has "Special Rules" that apply to diverse groups such as accountants, attorneys, casual labor, dentists, doctors, family members, insurance agents, officers and directors, partners, certain students, and some other workers.

If this seems just a bit complicated and you don't want to just roll the dice and hope for the best, then small business owners may submit relevant information on IRS Form SS-8 and request that the IRS determine the situation.

More information on this topic is available in Chapter 7 (Taxes) and in IRS Publication 15, Employers Tax Guide, at http://www.irs.gov.

Writing the Job Description and Defining Requirements

This book assumes that, unlike General Motors, your company does not have professionally constructed job descriptions and titles. The recruiting process must begin by defining staffing objectives and the associated skill sets carefully. This impresses the recruit, crystallizes management thinking, and forces the small business to outline exactly what is expected of the new hire. Much of this list will later guide interview questions and fit into the employment contract. A common mistake made by many small business owners is hiring an employee for one purpose and then changing the job later. Many employees will not take kindly to this spurious kind of thinking. A well-thought-out job description avoids this problem.

We approach this by solving two problems at once: deciding the type of person to hire, and writing a help-wanted advertisement to post in a local newspaper, trade publication, or on the Internet. All should go through this process even if there are no plans to advertise for the position, because it helps define exactly what is needed. There are three parts to the help-wanted ad: a job description, the job requirements, and information on how to apply.

For the job description, write down a wish-list of every area in which the small business needs extra help (this should be a continuing effort, so the next time more help is needed, begin again with this same list). Let's say you are unable to keep up with sales, and primarily need help in this area. Write down all sales-related tasks, but include other areas of concern in the list as well:

List 1: Help-Needed Wish-List

Represent us at trade shows and chamber meetings.

Add new features to the Website.

Make 50 outbound calls per day to local businesses.

Figure monthly commissions.

Visit customers and demonstrate products.

Monthly bank reconciliation and daily entries.

Design new marketing brochure.

Prepare proposals.

Prepare customer agreements.

Call customers to collect on delinquent accounts.

Enter calls, e-mails, letters, etc., into our customer ACTIV database.

Now make a second list—an outline of the job description—by paring down the first list. Include in the second list only the duties reasonably expected of the new hire. Someone else will need to do the other tasks, or this may reveal that even more help is needed. But for the moment, focus on the sales recruit:

List 2: Job Description Outline

Represent us at trade shows and chamber meetings.

~~Add new features to the web site~~

Make 50 outbound calls per day to local businesses.

~~Figure monthly commissions~~

Visit customers and demonstrate products.

~~Monthly bank reconciliation and daily entries~~

~~Design new marketing brochure~~

Prepare proposals.

~~Prepare customer agreements~~

~~Call customers to collect on delinquent accounts~~

Enter calls, e-mails, letters, etc., into our customer ACTIV database.

From this pruned-down list, write a job title and description—and make it sound exciting! Remember, this is a big move for potential candidates. You want the best to apply. Don't mention compensation at this point. Also, tell candidates how to apply. Consider: e-mail (fast, easy, and indicates some technical abilities), fax (be careful—dozens of spammed resumes may empty out the machine), or mail-in letters (some candidates will not respond this way). Also, note whether employment agencies may respond; if nothing is mentioned in this regard, expect a large number of agency-sponsored candidates. By writing out the list above, something like this will result:

Sales Rep Needed

Breakthrough Computer Service Product

Our company is expanding! Are you familiar with the problems faced by local businesses as they struggle to maintain their computer networks? We've got a great new product to maintain servers and workstations remotely. If you love to talk computers with 50 prospects per day, prepare customized proposals, and meet and help business owners, e-mail your resume to opportunity@aaaardvarkcomputer.com.

With this job description, the job requirements section of the ad will be easy to prepare. The job requirements should flow out of the work already accomplished. Think of the education, background, and experience levels needed, based upon the job description. In our example, we've settled on a more experienced type, who will hopefully arrive with some ready-to-book business contacts. Of course, this will cost more but save us time in training.

Requirements

Two or more years of local computer services sales experience.

Two or more years of success in business telemarketing.

Comfortable with local travel to visit customers, demonstrate our products, and attend local trade shows and business events. (Must own automobile and have a driver's license.)

Fluent in computer programs such as word processing, spreadsheet, presentation software, e-mail, and ACTIV.

Two years of college, including 18 credits in business / computers.

Put all this together, and we've decided exactly what our new hire will do, your requirements, and how to apply. The help-wanted ad is ready to go. Later on, we'll use these same materials to prepare a list of interview questions, and much of this will end up in the offer. Here is our completed help-wanted ad:

Sales Rep Needed

Breakthrough Computer Service Product

Our company is expanding! Are you familiar with the problems faced by local businesses as they struggle to maintain their computer networks? We've got a great new product to maintain servers and workstations remotely. Required: min 2 yrs computer svs sales, B2B telemarketing, trade shows, on-site demos, fluency w/word-proc, e-mail, laptop-based demos, and ACTIV. If you love to talk computers with 50+ prospects per day, prepare customized proposals, and meet and help business owners, e-mail your resume to opportunity@aaaardvarkcomputer.com.

Ads in printed publications are often edited down to conserve on words—and the budget. The more you say, the more you pay. On the other hand, some firms prefer big ads because they attract more attention.

Internet-based ads usually cost a fixed price, but they can be up to 2,000 words in length (more than is needed because few recruits will read this much) and may include graphics, logos, color fonts, and customized layouts. Internet-based ads usually allow candidates to press a link and immediately e-mail a resume and cover letter. Note that the average respondent to an Internet-based ad is a bit more technically savvy than respondees from printed publications. While it may take a while for a printed publication to go to press and be distributed, responses from the Internet may begin within hours.

Don't hesitate to spend money on recruiting—it's better to get a good selection of people than to train and hire the wrong person. Any extra money spent on recruiting is quickly regained in the productivity of the new hire.

Where to Recruit New Employees

Now that you've written a great help-wanted ad, it's time to consider whether to use it. Remember that half of the purpose of writing the ad was to determine exactly what the new hire will do, their credentials, background, and experience. Help may be recruited from many sources, including the following.

Local Newspapers and Trade Publications

A great tip: Pretend you are looking for a similar job, and see if anything related is listed in local newspapers or in trade publications. It's always a good idea to watch what competitors are doing. If lots of similar listings are seen, then maybe this is the right place. Key questions to ask printed sources: What is their circulation (number of readers)? In what geographic areas do they appear? and How long until readers will see the ad?

Resume File

After the job hunt closes, I always keep interesting resumes, and this can be a fast and inexpensive way of finding the right person. Remember that after the right person is recruited, the other candidates haven't moved to Antarctica. You will be surprised at how receptive people are when called and introduced to a new opportunity:

> Hi, you sent your resume in here a while ago and we couldn't respond at the time, but I was impressed with your credentials and would you be interested in learning about a new opportunity here at Aaaardvark Computer? Not right now? Well then do you know of anyone else that might be looking for a new career with a fast-growing business?

If enough calls are made, it's only a matter of time until a great recruit is located.

The Internet

Sites such as Monster.com, HotJobs.com, CareerPath.com, and DICE.com are well-known and effective means of locating new employees. There are differences in their approaches. For example, Monster.com is the monster among employees searching for jobs, and just about everyone spends time here. HotJobs.com (now owned by Yahoo) also has immense traffic. CareerPath.com is associated with the listings in many major newspapers; DICE is frequented by computer types. Of course, pricing varies greatly also. Read up and see which is best for your situation. Additionally, there are thousands of other Internet-based job sites that specialize in particular industries or geographic areas, and some are free. Maybe there is one that is "the place to go" for your business.

Since you have already written a great help-wanted ad, it will be easy to "copy and paste" this into the forms at various Websites. A new ad can be available to everyone on the planet within an hour or two, and responses may begin within hours. Most sites are very easy to use as long as a credit card is handy and special computer skills or languages are not needed. Just enter the text and press the appropriate buttons. Color, pictures, and snazzy layouts may also enhance the ad's appeal. It's also easy to post lengthy job descriptions and gushing praise of your small business, because Internet ads have loose restrictions on ad size. On the Internet, your ad stands equal to those of bigger competitors. If size matters, yours will be as big as theirs. Finally, note that respondees to Internet-based ads have pretty much proven that they have some technical expertise. An idea of their word-processing capabilities can be garnered by looking closely at the resume.

Ask Around

Asking friends, employees, chamber of commerce members, and colleagues may also be effective in recruiting—especially if there is a well-thought-out job description, as we have already accomplished. If enough calls are made, it's only a matter of time until a great candidate is located. E-mail or fax the job announcement to anyone that may help, and call later for follow-up because many will forget. Note that it's actually better to hire a friend's brother's girl-friend's cousin than your friend, because things can get complicated with direct acquaintances.

Most recruiting pros say that the best results come from being a bit subtle, saying "I am asking to see if you know of anyone..." rather than, "I wanted to see if you would be interested..." in this opportunity.

> **Where the employees are, someone waits for...**
>
> Connie Francis sang about finding boys, but about 80 percent of jobs are found through networking and personal contacts. Only about 20 percent are filled through traditional printed ads and the Internet, even though responses to these announcements are often huge.

Recruiters

Also known as employment agencies, placement agencies, or "headhunters," recruiters earn fees from you, the employer, after they find and you hire an employee. Since a lot of work is involved in this and small business owners may change their minds without obligation, the first step may be to convince the agency that help is needed, and fast. Money is not a major factor.

Rates are usually 15 percent to 35 percent of the new employee's first-year salary (not including commissions, benefits, or bonuses). Small business owners will be asked to sign a contract, which is often negotiable. For example, some agreements state that the recruiter's fee is earned and payable on the employee's first day on the job, but this is often changed to 90 days. If a new employee quits quickly after being hired, many recruiters will consider that they have done their job and earned the fee, and maybe your company is not such a great place to work. If a recruiter says, "I can't change the language to 90 days, but I will quickly replace anyone that quits for free"—don't expect this to happen. Beyond this, look for recruiters who have experience, and a reputation, in your industry. Also, don't assume that the recruiter has done a thorough background check of the new employee. If background, experience, education, and references are important, double-check this using internal resources.

Temp Agencies

Temp agencies are great for quickly filling certain positions where there is a large demand for common skills, such as secretarial, receptionist, accounting, and labor positions. The great thing about temp agencies is that they can provide competent people with the needed skills quickly, but the flip side is that it is often hard to let these people go—and the fees can really add up.

Also note that although it may seem expensive to pay $40 per hour for a Quickbooks accountant, the temp-accountant may not be wild about receiving $18 per hour from the agency. Ask up-front for a "buyout" agreement where a great temp may be converted to full time for a price. Otherwise, many staffing firms require a wait of at least 180 days before a small business may directly employ or contract persons introduced by the agency.

Finally, be careful about temps who stay around for more than 12 to 16 weeks, because the IRS may later deem this an employment relationship.

Competitors

A time-honored tradition is to raid the staffs of competitors when it's time to expand. Many firms love this idea, because these recruits may bring along know-how and business contacts that would otherwise be difficult to obtain. Vendors and other business partners are often tapped for these same purposes. Make sure the new recruit does not have a "non-compete" clause in previous employment agreements, because this could mean that they are not allowed to do the work that is important to you.

Local Government, Universities, and Schools

This approach may be effective, especially if entry-level or clerical/labor skills are needed. Many of these services and sites are free. Also, organizations such as SCORE may provide extremely experienced executives without charge. The downside is that this often takes longer than other alternatives.

Employee Leasing

Employee leasing is where a third-party company hires away the staff of a small business and then leases them back. Future recruits may be sourced from either the employee leasing company or from efforts by the small business.

This alternative may be more of a financial-headache outsourcing ploy than a means of locating and recruiting new employees. Employee leasing firms are mostly interested in acquiring existing staffs under lease-back arrangements. The leasing firm then administers payroll functions including withholding, medical and other insurance benefits, retirement plans, and more. Large employee leasing firms will pay smaller rates for all of these programs than most small businesses because all these costs are aggregated over many employees, resulting in better pricing. Also, the employee leasing company is relieving its small business client of many headaches when personnel administration tasks are taken away, such as employee handbooks, wording of notices, benefits administration, compliance with hiring and firing laws, background checks, record-keeping, and more.

Employee leasing is an unlikely alternative until a small business reaches about 10 employees because the pricing will not make sense to either party.

Employee leasing should be considered by small businesses employing more than 10 regular employees, and where the leasing company has expertise in providing quickly a steady stream of quality recruits with important skills sets.

Leasing rather than hiring employees is sometimes considered a way to avoid or circumvent employment laws and benefits requirements, but this is not correct. The same laws apply, except the employee leasing company is paid to accept compliance responsibilities. At the end of the day, however, the small business is still responsible, just as before.

Promote Current Employees

Don't forget current employees. Many have skills from previous jobs that the employer has long since forgotten but the employee is still keen to develop. Employees are delighted when their help is needed and their capabilities are recognized. There are lots of great reasons to promote from within and then back-fill by hiring less-experienced persons to fill the void.

Recruiting is not a one-time process, but a continuing effort. Hopefully, much of this will be needed in the near future. Always be on the lookout for the right people, and keep a file on potential new employees. When the time is right, your small business will be ready to begin calling immediately, and recruit the best.

Employee Documents and Files

Upon hiring the first employee, your small business has entered a new legal realm; much of this is described in this chapter. As part of your new responsibilities, you need to keep detailed, accurate, consistent, and timely records on all employees from the time of application until termination, and to communicate certain information to and from employees with the following documents.

Application for Employment

Most well-managed businesses require that all candidates under consideration complete a job application, even if a good resume is available.

The application allows the employer to ask certain questions and gain information that may not be on the resume ("Have you ever been fired from a job with cause?") and that requires the applicant to agree that information may be verified and that false statements may result in immediate termination at any time after employment commences. Employers should also inform applicants if successful results in credit and criminal background checks or drug testing are required before hiring.

The completed job application is the first piece of work produced by the aspiring employee for your small business. So far, it's free. Look carefully for neatness, spelling errors, sloppiness, and grammar. Their work will not get any better than this later.

A sample application for employment is available for review or download at www.TheSmallBusinessOwnersManual.com.

Conditional Offer of Employment Letter

Many potential employees will be impressed by a conditional offer of employment letter, outlining the terms of the new employment opportunity.

The letter is a one- or two-page document from the small business owner or another authorized officer of the company, explaining:

- This is an offer of employment (full-time, part-time, or from/to dates).
- Start date.
- Anticipated work schedule or hours.
- Title and work description.
- Reporting manager.
- Salary and related compensation (state salary in terms of the normal pay period; never use annual salary—problems may occur later if the new employee is terminated.
- Benefits.
- Whether the employee will be treated as exempt or non-exempt per the FLSA.
- The offer is contingent upon passing a drug test; a satisfactory credit and criminal background check; satisfactory reference checks; and verification of previous employment, work experience, education, and related credentials (all optional).
- The offer must be accepted in writing by the candidate and returned to the small business by a certain date or time; otherwise, the offer is withdrawn.

A sample offer of employment letter is available for view and download at www.TheSmallBusinessOwnersManual.com.

Credit and Criminal Background Checks

Before hiring, consider a credit and criminal background check. These reports may intimidate some candidates, but in our security-conscious world, the need for this information is increasingly understood. Good candidates will be unfazed by all this, and those who decline often have something to hide.

The reports should be ordered upon extending an offer letter, where the offer is contingent upon a satisfactory record. "Satisfactory" should be rethought and redefined for different types of workers, but the definition must remain the same for new employees performing the same job unless there is cause for change (which should be documented). Be careful in approaching this, however, since it may be reasonable to demand a record clear of drunk-driving convictions for limousine drivers, but not for bricklayers. Again, small business owners often fear that they will be accused of not employing certain persons for discriminatory reasons.

Credit and criminal background reports are available from many local companies for about $50 to $150. These firms tap the national credit databases and search local court records. The reports sometimes take a few days, because local court records are checked and duplicate records of people with common names may exist.

To find a provider of this information, ask a colleague for a referral, or search for "credit and criminal background check" on a favorite search engine. A personal relationship is hardly necessary.

The job candidate must sign a statement (normally supplied by the report provider) allowing your small business to order this report. The recruit should be given a copy of the report whether hired or not.

When the report is received, what should be of concern? Obviously, any criminal record may be a problem; but just as important, did the candidate lie about anything in the application or in an interview? If so, this person cannot be hired, or the stage has been set for problems:

> So Mr. Jones lied to you about his criminal record and you still hired him? Then you knew he was dishonest when you employed him, didn't you?

or

> So Ms. Longlegs is being fired for dishonesty—but then you hired Mr. Jones after he lied to you. So if dishonesty is okay at your company, why did you really fire Ms. Longlegs?

On the credit report, look for addresses from cities not disclosed on the resume, indicating previous residences and employment—and perhaps the need to search local court records.

If credit problems are noticed, consider how it is possible that a candidate claims to be making big money but can't pay their credit card bills. Is their current income really correct? If so, why can't they pay their bills? Could there be a substance abuse problem? Be attentive because from the moment this person is hired, their problems become your problems, too. Your small business may be responsible immediately for medical treatments, and your inventory or assets may be a handy way for someone with a substance abuse problem to finance the habit.

If there are judgments on the record, get a copy to learn what really happened. Was a judgment issued because a candidate could not pay for her mother's medical problems, or did this person commit fraud at a previous workplace?

Finally, don't demand perfection here or anywhere else in recruiting new employees. Determine what level of problems are not appropriate for the position being staffed, and consider that anything else will be just fine.

Credit and criminal background checks may be immensely useful in protecting your small business from the damages caused by the wrong types of people, but all actions taken in this area must comply with the Fair Credit Reporting Act (http://www.ftc.gov/os/statutes/fcra.htm). It is not difficult to run afoul of this complex, employer-unfriendly 2002 legislation, so extreme care should be taken if credit and criminal background checks are necessary.

A sample "Credit and Criminal Background Report Release" form is available for download and a sample credit and criminal background report may be seen at www.TheSmallBusinessOwnersManual.com.

Drug Testing

This is another area where small business owners have a legitimate cause for concern. Employers have the right to insist upon a drug-free workplace, but must tread gingerly not to run afoul of privacy laws and ADA. A recent consulting study found that employees with drug or alcohol abuse problems cost their employers an average of about $7,000 extra per year in various losses.

Similar to credit and criminal background checks, drug testing takes place after a conditional offer of employment letter has been extended and the candidate signs a release authorizing the test. In this regard, the offer is conditional upon the applicant's: (1) signing a consent to taking a drug test; (2) actually taking the drug test to the satisfaction of the testing laboratory; and (3) receiving a negative drug test result. The preemployment drug test should be conducted less than 30 days prior to the applicant's expected first day of employment. The conditional offer of employment letter should state that the offer is withdrawn if any of the above conditions are not met, and that applicants who submit to a preemployment drug test and receive positive results may not reapply for any positions at the small business for at least 180 days. Further, applicants should be informed in the conditional offer of employment letter that samples provided by applicants are also analyzed for adulterants (chemicals intended to obfuscate drug testing). If adulterants are found, the offer for that applicant is withdrawn.

Apart from employment, it is important to inform applicants in the conditional offer of employment letter that they are not entitled to participate in any employee assistance or rehabilitation programs offered by the small business until employment commences. In other words, applicants who apply and fail the drug test were never employees, and are therefore not entitled to any employee benefits.

Regarding confidentiality and privacy, the conditional offer of employment letter should say that all drug test results shall be considered confidential information, shall be appropriately labeled and managed as such, shall be retained in a secure location with controlled access, and shall not be kept as part of the applicant's employment record.

Finally, your small business should contract with a third-party service supplier to make sure everything is done correctly. These firms provide the administration, collection, testing, verification, and reporting of samples for preemployment drug testing purposes and ensure that all aspects of the testing process are private and confidential and comply with applicable federal and state laws and regulations.

The Employee Handbook

Many new hires consider the employee handbook to be just another curious pile of papers heaped on during the first day of work. Many end up on the bottom of desk drawers, never read, because it seems easier to ask other employees questions such as, "What's the deal around here if I get sick?"

Nevertheless, employee handbooks carry real legal weight and should be considered by growing small business owners because a current, well-thought-out handbook:

- Makes the small business look more professional and serves as a welcome letter to anxious new employees

- Clarifies potential misunderstandings within the company and in legal realms because it serves as the "go to" source for many employment-related issues

- Allows employees to spend less time asking and answering the most common questions

- Lays down important rules and outlines behavioral expectations

- Outlines company benefits, who is eligible, and when

- States that the small business complies with government requirements such as Title VII of the 1964 Civil Rights Act, the Age Discrimination in Employment Act (ADEA), the Labor Standards Act (FLSA), the Family Medical Leave Act (FMLA), the Americans with Disabilities Act (ADA), the Federal Electronic Eavesdropping Act, the Fair Credit Reporting Act (FCRA), the Drug Free Workplace Act, and other federal and state legislation (yes, that's a bit much for most small businesses to take seriously, but at least pay lip service to all of this in the handbook, which also states that the company consequently requires that employees must act in accordance with these various regulations).

Although an employee handbook is not really required, it serves many useful purposes, and there is a strong argument that as the small business adds its fourth or fifth recruit, this document would be beneficial. For example, compliance with the FMLA must be discussed somewhere, so why not in the expected place, which is the employee handbook?

Here are the sections to include in the employee handbook. They can be in any order that suits a particular small business.

Company Background and Overview

In this introduction, start off in a welcoming manner, providing a brief history of your small business, its founders, its current Unique Selling Proposition, and other background information that may not be readily available.

Compensation

Explain how employees are paid, and when. Describe direct-deposit options and how employee contributions to benefit programs are deducted from paychecks. Define the difference between part-time and full-time employment. Say that there will be no guarantees as to the minimum number of hours for part-time workers and that benefits are provided only to full-time employees.

Outline of Benefits, Vacation, Holidays

Here is where any benefits offered by your small business are described. Include life and health insurance coverages, and ERISA (Employee Retirement and Income Security Act) plans. Make sure that employees know about mandatory benefits, too, such as disability, workers' compensation insurance, and unemployment insurance, because employers are required to pay for this. Also describe when benefits such as paid vacation and medical insurance become available. Provide a list of recognized company holidays (but supplement this with an annual memo listing the exact dates). Remember that for the most part, the same deal must be offered to everyone (including you, the owner), so this is a good place to summarize everything. All this should be summarized very briefly, with referrals to the actual documents published by the benefit providers; there is no need to retype and reword what they have already done.

Take care that the employee handbook remains consistent with the requirements of the benefits providers. For example, if medical insurance arrangements are changed to allow that full-time employees (working 30-plus hours per week) are covered after 60 days of employment, this must be changed in the employee handbook, too, or the small business is probably liable for any problems.

If your small business employs more than 50 people, the FMLA generally requires that employees who have worked at least 1,250 hours be granted an unpaid leave for up to 12 weeks over any 12-month period to:

- Attend to personal health matters affecting job performance
- Provide care for their children, parents, or a spouse with serious medical problems
- Care for a daughter or son during the first 12 months of life

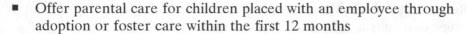

- Offer parental care for children placed with an employee through adoption or foster care within the first 12 months

State laws may impose additional requirements.

To avoid litigation, it may be wise to include a few words about severance pay. If there is a specific plan, describe the plan and its provisions. Perhaps the best advice for most small businesses is to say explicitly that there is no severance pay, and changes regarding this policy are not binding unless communicated in writing from the small business owner.

General Attendance and Employee Behavior Rules

Describe here company rules regarding the attendance policy, tardiness, absences, job performance, disorderly conduct, honesty, insubordination, theft of company property or use of company property for personal purposes, and falsifying records. It is important to detail how, when, and who employees should notify when tardiness, early leave, or absences occur.

To avoid a situation where an employee says, "The employee handbook doesn't say anything about keeping my pants zipped up," introduce the section with a statement such as:

> The Company expects all employees to exhibit normal and good judgment in all situations; however, the following are examples of special situations . . .

Finally, it is important to spell out policies and procedures invoked when problems occur, so that employees may see that a particular situation must be handled in a certain manner, no matter who is involved.

Recording Time and Hours Worked

The FLSA requires that employees be paid at least the federal minimum hourly wage. This is obviously not an issue when it's time to hire, but, rather, when it's time to fire. Displeased employees may claim that the medieval practices in use at your small business required huge amounts of off-the-clock overtime, and their generous compensation divided by hours worked really resulted in a per-hour rate less than the minimum wage. The Department of Labor and the disaffected employee would then feast on your small business for "lost" hours at 1.5 times the hourly rate, damages in the same amount, and everyone's attorney fees.

The remedy for this begins with the employee handbook. Provide a policy and describe the means for reporting all hours worked; describe exactly who may authorize overtime; and detail the time frame and manner in which to report problems. Also, demand that time-reporting is immediate (not estimated a week later), accurate, honest, and accomplished solely by the employee (no log-ins/log-outs by coworkers). Further, state the resulting disciplinary actions taken if problems occur.

Job Descriptions

Small businesses are often averse to casting job descriptions in stone, because things change so quickly. If the situation is relatively stable at your company, the employee handbook may be used for this purpose.

Care should be taken in this area, however, since small businesses may inadvertently run afoul of ADEA, ADA, and state legislation. This can be avoided by being as inclusive as possible in job descriptions, or by not discussing job descriptions at all.

Confidentiality of Information and Conflicts of Interest

Employees must know from day one the definition of "confidential information" within your small business. Define this in the employee handbook and describe that this means information cannot be disclosed to outsiders except in limited circumstances, such that the information becomes generally available to the public, or if demanded by the legal system. It may also be relevant to include a "conflict of interest" section, requiring that employees not work in competition with your small business, directly or indirectly, during the period of employment and for a period of time afterward. Of course, it is another matter whether the courts will allow this.

Work for Hire

For programmers, developers, creative types, engineers, and others, the agreement must describe that anything produced during employment with your small business belongs to you and not to them, and that the compensation paid is payment in full for such work. This should also be in employment agreements, if they are used.

Grooming Requirements and Dress Code

Considering interaction with customers and the public as well as safety and legal and contractual requirements, set forth your dress code, covering topics such as facial hair, hair length, jewelry, and makeup. This area may be dicey, because certain employees may think that gender or racial discrimination is really at work here. Nevertheless, the legal system has generally understood and supported employers in this regard. Of course, developing a policy after problems surface puts you in a weaker position.

Privacy and Employee Use of Company Property for Non-Business Use

Here, small business owners should describe policies required if and when it is necessary to:

- Restrict the use of company assets such as computers, telephones, fax and copy machines, tools, etc. The best policy is to disallow the use of any company property for any non-business use. This is stark but clear;

otherwise, company assets will soon be considered at the disposal of employees for personal purposes, and you will soon wonder if certain employees are working for your small business or themselves.

- Examine employee property such as purses, clothing, or gym bags (which may well be separately required for security purposes).

- Enter areas such as restrooms, lockers, or changing areas, to the extent that company policies may affect employee rights to privacy.

- Monitor employee telephone calls or e-mail. In this area, small business employers must be aware of the requirements of the Federal Electronic Eavesdropping Act prohibiting interception of certain communications; both criminal and civil penalties may be imposed upon violators.

Safety and Health

This section deals with issues such as:

- The policy on smoking, smoking on the premises, the use of prescription, non-prescription, and illegal drugs, alcohol usage, and drug/alcohol testing. Some employers recently have required that employees not smoke, even when away from the workplace on personal time. It is not clear if this will be universally allowable.

- Many small businesses involved in the construction, production, testing, medical, and many other industries have special safety requirements, mandated by OSHA, state agencies, insurance providers, or business partners. Safety policies may all be described in the employee handbook, including the requirements, when and where the requirements apply, who must comply, and actions taken for non-compliance.

Additionally, employees should be told that although it is the employer's policy to maintain a safe and healthy workplace, employees are ultimately responsible as well.

All employee handbooks should also say something about emergency exits and procedures, the location of fire extinguishers and first-aid equipment, and a formal process for reporting medical problems, damage to equipment, and new safety hazards, such as broken equipment.

Finally, a form should be provided where employees provide the names of individuals to contact in case of emergency or medical problems. Employees should also be admonished to report workplace injuries and property damages immediately to avoid the risk of losing workers' compensation and other benefits.

Sexual Harassment, Equal Opportunity

All small businesses must do what is possible to avoid complaints and litigation regarding sexual harassment or discrimination, especially in today's legal-lottery environment, where unhappy employees and ex-employees may roll the dice and sue your small business with little downside but a handsome upside. The place to begin is the employee handbook, which should state that:

- Prohibited behavior includes sexual advances, requests for sexual favors, and otherwise creating a sexually charged or intimidating environment. Note that the policy should also say that personnel decisions shall not be affected if employees accept or reject such advances. This precludes an employee from demanding a raise and promotion for providing sexual favors.

- Complaints are made to specified persons, hopefully not to a direct manager of the aggrieved.

- The small business must affirm its commitment to non-discrimination and to treat all employees equally.

Yes, this is incredibly vague, which is why a professional and/or attorney is often needed to get the right language here, and even then there are no guarantees about the language. Nor are there any guarantees that your company will not be sued. And your small business may still get hammered for a huge judgment, allowing both victim and attorney to live comfortably for a long time.

Both sexual harassment and non-discrimination policies should provide a channel for reporting problems other than through the purported victim's manager, because the manager may well be the alleged violator. This is often difficult for very small businesses with only a few employees.

Alternate Dispute Resolution (ADR)

Litigation costs against employers have grown at astonishing rates over the last couple of decades, and no end is in sight. Many frivolous lawsuits have been filed, resulting in business bankruptcies and major reallocations of time, attention, and funds away from productive purposes.

Some small businesses sometimes seek to mitigate this threat by handling grievances internally, and if this fails, through binding arbitration. Binding arbitration requires that both parties waive their rights to resolution through the legal system in advance, and agree to be bound by the decision of an impartial, experienced, and mutually agreeable mediator. Many small businesses feel that binding arbitration is cheaper, faster, and less capricious than the legal system, although not everyone agrees. There are many firms and individuals offering services in this area.

Employees must agree to this during the application process, since it is not proper to demand that new hires give up their rights to use the legal system after employment commences. More specific information should be communicated in the employee handbook.

Courts have generally found that employer policies demanding the use of binding arbitration are legally enforceable, but this area is complex, varies from state to state, and many small businesses will have different needs in this area. For these reasons, it will be necessary to consult with legal counsel to decide what is best for you.

Employer Caveats

Three important caveats should be included in the employee handbook:

1. First, language should be included allowing the small business in its sole determination to change, amend, replace, or delete sections of the employee handbook without notice, and without employee consent, at any time.

2. Second, in a previous discussion we noted that employment in most states is generally considered at-will, meaning that employees may be terminated at any time for any legal reason, or no reason. This is good for employers. But this may be compromised if the employer later makes intentional—or, most commonly, inadvertent—assurances regarding continued employment. This problem may be addressed by disclaiming such assurances and stating that

   > ...employment is at-will, not guaranteed for any specific period of time, and employment may be discontinued by either party at any time, for any legal reason, without cause, and without notice...

   Place this language prominently in the employee handbook and in other relevant places as needed to avoid loss of at-will employment status.

3. Finally, state that nothing in the employee handbook may be changed unless communicated in writing by specific management of your small business.

Proof of Receipt

When trouble occurs, some employees may claim that they never received a copy of your carefully drafted employee handbook. This problem may be avoided by:

- Having your CPA or a credible independent third party give a copy of this and other employment documents to the new hire, logging the act, and asking the employee to cosign a log book or related document.

- Asking the new hire to immediately sign a statement affirming receipt of the copy.

- Asking the new hire to initial each page of the employee handbook, make a copy, and then return a copy to you.

Yes, this is intimidating, and there is much potential for costly missteps. But the good news is that this may be accomplished more quickly, easily, and inexpensively than before, thanks to the Internet. For beginners, just search for "employee handbook" at your favorite search site; many great on-line templates are available that can be downloaded in Microsoft Word format. Do your best to customize this to fit the situation at your small business, but also give it to an attorney or experienced HR specialist for review and finishing touches.

A sample employee handbook is also available for view and download at www.TheSmallBusinessOwnersManual.com. An experienced provider of employment agreements is Petroff Consulting (http://www.petroffconsulting.com).

Although all of this may seem harsh, try to keep the tone of the employee handbook as positive as possible because this important document is needed for both legal, informational, and motivational purposes.

Employment Agreement

When a new employee is hired, all seems well in the world as employer and employee enjoy a period of romance (well, business romance). It seems the other party can do no wrong. That may change, and when things get difficult, a written employment agreement may quickly and definitively solve many problems. The employment agreement spells out compensation, but just as important, it describes the employee's responsibilities, schedule, and other details. The great thing about written agreements is that when there is a disagreement, it doesn't matter what somebody thinks or said or feels; only the agreement is important.

Employment agreements should be used sparingly and not offered to all. They are especially effective when the employer wants to offer extra security to an employee with special skills or experience.

The agreement does take some time and requires careful thought. It can be changed as needed for each new person, but the most difficult part is deciding exactly how to describe the job and its concomitant responsibilities. The benefit is that it forces the employer to crystallize and define the exact expectations of, and compensation to, the new recruit.

Most agreements are for a one-year period. Don't forget to renew 30 to 60 days in advance of termination. Also, be sure to work with your employee to make relevant changes as the company changes. Failure to update the agreement in some areas will make other important areas look outdated, too.

Note that employment agreements are not required, but when they are used, the employment may no longer be considered at-will.

Employment agreements serve many purposes, but the two most important are to protect the small business and to motivate the new recruit. These documents are complex and vary greatly in different states, industries, and among companies, but all should include clear language and articulate the following essentials:

- ☐ **Clearly define the position,** so that the new recruit will know exactly what is expected beyond the hype of interviews and recruiting meetings. This should include the job title and a list of tasks, responsibilities, and objectives, thought out clearly in advance so that the new hire's actions provide maximum benefit. This section may be quite lengthy. A disclaimer for later changes should be included so that the job definition may change reasonably as business needs change (but don't push it too far here, or promising new candidates may fear that the situation is unstable). This section should also include work hours and the person to whom the new hire reports.

- ☐ **Compensation.** This section is usually of paramount interest to the new hire. Here is where salary, bonuses, commissions, expenses, benefits, and any other money, perks, and other compensation are defined. For sales people or anyone working on incentive pay, great care should be taken to think this out carefully because livelihoods often turn on this issue. If a mistake is made that obligates your small business, be prepared to pay; it's not acceptable to change the deal later. On the other hand, if misunderstandings occur in your favor, the new employee may become disenchanted and quit. Having said this, the small business should have the right to make changes unilaterally as business needs change. Be careful here, because employees may become discouraged by continually changing comp plans.

- ☐ **Confidentiality.** A common provision these days is that employees must not divulge or attempt to benefit from information that is proprietary to your small business—such as trade secrets, customer lists, and production methods—during the tenure of their employment and for a specified time afterward.

- ☐ **Work for Hire.** For programmers, developers, creative types, engineers and others, the agreement must describe that anything produced during employment with your small business belongs to you and not to them, and that the compensation paid is payment in full for such work. This should also be in the employee handbook.

- ☐ **Term, Renewal, and Termination.** Like any agreement, beginning and end dates must be included. Employment agreements may also describe (1) the employer's right to renew or renegotiate, (2) automatic termination or employer's option to terminate upon the occurrence of certain events, or (3) automatic termination on a specific date. Reasons for termination often include completion of a project, death or disability of the employee or small business owner, or sale of the company. Assurances may also be given here that termination will not occur if certain events occur (for example, "Small business may not terminate this agreement for a one-year period following any quarter in which sales objectives are met"). This provides security to the employee, especially in at-will employment states, builds morale, and reduces turnover.

- **Performance "Out" Clause.** Employers may need the ability to terminate for material breaches of the employment agreement. For example, if a new production manager agrees to increase output of welding tools by 50 percent but production instead declines, the small business must have the right to terminate Mr. Incompetent and thereby free up funds to hire the right person.

- **Non-Compete.** Many employment agreements also demand that employees may not compete against the employer for a period of perhaps six months to five years following termination of employment. This requirement is often not taken seriously by employees, competitors, and, most important, by the courts.

- **Truthfulness.** Here, the small business requires that the recruit have been honest in describing previous experience, background, education, and other matters. To support this, include a copy of the resume as a formal attachment to the employment agreement. If material discrepancies are later discovered, this is usually reason for immediate termination "with cause."

- **Disputes.** Many employers demand that employees agree to binding arbitration as the means to settle disputes, rather than roll the dice with less predictable judges and juries.

- **Attorney's Fees.** A standard provision in almost all agreements allows that if legal action is taken, the loser pays for the winner's legal and enforcement fees.

- **Entire Agreement.** Employment agreements, like most others agreements, should have language to the effect that

  > This agreement constitutes the entire agreement between the parties and supersedes all previous agreements and understandings. It may not be changed orally, but only by an agreement in writing signed by the parties hereto...

  This is important so that employees may not later claim, "I don't care what the agreement says, they told me in a meeting I would get paid the maximum amount as long as I showed up for work."

- **Non-Compliance with Laws.** The agreement should also allow that if one or more parts are found to not be in compliance with the law, the entire agreement is not thrown out by the courts. This is also standard language in many commercial agreements.

Some of the items described here—such as confidentiality, work for hire, alternative dispute resolution, truthfulness, and others provisions—may be included in the employee handbook instead of in employment agreements. This is likely the case if the concern applies to all employees, not just a few.

Note that one of the main purposes here is to establish that the new employee is indeed an employee and not an independent contractor, agent, or vendor. This automatically subjects your small business to many statutory, tax-reporting, and payment requirements, which is presumably what everyone wants here.

The employment agreement includes specific understandings between employer and employee. The employee handbook (as discussed) covers company policies and procedures that apply to everyone, such as recognized holidays.

Finally, the protocol here is that the employment agreement or "written offer," is sent to the new recruit, who must sign and return within a specified number of days along with an acceptance letter. Once the letter is released to the new hire, your small business will likely be held liable even if it not signed by the employer. Problems could occur if the recruit leaves a current job and then learns that your offer is not really there.

Employment agreements are notoriously complex. The small business owner should draft parts of this related to specific areas outside of the legal realm but then ask legal counsel to review everything to make sure it properly protects the company and remains in compliance with the law.

U.S. Government Forms W-4, I-9, and Other Needed Documents

The U.S. government requires that employees communicate their desired income tax withholding on IRS Form W-4. Immigration status is reported on Form I-9. Both of these forms are detailed further in Chapter 7.

Some states need additional information on new employees, and companies providing insurance and benefits need relevant information for coverages to be effective. Make sure this is all organized and ready to go. Ask your CPA to make a list and supply whatever additional forms and documents are lacking. Professionalism in this area will positively affect the morale of nervous new employees and allow these burdensome tasks to be discharged quickly with minimal headaches.

The new employee should complete and return this information on the first day of employment. Also, be sure to provide the employee handbook (as discussed) and information on specific coverages as supplied by insurance and benefits providers.

The Hiring Process

Now that we've written the job description and recruiting advertisement and all the paperwork is figured out, it's time to hire someone.

Review Resumes and Call

A large number of e-mail resumes are, hopefully, in your in-box as responses to the recruiting ads. Begin reviewing these immediately; there is no need to wait for laggards.

The first part of this process is to eliminate the majority of responses. This is usually quite easy because many respondents send out their applications by virtually spamming their resumes to as many opportunities as possible. As a result, most responses will be grossly inappropriate.

Focus on the serious, sincere responses by carefully reading cover letters and resumes, but concentrate on eliminating all but perhaps 10 persons. When reviewing, think hard to determine whether the candidate:

- Meets the requirements described in the ad and is not under or overqualified
- Lives within a reasonable commuting distance
- Appears to be stretching the truth or is unnecessarily vague
- Exhibits acceptable grammar, spelling, computer skills, and communications abilities

> ### Joe Learns New Code Words
>
> Employment practices may be a minefield of problems. Many code words can lead to problems. Here are just a few:
>
> "Overqualified" may be interpreted as age discrimination.
>
> "Permanent Employee" may be interpreted as a life-long commitment, thereby weakening the argument that an employee is at-will.
>
> "Performance Bonus" may be considered unfair to employees not working while exercising their FMLA rights. Small businesses may need to pay Performance Bonuses to hapless workers who were denied their right to earn these extra amounts.

With the in-box now reduced to a small number of interesting candidates, pick up the phone and begin calling. Be careful about leaving revealing messages at any telephone number. Saying, "I am calling about the e-mail you sent earlier today to our aircraft bearings company" should be enough.

The purpose of the phone call is to further qualify and decide whether time is well-spent by going the next step in the interview. Another purpose is to raise enthusiasm about opportunities at your small business. To do this, first put the person at ease. Start by providing some description of your company and the specific opportunity, and then confirm facts and gain more detail, especially regarding the questions already discussed. If things still look good, agree upon an interview time immediately, even though it may be best to schedule the interview for one or two weeks in the future. If things are less certain, simply say:

> Thanks for your time. We are considering you along with a few others that we still need to speak with, so hopefully we'll be able to talk again soon.

Interviewing Potential Employees

As good candidates are discovered through responses to help-wanted ads, don't wait. Begin calling and interviewing right away. This takes longer than you think, and the best candidates may be far along in the hiring process with competitors.

Interviews should be structured and formal, even if your small business is really small. Job seekers may become uncomfortable in informal situations. If the interviewer seems unprepared, unclear of exact needs, less than excited, distracted, or vaguely familiar with a candidate's credentials, this will only reinforce fears of working for your company. You are being interviewed, too, so dress well, hold the interview in the most impressive possible surroundings, don't allow outside interruptions or phone calls, have a list of questions ready, and study the candidate's resume in advance.

It is ironic that even in larger companies, most managers who hire are not hiring managers. Many are good at one function or another, but they are poorly prepared for job interviews. Impressive corporate surroundings and a well-known reputation are often squandered when a busy manager hurriedly reviews a resume for the first time as the candidate sits down for the interview, a discouraging sight to eager candidates—and a waste of your time and money.

There are five steps involved in conducting an interview.

Welcome

Greet the candidates, thank them for coming, and make them feel welcomed. Avoid making them wait in the reception area. Suggest that this meeting is an important part of your day. Make small talk about traffic, weather, sports, or whatever. Avoid news or politics or anything controversial. Of course, don't even mention subjects like race, religion, sexual preferences, etc. But also, do not dare ask questions about family, children, health, background, friends, or other areas that concern a candidate's personal situation. If the candidate leads the conversation into this area, gently direct the talk into a neutral area. No business yet.

Introduction

Now it's time for business. Talk about the company, its glorious history and position in the market. Don't talk about the job opportunity yet.

Interview Questions

It's time to get more specific. In a give-and-take manner, tell a little about the opportunity and then ask a question or two. A great list of interview questions may be downloaded from www.TheSmallBusinessOwnersManual.com. Consider these questions against the "Job Description Outline" and "Requirements" sections presented previously.

It's not fair to ask too many questions when the candidate doesn't know any more than what was described in the help-wanted ad. On the other hand, don't lay out the whole situation such that the candidate knows exactly how to answer the interview questions. Explain a little, ask some questions, explain a little more, and so on.

Candidate Questions

Ask the candidate if they have any questions or if they need further clarification. Ask sincerely, and not in the manner of, "I am sure you do not have any questions because I am finished with you." Much can be garnered from the questions asked by applicants, and this is also a time to build further rapport. If the candidate has no questions, well—then that says something, too. Expect to be asked about compensation. At this point, give a range, but not a precise number.

Conclusion

By this time, you will know whether to continue considering a particular person. If there is insufficient interest, thank the applicant for coming and later send a polite letter declining further consideration. If there is further interest, this is the time to tell the recruit the additional hiring procedures and express enthusiasm about his or her credentials. Say something such as:

> Well, I am very impressed with your experience in this area, and you are certainly one of the more interesting candidates I have met. So I hope we can continue exploring this, and I want to let you know right up front how we proceed from here. After this interview, I want you to speak with one of my colleagues, and then we to test your computer skills. Then, I would like to speak with three of your references for a few minutes, including a former manager. Someone will also verify what you told us on your resume about your employment and educational background. If all goes well, we'll have a conditional offer of employment for you within 24 hours. Now the "conditional" part means we get what's called a satisfactory credit and criminal background report, and the resume verifications must check out. Now I don't care if there are some minor credit issues, but of course we need to make sure there are no major problems because you will be handling valuable inventory. So as we proceed, please be assured that I am being 100 percent truthful with you, and I need the same in return. I want this to work out because it looks like this could be a great opportunity for both of us. So does this make sense to you?

The purpose to this statement is to let the candidate know that this may be a small business, but you know what you are doing. The credit and criminal background check is increasingly important in today's security-conscious world. The process for ordering these, and what to look for, has already been described. Now it's time to move on to the next step in the hiring process: checking references.

A Few Do's and Don'ts:

☐ Do use a checklist of questions.

☐ Don't hold it against people if they are not perfect. In the hiring process, everyone will come up short in some way. You won't find the perfect employee in this lifetime.

☐ Do ask others to interview the candidate, asking the same questions in different ways. Later compare answers to gauge consistency. You will be surprised at the little things coworkers saw that you missed.

☐ Is this a physically attractive candidate? Don't even consider this factor. In today's business environment, it's better to work hard with people that you feel comfortable with and pursue other interests elsewhere. Don't find your honey where you make your money!

☐ Do credit and criminal background checks, and perhaps drug testing, as described in a previous section.

☐ Don't believe everything the recruit says. It's impossible to check everything, but get to the bottom of a few selected items. If a small item was grossly exaggerated, chances are, bigger items were also misrepresented.

☐ Do use the exact same process in hiring every employee. Consistent practices are necessary to avoid legal tangles.

The New Hire Celebrates by Giving His Boss Joe Some Illegal Drugs

I am always on the lookout for great salespeople and could not believe my good fortune when a business colleague referred me to a seasoned person from my industry who had just moved into town. He had great experience in another city, and although his reasons for moving were a bit vague, I was won over by his zealousness, industry knowledge, and promises that he would walk in the door with a big book of business. I decided to cut short my usual processes, and after only two interviews over two days and a scanty background check, I found myself walking around the office and introducing all to this challenging new salesperson. I had to cut the introductions short as Mr. Perfect jumped on the telephones, eager to tell the world they could now do business with my company.

At the end of the day, he asked me for a ride home. I was not clear on what happened to his car, and as we drove, I barely listened to his confusing story about why he needed to be left off at a street corner in a somewhat seedy commercial district. Feeling good about the whole situation, I complied.

After driving home, I exited the car and dropped a pen between the two front car seats. I used a powerful flashlight to help locate and remove it, but found something else that stopped me cold. Under the front seat where Mr. Perfect had been sitting were about a dozen pills, which I immediately recognized as illegal drugs.

Now I had to unhire a very bad employee who would never have made it through my own employment process—if I had stuck to my own rules.

Reference Checks

Conducting reference checks is a standard part of the hiring process, and if the situation looks promising, it is appropriate to ask for at least three references. It may not be appropriate to call the candidate's current employer, but

---

Joe's Spooky Manager From the Virtual Ether

The company was expanding rapidly, and we had an immediate need for a manager to generate revenues directly and open new offices across the Southwest. The perfect resume was on my desk.

After conducting the first interview, I was enamored of this new candidate, who had just moved to the area. In her previous post, she began as a sales rep and reported through two management levels to the three owners of the company. Her husband was not involved at all, she said, because he was working out of state. In only three years, she had increased revenues dramatically and then waltzed around the western U.S., opening offices in major cities, staffing for more business, and then moving on. She was making a fortune but had to leave because her husband was transferred to our city. There was a good chance her husband would become her first customer at our company.

I wanted to jump ahead and make an offer, but reluctantly began checking her background and references. She seemed a bit flustered when I said, "By the way, I can't seem to find the phone numbers of the offices you opened in Phoenix and Denver. Can you tell me what they are?" After some delay, I received the two numbers with an explanation that the offices were not really that busy now; things had slowed down since she left. Indeed they were. Both telephone numbers connected with personal answering machines. The red flags were up.

Other discreet checks were not coming out as expected, but the finale came when I asked in a telephone call, "Susan, I looked up your business address on the Internet, and it looks like a residential area. So was the business (employing 30 people) run out of your home?"

"Uhhh, no," she replied, "that is an office building." She seemed unsure.

I continued. "Well, I called the secretary of state there and was told that the business was registered in the name of your husband. So I was wondering, how do these other three people fit in?"

There was a long silence, and then she responded in an uncertain voice, "My husband is such a jerk. I can't believe they would make him an officer of the company and no one even told me."

"Your husband was made an officer of a company in which he wasn't involved at all, and he didn't tell you?" I said.

"I don't know what's going on," she said nervously, "I'm going to ask him tonight what's going on and then I'll tell you."

"Sure," I said, "call me."

Her story was unraveled, and that was the last conversation I had with my promising new manager.

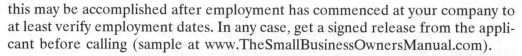

this may be accomplished after employment has commenced at your company to at least verify employment dates. In any case, get a signed release from the applicant before calling (sample at www.TheSmallBusinessOwnersManual.com).

Many in the business world these days are leery of providing references because there is little upside but plenty of scary stories about references and lawsuits against nice people who talk too much on the phone. Begin the call by warming up the other person with a short and friendly introduction to the situation and stress informality. Then ask safe questions, such as dates of employment, job titles, and responsibilities. A list of good questions to ask is available at www.TheSmallBusinessOwnersManual.com.

One common technique used by good recruiters is to mine references for additional references. For example, if Roger Recruit helped both the finance and MIS departments, whom in MIS did he work with? Because a recruit can hardly be expected to provide anything less than the most complimentary references, the second reference may be more candid than the first.

Finally, if several candidates are being considered, be sure to ask the same questions of all references for all candidates. This will allow a more accurate apples-to-apples comparison and avoid accusations that you were unfairly suspicious of particular applicants.

Stop, Think, Then Make the Offer

Now that all the information is gathered, sit back and see if everything is in accordance with the original plans (as discussed earlier in this chapter). Does everything makes sense? Hopefully, many candidates were evaluated, a few were interviewed, and now one is selected. But consider that it may be possible that no one is really a good fit.

Further, consider that hiring a new employee is a serious matter and greatly affects both the life of the new recruit and the character of your small business. There are also many legal responsibilities that commence immediately upon employment and don't go away easily.

If the pressure is on and it's time to grow, then make sure everything is ready, prepare the offer letter (even if it is short and simple), and call your new employee with the good news. Now you are in sales mode again, so be positive and enthusiastic to increase the chances of acceptance.

With permission from the new recruit, send the offer letter and allow some time for consideration and response. This is usually three to 14 days. Further time may then be needed so that the new employee may provide notice of resignation to the previous employer (usually two weeks). If the employee says that notice is not needed, be alarmed and expect the same treatment when troubles arise at your firm.

Keep all other options open as much as possible, since the deal is not complete until the new employee shows up for work on the first day. There is a good chance that the current employer will fight to keep good employees from leaving, there is a chance that another company will come through with a better offer, and there is a chance the new person will just get buyer's remorse and not show up.

Document All Hire, Fire, and Other Employee-Related Issues

Now that things are underway with new employees, it's time to learn a few things about management and administration. Many books are available on these subjects, so just a few words are offered here.

Just to be safe, always keep a wary eye on communications with employees, including the handbook, letters, e-mails, etc., and make sure that unclear language does not allow anyone to claim that an agreement or understanding was in place and that their job was secure. Terminated employees are often angry at the ex-employer and may team up with litigious attorneys and attempt a shakedown. Careful actions in this area will preclude situations where your expensive attorney concludes:

> We can settle now without a trial for $25,000, but if we go to court, your legal fees will be more than this anyway and we may get hammered with a wrongful-termination judgment for $100,000 plus legal fees.

Moreover, it is important to manage all employees consistently; apply the same rules to everyone without exception, or drop the rule. Otherwise, employment-related actions appear capricious and your small business is exposed to claims of wrongful termination, discrimination, and other complaints. Develop, communicate, and review performance measurements for all employees, and consistently enforce them.

Every employee-related event should be documented, consistently, for all employees. This includes tardiness, sick days, vacation days, early leave for family events and doctor visits, work problems, and employment-related conversations. It's best to have a neutral person or an automated system record much of this, since an irate employee will disclaim your observations in court. For example, it's easy to say, "I was on time for work every day and never left early. My employer is lying, and they're really firing me because I am of a different religion." It's harder to claim this if arrival and departure times are recorded by a time clock, by receptionist records, or with the time stamp in e-mails that employees must send as the method of clocking in and clocking out every day.

As part of this process, develop performance review meetings and associated disciplinary policies. When giving reviews, be fair, candid, and not overly patronizing. Immediately after this, while memories are fresh, take time to enter the meeting notes into a memo and include the date, names of persons in attendance, agenda, problems discussed, and actions taken. Then, within a day or two, ask the employee to sign the memo. The signature line may look something like this:

> ... Finally, we discussed that you were seen taking pencils from the office supply room and into your car.

_____

Joe Capitalist,

President, Small Business, Inc.

_____

Joe Smith, Employee (please sign and date)

My signature above means that I have received a copy of this memo.

(A sample employee review memo is available for viewing and download at www.TheSmallBusinessOwnersManual.com).

If the employee refuses, trouble is coming, so hold the meeting again but this time with another person present, who can later serve as a witness. Otherwise, the employee will claim that the meeting never happened and that he was shocked at later being fired.

All this may sound somewhat ominous, but keep it light. Don't let the tone of the meeting approximate that of a war-crimes trial unless major problems are at hand. Nothing lightens up a meeting and improves morale better than sincere compliments about all the things that are going right. The majority of review meetings should be pleasant for everyone.

Note, however, that even "good time" performance review memos can later become important. In many cases, if employees claim that they screwed up consistently right from the beginning, your small business may well be found culpable for making the mistake of hiring such a person. But if good, and then bad, behavior can be demonstrated, it appears that the employee has the ability to do the job, but now has other problems, which are not your fault.

Good, consistent documentation is usually the enemy of litigious attorneys.

Finally, regulations from all the different federal and state agencies described in this chapter regarding preservation of records are immensely complex. Problems may resurface years after employees have left the company, or records may be needed as proof of your consistency when new employees have problems. For example, small businesses may be required to produce information for up to 30 years in cases where workers claim exposure to hazardous materials. The safest advice is to therefore to keep all employment-related records forever.

How to Lose Employees: Resignations and Terminations

There are four basic ways employees can leave the employ of your small business. The manner of saying good-bye has consequences regarding the unemployment insurance rates charged to your company and may affect other matters such as employment agreements. The right classification is important because small businesses with a record of firing many employees without cause will pay higher unemployment insurance rates.

Additionally, employment terminations must be carefully planned because of the severe psychological and financial impact this event may have on ex-employees. Many shocked and angry ex-employees will seek revenge in a fast and powerful way, and these days, this often amounts to a lawsuit or legal shakedown.

You, the small business owner, must approach employee terminations in a non-emotional and objective manner, no matter how charged the situation. Usually, this can be accomplished by dealing with the matter as a sincere effort made by both parties, but one that is just not optimal for the company. Or describe termination as a task that must be undertaken in order to be consistent with company policies. Perhaps you might also suggest that it is not entirely to your liking.

In the case of layoffs, it may be appropriate to be more forthcoming and communicate that the employee's efforts were good and greatly appreciated, but it is a matter of money and survival.

Four Means of Employee-Employer Separation

Terminated With Cause

The employee cannot fulfill the job requirements; for example, he or she fails to meet a production quota (expect this to adversely affect the unemployment insurance rate) or is caught doing something bad, such as stealing (employees are rarely eligible for unemployment insurance in this case).

An important exception occurs often when a small business makes a "mistake" in hiring someone who was not capable in the first place. For example, if a secretary is fired for inability to create original legal agreements, the employer is likely to be cited as having made a mistake for hiring this person in the first place. This can be avoided if there is a written record of positive employee reviews at the beginning of the employment tenure to establish that the employee can indeed do the job, followed by increasingly negative reviews establishing that performance declined, the employer attempted to fix the situation, but the once-promising employee just did not respond.

Terminated Without Cause

This is an exercise of the employer's rights in regard to at-will employment status, and basically allows that the employee may have performed well, but the company just wants someone else. Layoffs are also considered "termination without cause." In this case, the unemployment insurance account of the small business will likely be charged, and UI tax rates may increase.

Sometimes, the small business owner may want to pave the way for unemployment insurance benefits approval by writing a letter to the hapless ex-employee, saying something such as:

> ...despite your best efforts, which were of value and appreciated by this company, we are experiencing a general business slowdown that necessitates termination of your employment...

Resigned With Cause

Watch out for this one. This is where ex-employees say they are quitting because of an employment-related event they didn't like.

The ex-employee may also make the accusation of "constructive discharge." This means that the employer desired to fire this person but instead created an unbearable work environment to force the resignation.

In this case, get ready for a call from a local attorney who wants to discuss discrimination, harassment, a bad work environment, unfair treatment, or something else that's not pleasant.

Resigned Without Cause

Employees often leave their positions because they get a better job somewhere else, or for no known reason. Here, they have voluntarily left their employment and are therefore not eligible for unemployment insurance. The employer's unemployment insurance account is not normally charged.

Note, however, that if the meandering worker is later laid off by his or her next employer, the unemployment insurance account of your small business may well be dinged.

The Termination Meeting

When the final day comes and the termination meeting begins, it is important to have a trusted and credible witness present. Also, have a letter ready for the employee to sign, acknowledging that you made certain statements in the meeting such as the fact that this is a layoff, or perhaps that the employee could not adequately perform as expected. Say what needs to be said in a non-emotional manner, and then ask the now ex-employee to sign an acknowledgment memo.

There may be resistance to this, so stress that signing the memo means only that the ex-employee has received a copy of the memo; not that he or she agrees with the reasoning. The purpose is to preclude a situation where the terminated employee claims that something entirely different was the reason for termination ("I didn't like the constant lewd jokes") or that no termination meeting was ever held at all. That is also the reason a credible witness should attend the meeting. The memo may say something like this:

> Dear Mr. Incompetent:
>
> This company regrets that your employment here is being terminated, effective immediately, for failure to perform the job requirements to the levels we expected of you. Please sign below to acknowledge that you have received a copy of this memo.
>
> Sincerely,
>
> _____
>
> Joe Capitalist,
> President, Small Business, Inc.
>
> _____
>
> Ima Incompetent, Employee (please sign and date)
>
> My signature above means that I have received a copy of this memo.

Note that the biggest concern here is not the unemployment insurance but the fact that the ex-employee is now madder than a hornet and wants to get a mean lawyer to grind you into the dirt like a cigarette butt. In a one-on-one employment termination meeting, it's your word against the "ex" and there's a good chance the evil employer will lose. But if the stage is set as described, there is less chance of lingering legal consequences.

Retaining and Hiring HR Professionals

Hiring and firing and weeding and seeding are perhaps the most important activities undertaken by small businesses, but as we have seen, this can be enormously complex. Well-meaning entrepreneurs may easily run afoul of state and federal laws. Human resource (HR) administration is equally complex, and, of course, everything continues to change. It is just impossible for mere mortals to keep abreast of every possible requirement and exposure.

For these reasons, most small businesses should outsource much of this to professionals as employment grows. HR professionals may be retained to help on an ad hoc basis for the smallest of situations, and this, along with a good CPA and legal counsel, may work well until total employment reaches about 50 persons. At this point, small businesses become subject to even more regulations, and nothing short of a full-time HR manager will do.

Petroff Consulting Group (www.petroffconsulting.com) has a good deal of experience in most of these areas, or search under the specific topics already discussed, because many of these specialists offer a full range of human resources consulting services.

Despite all these employment-related issues, many small businesses continue to prosper and grow. There is a way though all this for small business owners who are diligent and are able to navigate their way through the challenges of growing the company with a well-managed, productive, and contented workforce.

Chapter 7

It's Okay to Hate Taxes

Government has blessed small businesses with a cornucopia of taxes. There are taxes on just about everything imaginable, and civil servants continue to think of complicated new taxes, fees, penalties, and charges to impose on all of us.

For most small businesses, taxes represent the largest single expenditure. For many firms operating under the high-volume/low-margin model, the government makes a lot more money on a sale than the small business. Consider, for example, a consumer electronics firm that sells most goods on a 10 percent markup. In some states, sales taxes are 8 percent of revenues, and income taxes are 40 percent of the margin. Without looking very hard, the government makes 12 percent on a sale and the small business makes only 10 percent.

Most small businesses are always interested in ways to minimize their largest expense: taxes. That is what we will talk about here.

There are many types of taxes, and a detailed discussion would fill many boxes of huge, boring books. Further, understanding and preparing income, payroll, sales, and other forms of taxation are separate areas of study that cannot be covered responsibly in just one chapter. We review here the major forms of business taxation, summarizing information most relevant to small business owners.

- Description (not justification) of the tax
- Rates
- How to pay (forms to use)
- When to pay (schedule)
- How to minimize

Income Taxes

Description

The federal government (IRS) and all states except five charge income taxes to incorporated small businesses. (Nevada, Washington, and Wyoming do not have state corporate income taxes; Michigan uses a "business activities tax," and Texas imposes a franchise tax.) Rates are from 0 percent to a high of 9.99 percent of income in Pennsylvania.

If your small business is a proprietorship, partnership, Sub S-Corporation, Personal Service Corporation, or Professional Corporation (all described in Chapter 2), income from the business is not taxed but flows to personal tax returns; some aspects of this are discussed here, but personal tax rates are not.

Rates

At the federal level, income taxes are basically "revenues less expenses equals taxable income." This is where the simplicity stops and complexity begins (although complexity can be advantageous to the small business, as we shall see soon). At this point, most corporations figure their tax by using the following schedule.

Federal Corporate Tax Rate Schedule

Taxable Income			
Over—	But not over—	Tax is:	Of the amount over—
$0	$50,000	15 percent	$0
50,000	75,000	$ 7,500 + 25 percent	50,000
75,000	100,000	13,750 + 34 percent	75,000
100,000	335,000	22,250 + 39 percent	100,000
335,000	10,000,000	113,900 + 34 percent	335,000
10,000,000	15,000,000	3,400,000 + 35 percent	10,000,000
15,000,000	18,333,333	5,150,000 + 38 percent	15,000,000
18,333,333	————	35 percent	–0–

In most cases, the state taxes begin by taking the federal corporate tax return, making certain adjustments, and then applying the state corporate income tax rates. Note that many states charge a minimum fee, ranging from $10 in Oregon to an $800 franchise tax fee in California. Further, most states do not allow federal income taxes to be used as a deduction before paying the state rates. Thus, a corporation with $1 million in taxable income operating in New York, for example, will pay federal income taxes of $340,000 (34 percent) plus $750,000 (7.5 percent) at the state level, totaling 41.5 percent.

How to Pay (Forms to Use)

A corporation generally must file Form 1120 to compute its income tax liability. However, shorter and nicer Form 1120–A may be used if gross receipts, total income, and total assets are each under $500,000 and certain other requirements are met.

Estimated income tax payments are usually submitted by dropping off a check and a Form 8109 "coupon" at your local bank or other authorized financial institution; these are not sent directly to the IRS.

Generally, all corporations in existence for any part of a taxable year (including companies in bankruptcy) must file an income tax return, regardless of whether or not they have taxable income.

When to Pay

Corporations must make installment payments if estimated taxes for the year are $500 or more. As always, if the payments are even a day late, an underpayment penalty is assessed. To avoid this, make installment payments by the 15th day of the fourth, sixth, ninth, and 12th months of the corporation's tax year. (For most small businesses, this is the 15th of April, June, September, and December.)

After making the estimated tax payments, most corporations need to file the complete income tax return (Form 1120 or 1120A) by the 15th day of the third month after the end of its tax year (for most companies, this is March 15). A new corporation filing a short-period return must generally file by the 15th day of the third month after the short period ends.

It is probably apparent from all this that filing federal and state corporate income tax returns (or the equivalent forms for small businesses that are not incorporated) is a task for professionals. There are many opportunities for the busy small business owner to screw up and get pounded with penalties, taxes, and interest. The best advice is to focus on growing the business, and let an expert do the taxes.

For those who must do everything, however, volumes of information on corporate taxes are available in print and on-line, so small business owners needing extra detail should consult these sources. Begin with Publication 1066 (Small

Business Tax Workshop Workbook) and Publication 542 (Corporations). The IRS has done a great job of preparing these simple-to-read compilations of a difficult-to-understand area, and these publications can easily be found on-line and downloaded at www.irs.gov or can be obtained by calling 1-800-829-4933.

Minimizing Business Income Taxes

The complexities of income taxes for corporations and other business forms offer great opportunities to minimize, defer, and avoid taxes. This subject area is vast enough to employ battalions of business tax specialists, but the most common techniques and areas of concern are reviewed here. In general, use the business to pay as many personal expenses as possible. This increases deductible business expenses and reduces taxable income. The most commonly used deductions for this purpose are as follows.

Business Use of Home

Small business owners may be able to deduct certain expenses for part of the home, even if it is not the primary business location.

The IRS considers deductible expenses for business use of the home to include the business portion of personal expenses such as depreciation, maintenance, insurance, mortgage interest, real estate taxes, rent paid, repairs, and utilities. If a home office, for example, is 15 percent of the square footage of the home, the small business owner as an individual may submit an expense report to the company for 15 percent of these expenses and receive reimbursement. The company's taxable net income and income tax expenses are reduced, but neither the owner nor the company incur payroll taxes on these amounts.

To deduct these expenses, IRS rules require that the home be used "regularly and exclusively" as one of the following:

- The principal place of business for a small business [this means that the home is used "exclusively and regularly for administrative or management activities of your trade or business; and you have no other fixed location where you conduct substantial administrative or management activities of your trade or business" (Reference: IRS Topic 509, Business Use of Home)]

- The place where you meet and deal with patients, clients, or customers in the normal course of the trade or business

- A separate structure that is not attached to the home in connection with the small business

Be careful that no personal activities are apparent in the room, because this would foil the requirement that the room or structure be used "exclusively" for business. For example, if a library of family photographs resides on bookshelves or on the computer in a home business office, this may cause a problem.

Be sure to keep records, bills, checks, and worksheets used to calculate these deductions.

As a practical matter, many small business owners use portions of the home for business and take liberal deductions even when the allowance is questionable.

Use IRS Form 8829 to calculate "business use of the home" deductions. This amount is then carried as a deduction to the appropriate business income tax return statement. IRS Publication 587 has detailed information on rules for the business use of the home (available at www.irs.gov, or call 1-800-829-4933 and receive free copies by mail).

Travel and Entertainment Expenses

This category includes payment for entertaining clients and employees, meals, travel by auto, air travel, baggage handling fees, taxis, hotels, parking, gifts, car rentals, taxes on these items, and other related expenses. The IRS generally allows a deduction for business-related travel and entertainment expenses; however, although employees may receive reimbursement for all their meals and entertainment expenses, only 50 percent of these amounts may be used as a deduction for business income tax purposes.

The IRS has complex and intricate rules regarding this. In IRS Publication 463, for example (Travel, Entertainment, Gift, and Car Expenses), small business owners may learn all about the precise definition of a "Bona Fide Business Expense," "Lavish or Extravagant" meal expenses, the "Directly Related Test," the "Associated Test," and much more.

Further, accurate records and receipts must be kept explaining the date, business purpose, persons met, and amounts associated with each travel and entertainment expense. This is best accomplished using spreadsheets such as Microsoft Excel; however, the report must be printed and signed periodically.

In general, small business owners want to report expenses of this nature liberally to increase business expenses, reduce taxable income, and thereby reduce income tax expenses. The reality is that many small business owners consider virtually all travel and entertainment expenses to be business related. Many small businesses simply pay off the credit card of the owner and the top officers each month, and everything is wedged into one expense line item or another. As far as recordkeeping is concerned, many consider the credit card statement enough for the IRS, although this would not suffice for an audit. These companies are obviously taking the position, "If I get audited, I will explain it all, and if they don't believe me, so what? I won't go to jail."

I have heard of some rather extravagant interpretations of "travel and entertainment expenses" over the years, but have never heard of a situation where the IRS challenged a small business owner for incorrectly classifying personal expenses as business-related travel and entertainment expenses.

For more information, see IRS Publication 463 (Travel, Entertainment, Gift, and Car Expenses), www.irs.gov, or call 1-800-829-4933 and receive free copies by mail.

Automobile Expense and Mileage

Automobile expenses are usually treated in one of two ways, depending upon which offers the most advantage to the small business:

- Businesses may deduct estimated automobile expenses by charging a standard mileage amount of $37.5 cents per mile. This is normally accomplished when employees or owners submit an expense report to the small business and receive expense (no payroll taxes) reimbursement. At year-end, the small business claims these expenses as deductions on the business income tax return. Note that if reimbursement amounts are more than 37.5 cents per mile, the difference is taxable income to employees or owners. There are several situations where this standard allowance may not be used, such as when two or more vehicles are used in the business.

- Small business owners and employees total all of their automotive expenses (such as gasoline, maintenance, parts, fees, depreciation, interest, etc.), figure the percentage of business use, and receive reimbursement from the small business. At year-end, the small business claims these deductions on the business income tax return.

Joe's Colleague Has More Mileage Than He Thought

I once attended a meeting of a small business colleague and his CPA, where we computed corporate taxes for the previous year. The CPA was a large, jolly Santa-Claus type of person, always generous in giving away the government's money. My colleague was rather detail-oriented and had a good accounting background.

We got to the part about automobile expenses. The CPA asked my colleague, "So how much did you use your car for business this year?"

He replied, "Well, I kept a spreadsheet of my mileage, and it's either 45 percent or 55 percent of my total mileage this year, but I wanted to ask you a question to see if this one type of use is allowable."

The CPA grimaced and said, "I don't like either of those numbers. I like 80 percent because it's a nice number and everyone is using it these days."

"But I don't have records to support that," protested my colleague.

"It's okay. Everything will be fine and I'm sure no one will ever look at your records anyway," responded the CPA.

And so 80 percent it was. And we never did hear from the IRS.

Once again, the IRS has complex and intricate rules regarding this (see IRS Publication 463, Travel, Entertainment, Gift, and Car Expenses), where the proper deduction may be calculated for when the owner leaves home, drops a child at school, goes to a business appointment, and then to the office.

The IRS requires those who use this deduction to keep accurate records of each deductible trip, including dates, miles, business purpose, and persons met.

As a practical matter, however, many small business owners keep very thin records, or none at all, and simply report 100 percent of their automobile expenses as business related. Again, many seem to take the position, "If I get audited, I will explain it all, and if they don't believe me, so what? I won't go to jail."

For more information, see IRS Publication 463 (Travel, Entertainment, Gift, and Car Expenses), www.irs.gov, or call 1-800-829-4933 and receive free copies by mail.

Retirement Plans

The federal government now allows tax benefits under a wide range of retirement plans available to small businesses, and small businesses have taken notice. More than 1 million firms of 100 or fewer employees now offer one of the many retirement plans available, and over 80 percent of the employees in these companies have chosen to participate. The tax advantages to these programs have been increased recently, which is all the more reason for small business owners to take notice of this tax minimization opportunity.

Employer-sponsored retirement plans are popular because this benefit helps in recruiting and retaining better-quality employees, and improves employee morale. This is a great way to gain an even deeper commitment from a good team.

Retirement plans were created primarily to encourage savings by offering employers and employees the opportunity of deferring taxes, and that is what we discuss here.

Small business owners gain a double benefit from setting up and investing in company-sponsored retirement plans, because (1) business income taxes are deferred (that is, pushed into later years, but not avoided), and (2) entrepreneurs actually pack away significant funds for later years. Retirement savings are not taxed at current rates, but accumulate untaxed until they are later distributed back to the participant. This means that bigger nest eggs are available at retirement (because income was earned on the deferred taxes for many years). When the plan begins distributions back to the participant, overall income—and taxes—will likely be less than now.

For example, let us assume that a New York manufacturing company finds that taxable income will be about $115,000. This small business owes the IRS $28,100 and the state of New York $8,625 (totaling $36,725). But if the business contributes $20,000 to SEP-IRA's (including *your* SEP-IRA), taxable income drops to $95,000, and total taxes drop to $27,675. But the balance in the small business owner's retirement plan still increases.

Take note, however, that retirement plans offered by a business to employees must generally offer the plan to everyone, or no one. If a small business owner decides to contribute 10 percent of income to a retirement plan, the same amount must be paid in for other employees, too. A way around this is to set eligibility policies, such as "only employees with more than five years of continuous employment with the company qualify for the retirement plan."

Further, the IRS sets limits on employee contributions to these types of plans, to ensure that highly paid employees do not abuse these tax advantages, and we certainly would not want this to happen. These limits change annually. On the other hand, some retirement plans allow the option to reduce or even skip contributions in lean years.

Many companies kick in a percentage of what the employee adds to his or her retirement plan. For example, if an employee (including the small business owner) contributes $100 out of each paycheck to a retirement plan, and the company matches 50 percent of this, the total amount of tax-exposed income now shoved into these plans increases by $150 per pay period. Some plans allow employees to "roll over" the funds if they decide to leave your small business for a new job, so none of their savings is lost.

There are now a complete range of retirement programs for small businesses. Many are listed here. Some are not relevant to certain forms of business ownership (for example, sole-proprietorship or corporation). Specific plans that may be considered include:

401(k) Plans

A 401(k) is a type of retirement plan in which the small business owner and employees save and invest for retirement through regular contributions during the year. In contrast, many other options allow contributions only from the employer (SEP-IRA) or employee (IRAs), but not both. Under this program, employees authorize the employer to deduct a certain amount of money from each paycheck before taxes, and the employer may kick in a similar amount. These funds are then invested in familiar stocks, bonds, and mutual funds, under the company 401(k) plan.

Individual Retirement Account (IRA) Plans

There are over 10 different types of IRA plans now available, which are briefly summarized below.

A traditional IRA is available to those under the age of 70.5 who are currently earning income. Earnings are tax-deferred until withdrawal, and withdrawals must begin at age 70.5, or penalties are assessed. Contributions may or may not be tax-deductible, depending upon many factors, but the earnings grow tax-free over time. When it's time to begin taking distributions from the plan, however, amounts received are treated as taxable income (although tax rates in retirement will likely be lower than they are now). IRAs are mostly for individuals (as opposed to small businesses). In fact, employers may not contribute to IRAs, only employees.

A Simplified Employee Pension (SEP-IRA) is a traditional IRA set up by an employer for employees. Here, the small business may contribute to the employee's IRA a maximum of 15 percent per year of each employee's total compensation, if the employee qualifies, as determined by the employer (seniority, etc.). Employees may not contribute to their own plans; only employers. SEP-IRAs are one of my favorite tax-deferral plans.

A Savings Incentive Match Plan for Employees' IRA (SIMPLE-IRA) is actually not very simple. This is a traditional IRA initiated by a small business. The business must make a matching contribution, which is a percentage of employee pay (all contribution percentages must be the same).

A Group IRA, or Employer and Employee Association Trust Account, is a traditional IRA, but for larger groups, such as unions.

A Roth IRA requires that contributions into the account not be deductible, but distributions (that is, withdrawals) from the account are not normally taxable. IRAs are mostly for individuals (as opposed to small businesses).

An Individual Retirement Annuity is like an IRA, but is operated by a life insurance company through a special annuity contract.

An Education IRA (EIRA) provides funds allowing a beneficiary to attend a higher education program, or even for kindergarten- through 12th-grade education in public, private, or religious schools.

A Spousal IRA is funded by a married taxpayer, but in the name of his or her spouse. Here, one married partner usually has a regular income, and the other has minimal compensation. The working spouse may contribute to the Spousal IRA and to his or her own IRA. This allows a small business owner to defer more money out of the company.

An Inherited IRA is intended to be inherited by someone who is not the spouse of the now-deceased IRA owner. This is yet another mechanism to encourage savings through tax deferral. Note that 401(k) investors (as opposed to IRA investors) can usually defer much more income on a pretax basis, which then increases even more after employers kick in their portion. It happens that 401(k)'s are another one of my favorites.

A Rollover (Conduit) IRA typically refers to an IRA only used to receive funds from a different IRA plan distribution, which funds are then moved into another qualified plan at some point in future. They are used in special situations, normally requiring retirement fund transfers.

These retirement plans are obviously complex and are only summarized briefly in these pages. Check with an investment pro to learn what makes sense for your small business. Although this may seem daunting to most small business owners, large investment companies, banks, payroll services providers, and others who sell these programs make it easy. Simply sign a few papers and program administrators establish the plan, help select investments, explain how to pump money into the accounts quickly or automatically, provide information to employees, and then do the administration, carrying out a variety of tax-reporting and recordkeeping requirements.

Why do these investment companies want your money so badly? After all, it's merely on deposit and cannot be used for any purpose other than the specified investments. The reason is fees. The retirement savings of millions of small business are eroded because of high fees charged to administer small business retirement programs such as 401(k) plans. A recent study, for example, found that investors in plans with 50 persons or less paid an average of 1.4 percent per year in fees, and some paid as much as 3 percent. Large companies offering similar programs to 1000-plus employees paid only 1.17 percent. Note, however, that of the 400,000 401(k) plans now in operation, nearly 300,000 are plans with fewer than 50 employees. Since fees of this nature are not regulated, anything goes. This can make a huge difference over time, when the effects of compounding interest accumulate or when safer, low-risk investments are preferred.

The solution for some may be found among a new group of low-cost on-line plans such as Fidelity's "Online 401(k) or Invest N Retire's "EFT 401(k)" (through Charles Schwab Corp.'s brokerage services). (Christopher Oster and Karen Damato, "Big Fees Hit Small Plans, *Wall Street Journal*, 21 October 2004, Section D.)

Once the plan is set up, where should the funds be invested? Like some experts, I recommend throwing darts to decide among index funds, but that's another subject. Once the funds are in a retirement plan, investors will be able to choose just about anything already familiar, such as stocks, bonds, mutual funds, etc. The investment is the same—it's just held in a different type of account.

To find out more about the tax side of this issue, get Publication 560 (Retirement Plans for Small Businesses) and Publication 590 (Individual Retirement Arrangements) at www.irs.gov, or call 1-800-829-4933 and receive free copies by mail.

Medical Expenses and Insurance

Medical expenses and insurance may generally be deducted against the income of small businesses, but this can be a bit complex.

For sole proprietorships or similar situations where the effects of the business flow to the individual's personal income tax return (Form 1040), a deduction is allowed on Schedule A for the amount by which total medical care expenses exceed 7.5 percent of adjusted gross income (AGI). Remember that expenses at the personal level are considered after payroll taxes, so it's more advantageous for the small business owner to have the business pay these expenses. This is possible, because the self-employed health insurance deduction percentage is now 100 percent.

Offering medical insurance to employees is generally not required, but if a company offers medical insurance to anyone, the same deal must be offered to everyone. For example, the small business owner may not purchase a top-end policy for himself and a low-end HMO plan for other employees.

For sole proprietors, partners in a partnership, or shareholders in an S-Corporation, a deduction against income of up to 100 percent of medical insurance premiums may be allowed, and any remaining premiums may be tallied with other medical expenses as an itemized deduction on Form 1040, Schedule A (Personal Income Tax Return). This is not allowed in any month of eligibility in an employer-sponsored subsidized health plan.

The expenses incurred by you—the small business owner—your spouse, and your dependents are allowed.

What is a "medical expense"? This area is complex and easily could fill an exciting book. Generally, the small business owner can include just about anything that seems medical-related. In the unlikely event of an IRS audit and challenge, the small business would pay back taxes, a penalty, and interest on disallowed amounts.

Specifically, medical expenses include insurance premiums paid for medical coverage including accident, health, and qualified long-term care insurance. A deduction is not allowed for life insurance, for policies paying for lost income due to medical problems, or for policies that pay a fixed periodic amount when medical problems prevent a normal work schedule.

Medical expenses also include fees paid to doctors, dentists, chiropractors, psychiatrists, and certain other medical professionals. Payment for hospital services, long-term care services, nursing services, and lab fees are also allowed. Even expenses for services such as acupuncture, laser eye surgery, and substance-abuse (alcohol and drug) and inpatient treatment centers are deductible, along with the cost of items such as prescription eyeglasses, contact lenses, false teeth, crutches, hearing aids, wheelchairs, and more. The cost of insulin and prescription drugs is also deductible.

Expenses for fitness clubs, funerals, over-the-counter drugs, and most elective surgery are not allowed.

Don't forget transportation costs associated with getting the medical care, such as an ambulance, or fares for a taxi or bus. If a car is used, compute a deduction using the standard mileage rate, or use actual expenses such as a portion of your total annual fuel, oil, parts, maintenance, etc., as previously discussed. In either case, also include parking fees and tolls. You may even deduct meals and lodging charged by the hospital or medical service provider if the reason for being there is to receive medical care.

Be careful to deduct medical expenses actually paid during the year, regardless of when the services were provided. Total medical expenses for the year must be reduced by any reimbursements received from insurance companies or others, even if the reimbursement was paid to a doctor and not to you.

Archer Medical Savings Accounts (MSAs)

Medical Savings Accounts (now renamed "Archer MSAs") pay the costs of routine medical expenses for small business employees as well as sole proprietors. There are two elements to these plans: a medical savings account and a high-deductible health insurance policy. These may be especially useful to employees or owners of small businesses, because their medical insurance policies are often less generous than those of larger firms or the government.

If a small business has fewer than 51 employees, the employer can pay for everything or else let employees pay for the Medical Savings Account. If the employer pays for the entire cost of the plan, the payments are not taxable to the employee. The amount of employee (or individual) contributions can be claimed as a deduction on Line 29 of Form 1040.

Similar to an IRA, income in these accounts accumulates tax free.

When medical problems do occur, Archer MSA distributions are tax free if used to pay for qualifying medical expenses of the account holder, spouse, or dependents. Qualifying medical expenses are costs that could otherwise be used as itemized tax deductions on Schedule A.

Health Savings Accounts (HSAs)

Beginning in 2004, tax-deductible contributions were able to be applied to Health Saving Accounts (HSAs) to pay for medical expenses. Similar to MSAs, they are especially useful to employees or owners of small businesses, because medical coverage is often less generous than one gets through larger firms or the government.

An HSA is established either by an employer (for example, incorporated small businesses) or an individual (such as sole proprietors or the owners of corporations as individuals to supplement their company plans). They are set up as custodial accounts or tax-exempt trusts to pay medical expenses not covered by high-deductible health plans (the annual deductible is at least $1,000 for individuals and $2,000 for families). There are other rules of eligibility, too, so that these plans cannot be maintained by individuals who receive medical insurance through a spouse or Medicare. Also, HSAs don't exist by themselves—they must be combined with a high-deductible health insurance plan.

HSA rules are somewhat similar to rules concerning Individual Retirement Accounts (IRAs). HSAs, for example, are "portable," so that as a small business owner or employee moves among different insurance plans over the years, the HSA goes with the individual. HSAs are underwritten mostly by insurance companies and HMOs. Also, any eligible individual can set up an HSA in much the same way as IRAs: Permission or authorization from the Internal Revenue Service is not necessary.

Although tax deductions are limited to the amount of the annual insurance deduction (or the maximum deductible permitted under an Archer MSA), contributions to these plans are tax-deductible whether the individual itemizes or not. Also, employer contributions are tax-free to employees. After funds are in the account, earnings accumulate tax-free, and when medical problems arise, distributions from the HSA are excludable from gross income.

For more information see IRS Publication 502 (Medical and Dental Expenses) and Publication 969 (Health Savings Accounts and Other Tax-Favored Health Plans) at www.irs.gov, or call 1-800-829-4933 and receive free copies by mail.

Flexible Spending Account (FSA)

Another new tax-savings device is the little-known Flexible Spending Account (FSA). It's difficult to find information on this program, even at the IRS.

FSAs allow employees to take pretax dollars and deposit these funds into an FSA with their small business employer. When medical problems or many other related issues occur, employees submit receipts for reimbursement to the employer. Although the IRS has set the rules for FSAs, they are administered by (small business) employers, which leaves substantial room for hanky-panky.

FSAs are financially advantageous because certain health-care related expenses are paid for with pretax dollars. Unlike similar medical savings plans, these accounts are "use it or lose it" each year, so nothing accumulates. In other words, small business owners who set up accounts for themselves should spend all amounts accumulated within any given year.

Beyond regular medical expenses, the IRS recently added certain over-the-counter (OTC) medicines to the list of products eligible for coverage. Even common items such as allergy medicines, antacids, antifungals, botanicals, cough and cold products, dietary supplements, herbals, minerals, pain relievers and many other first-aid products are allowable. The general rule is that the IRS allows use of the FSA when these items are needed to treat a current illness, but not when used for general health purposes.

For more information, see IRS Publication 969 (Health Savings Accounts and Other Tax-Favored Health Plans), Publication 535 (Business Expenses), and Publication 553 (Highlights of Tax Changes) at www.irs.gov, or call 1-800-829-4933 and receive free copies by mail.

Section 179 Depreciation Allowance

Small businesses typically purchase items with a useful life of more than one year. This includes tangible property such as buildings (but not land), computers, furniture, production equipment, telephone systems, tools, vehicles, and even some intangible items such as patents, copyrights, and now even computer software.

It is often to the taxpayer's advantage to show the full amount of the purchase in the year of acquisition; however, the IRS requires that the cost of this depreciable property be spread out and deducted over a period of time associated with the useful life of the asset. Depreciation is a complex area not covered here. Instead of depreciating these assets, most small businesses will be able to take advantage of the "Section 179" deduction, where up to $100,000 in depreciable property may be expensed on IRS tax returns in the year of acquisition. This amount has been significantly increased lately, and many small businesses will be able to claim this deduction for virtually all of their asset acquisitions.

The advantages of using the Section 179 deduction are that it reduces taxable income and income tax liability in the year of purchase, and simplifies bookkeeping because depreciation schedules are not needed.

Using the Section 179 deduction is not always advantageous to the small business. Opting for this deduction instead of depreciating may adversely affect Social Security coverage and eligibility to claim earned income credits. Also, if business income is expected to increase in future years, expensing the asset under Section 179 will result in increased taxable income just when extra deductions are needed.

The total amount available under Section 179 is generally $100,000, but this amount may be modified under a number of rules, so small business taxpayers should understand how it works. Nevertheless, the $100,000 maximum is a dramatic increase from the previous figure of $24,000.

For more information, see IRS Publication 946 (How To Depreciate Property), Publication 551 (Uniform Capitalization Rules), and Publication 553 (Highlights of Tax Changes) at www.irs.gov, or call 1-800-829-4933 and receive free copies by mail.

Additional Employee Benefits

Small business owners may offer a wide range of other benefits that allow the company to purchase important goodies for themselves and their employees before amounts are subject to payroll taxes. Employees receive a double benefit because the various plans are paid for with pre-payroll tax dollars, and pricing for businesses is often better than pricing for the same services offered to individuals. Therefore, employees end up with a better plan. Still, entrepreneurs must think carefully about what employees really need and value, because the same package must often be offered to everyone or no one. These additional benefits may include:

☐ **Automobiles.** Discussed separately in this book *

☐ **Commissions and Bonuses.** These are treated the same as salary; there is no special tax advantage to calling compensation "bonuses," "commissions," "wages," or "salary". *

☐ **Dental and Vision Insurance.** The best deal is often to simply add this to the existing plan for medical insurance from the same carrier.

☐ **Dependent Care Assistance.** Small businesses may pay for employee dependent care and/or household services provided to employees subject to certain limits, and if the policy does not favor highly compensated employees.

☐ **Medical Insurance.** Coverage for the employee and his/her dependents (also discussed in Chapter 9).

☐ **Meals.** While meals provided to employees technically must be added to income and are taxable, this may be excluded from income if the meals are furnished at the main business location, and if meals are "furnished for your convenience."

☐ **Non-Medical Insurance: Short Term Disability Insurance, Long Term Disability Insurance, Life Insurance.** If a worker is injured on or off the job, these plans pay for some amount of lost income. In some states, minimal amounts must be purchased for any employee and paid for via withholding taxes (discussed further in Chapter 9).

☐ **Paid Time Off, Paid Holidays, Sick Leave, Parental Leave, Bereavement Leave, Personal Leave.** Offering pay during time off for situations such as these is not really a tax-deferral method but rather a way to keep employees happy, and can be part of the overall benefits plan.

☐ **Profit-Sharing Plans.** Profit-sharing plans allow a small business to distribute a portion of net income, gross margin, profits from a particular product line, or whatever best improves productivity and morale, through an informal company-designed plan. Profit-sharing plans can improve productivity immediately (if the payout is not too far off), but the distributions are treated as normal compensation and are subject to payroll taxes.

☐ **Stock Ownership Plans (SOPs).** Allow a small business to grant shares of stock to employees. The IRS does not require that this benefit be for "everyone or no one." It may be offered only to selected top officers. Corporations do not need to be publicly traded to consider this benefit. The IRS regulations regarding stock options and stock ownership plans are complex and depend upon a variety of factors. These plans can be used to defer income until the stock is sold and will help employees take a longer-term interest in the financial health of the small business.

☐ **Tuition Reimbursement.** Here, the employer pays for books, fees, supplies, tuition, and equipment as part of an "Educational Assistance Program." The courses must be relevant to the activities performed by employees, and part of a degree program. The Educational Assistance Program must also meet the following requirements: It cannot favor highly compensated employees; a maximum of 5 percent per year can benefit the small business owner; employees cannot receive cash instead of the education; and all employees must receive notice of the tuition reimbursement program.

☐ **Officer Loans.** Many firms defer taxes by setting up a loan through which the small business owner borrows money from the company. This may work to manage taxes, but ensure that everything is set up properly. Make sure there is a written loan agreement between yourself and the company, where interest is charged at market rates. Also, payments must be made back to the business in accordance with the agreement, including interest and penalties on delinquent amounts. Treat the loan as seriously as any other personal or business obligation. The IRS looks at the substance and not the form of the arrangement, and if they conclude that the loan is really a sweetheart deal between the small business owner and himself, the loan may be declared a sham. In that case, the IRS will recast the situation and declare that the "loan" is really either (1) income to the recipient (therefore subject to payroll taxes, but taxable income of the small business decreases accordingly); (2) a distribution of capital back from the small business; or (3) a dividend (subject to capital gains taxes to stockholders but not deductible by the company).

☐ **Retirement Plans.** Discussed in a previous section, retirement plans are a great way to manage taxes, improve morale, and accumulate savings. Also note that the cost of providing retirement planning advice and information to employees—including yourself—is deductible.

* These items may be offered only to selected persons rather than to all employees.

For more information, see IRS Publication 15B (The Employer's Guide to Fringe Benefits) at www.irs.gov, or call 1-800-829-4933 and receive free copies by mail.

An employee and fringe benefits package to minimize taxes and improve morale is another one of those areas where the entrepreneur may put a system into place that's good for everyone. Nevertheless, things change, so this area should be revisited every year or two.

Sales and Use Taxes

Description

Everyone is familiar with sales taxes, money collected by sellers as a percentage of revenues on behalf of state and local governments. What is a use tax? It is a means of ensuring that buyers who avoid sales taxes (usually by purchasing out of state) still pay the same amount. It does this by taxing their usage of a product in the tax jurisdiction in which the product is ultimately used.

For example, a fitness center opens in Tempe, Arizona, and purchases exercise equipment from all over the U.S. Equipment purchased in California and moved out of state is not subject to California sales taxes. The business must report the purchase to the state of Arizona, which then charges the buyer a use tax. This tax is normally the same as the local sales tax. Technically, the small businesses have no incentive to purchase out of state, and the local government gets a piece of the action either way.

As a practical matter, many small businesses purchase items out of state, do not report the transaction, and do not pay use taxes. Enforcement of use-tax laws is difficult because every small and large out-of-state purchase by consumers and businesses alike is subject to this tax, but taxing authorities have difficulty collecting this information.

Sales taxes are the inverse of use taxes: Small businesses must pay a certain percentage on the sale of most products (but few services) to the state, which then retains some of the funds and distributes the remainder to local governments. Businesses are authorized to collect this tax from buyers, but regardless of whether sales taxes are charged, the business must pay the appropriate amount to the state.

In addition to other business start-up and registration activities, all small businesses should check with their CPA or call a local sales and use tax office to see if a seller's permit is needed. More than one permit may be needed depending upon the products sold, and the locations of the business. With this, your company is on the radar of the state and will be able to submit and pay sales taxes. Otherwise, the business may not legally sell products.

Sales taxes can be especially complicated for small businesses that sell products in many locations. In California, for example, there are many different rates depending upon the county, city, and special district tax area, and so multilocation or traveling sellers must prepare a summary of sales in different jurisdictions. The situation may be a bit simpler for small businesses that ship products. Those sellers may usually charge a single, local rate on sales (less shipping charges), and not worry about the rates in use at the buying end *if* the seller has no physical presence in the buyer's area and *if* the product is shipped by a third party (and not company vehicles). Technically, the buyer (business or consumer) must report the difference to the state and pay the use tax, but few do.

Not all products are taxable. In Pennsylvania, for example, businesses do not collect sales taxes on clothing or food.

Further, small businesses do not normally pay sales and use taxes on items purchased for resale (that is, inventory), or for raw materials that flow into the cost of goods sold. In some situations, this is simple. For example, a toy maker should not pay sales taxes for plastic wheels purchased for toy cars—but what about the glue used to attach parts? The treatment of questions such as these may vary widely. Most states allow small businesses to submit these questions, and will research the matter and later provide a written ruling. This should be accomplished up front because otherwise, the small business might pay sales taxes unnecessarily, or owe for back taxes, penalties, and interest.

Sales and use tax regulations change frequently, and it is hard for most small business owners to keep up-to-date. Reporting sales taxes may also be complex. That is all the more reason to outsource the reporting and payment obligations to a CPA or other accounting professional, and focus on growing the business.

Rates

In many cases, there is a rate at the state level, augmented by other rates. Sales and use tax rates vary across localities, from zero (in five states) to 7.25 percent plus local surcharges in California. Further, many states do not charge sales taxes on food, prescription drugs, non-prescription drugs, or clothing. Information on the rates relevant to your small business must be obtained from local governments.

As an example, sales taxes for purchases in Los Angeles are:

State of California	6.00 percent
County of Los Angeles	0.25 percent
District tax	1.00 percent
Local tax	1.00 percent
Total	8.25 percent

How to Pay (Forms to Use)

Most states require that sellers submit a monthly or quarterly (depending upon sales volume) return describing revenues, exemptions, and sales and use taxes payable. If a quarterly return is needed, then estimated sales taxes are often required in the two interim months. In all cases, a monthly form (estimated or full return) must be submitted to the state along with payment.

When to Pay (Schedule)

The returns are usually due within 30 days of the close of the reporting period. As always, tax boards are always delighted when small businesses pay late, because penalties and interest are charged immediately.

How to Minimize

There are no significant strategies for minimizing sales taxes. The only way this could be accomplished would be to underreport revenues, or reclassify product revenues as services revenues (that is, sell the product for less money; charge a lot for shipping and handling). As a practical matter, however, this is rarely seen.

Regarding use taxes, many small businesses simply do not report equipment purchases and thereby avoid the tax. Care should be taken in this respect, however, since some large equipment purchases may show up in lien searches or through property-tax reporting systems.

Payroll Taxes

The third major area of taxation regarding small businesses is payroll taxes.

Employer Identification Number (EIN)

The first area of concern is the EIN. This is a special number issued by the IRS upon request from new employers. The EIN is used in virtually all communications with the federal government. A similar identification number is probably needed at the state level. If the business form of ownership is a sole proprietorship, then an EIN is not needed, since the sole proprietor's Social Security number is used instead.

The easiest and fastest way to get an EIN is to call the IRS at 1-800-829-4933 and the number will be issued immediately. Otherwise, fill out form SS-R (Application for Employee Identification Number) at www.irs.gov. The IRS will send back your EIN in about a month.

Every small business (except sole proprietorships) should get an EIN because it is needed for any compensation paid by the firm, including amounts paid to the owner.

W-4 and I-9 from New Employees

Immediately upon hiring new employees, small businesses should have the employee indicate her filing status (single, married, etc.) and the number of dependents claimed. This is accomplished though Form W-4 (available at www.irs.gov). The information provided here is needed to determine the proper amount of income tax to withhold. Of course, employees may change this whenever they desire. The employee, not the employer, is responsible for reporting correct information on this form.

Also, new employees must complete CIS Form I-9 (Employment Eligibility Verification, Section 1) no later than the close of business on the first day of work, and the new employer must finish Section 2 by the end of the employee's third day on the job. (CIS, or Citizenship and Immigration Services, was formerly known as INS, Immigration and Naturalization Services.) The employee must provide associated original identification documents to support the situation, and the employer should inspect these for authenticity and correctness and copy these to the employee file. Make sure your policy is consistent: Ask for the same information from everyone, regardless of appearances.

Form I-9 establishes that the new employee is authorized to work in the U.S. and that the employee who presents the employment authorization document is the person to whom it was issued.

Obtaining Form I-9 may be a bit difficult: First, poke around at www.uscis.gov or search at http://uscis.gov/graphics/exec/whereis/query.asp and see if the form is available online; CIS has been updating this form and has not yet established an availability date. If not, the next best alternative may be to ask your CPA or a colleague for a copy. Calling INS at 1-800-375-5283 could possibly be a time-consuming endeavor. An I-9 may be downloaded from www.TheSmallBusinessOwnersManual.com.

Employers must keep this information for three years after the date of hire, or one year after the date employment ends, whichever is later.

What Are Taxable Wages?

Wages include funds paid to employees for services performed, such as salary, wages, overtime pay, bonuses, commissions, sick pay, vacation pay, and special awards; but they may also include taxable fringe benefits and expense reimbursements where the expense is not an allowed IRS deduction. Further, all tips (cash and credit card) received by employees must be reported in accordance with IRS regulations.

Additionally, items such as clothing, books, tuition, inventory, equipment, or services ("Stay late and finish those reports this month and we'll pay for your expenses next month at school") are considered "wages paid in kind" and are treated the same way as normal wages. The value of a wage payment in kind is its fair market price on the day the payment is made. In the real world, it is difficult for the IRS to enforce this.

Not subject to payroll taxes are expenses paid by employees (including you, the small business owner) for the business. The best way to report this is to submit a monthly expense report to the company showing the date, expense, reason, and amount of all business expenses, signed by the employee (probably you) and also approved by the employee's manager or company owner (you again). Then, receive a check back from the company for this amount. This clarifies that the funds are for expense reimbursement and not taxable compensation. Some small business owners use the expense report as a way of having the business pay for personal expenses.

A business expense report in Microsoft Excel format is available for free download at www.TheSmallBusinessOwnersManual.com.

See Publication 15, Circular E (Employer's Tax Guide) for more information on wages, tips, and other compensation.

Form W-2, Form W-3, and Form 1096

All persons working with your Small business must be sent a copy of W-2 (for employees) or Form 1099 (for independent contractors) by January 31 of each year.

For employees, Copy A of Forms W-2 are tallied on Form W-3 (Transmittal of Wage and Tax Statements). This is then sent by the last day of February to the Social Security Administration (which then sends it to the IRS).

For independent contractors, Form 1096 (Annual Summary and Transmittal of U.S. Information Returns) is used to transmit Copy A of Forms 1099 to the IRS.

FICA, Social Security, and Medicare Taxes

Once an employee is on board, it's time to properly report and pay:

- **Income Taxes.** The employee pays this, but the employer must withhold the proper amount from each paycheck, according to compensation and the number of exemptions claimed on Form W-4.

- **Social Security Taxes.** The Federal Insurance Contribution Act (FICA) requires that employers withhold both Social Security and Medicare taxes from wages and non-monetary compensation paid to employees during each payroll period. The small business must withhold a matching amount. The FICA tax includes 6.2 percent for Social Security taxes, and 1.45 percent for Medicare. The Social Security portion is payable only until wages reach a certain limit, currently $84,900; there is no limit on the Medicare portion. Another way to look at this is that employers must withhold Social Security and Medicare taxes at a rate of 7.65 percent (6.2 percent up to $84,900, then 0 + 1.45 percent), but the employer pays 15.30 percent.

These funds must be deposited to certain authorized banks (ask your bank if they accept payroll tax deposits) along with Form 8109 (Federal Tax Deposit Coupon). Monthly or semiweekly deposits may be required. Rules governing the deposit schedule are complex, and IRS publications or a CPA should be consulted to determine the best fit for your situation. Otherwise, payment may be made with Form 941 instead of bank deposits if the net tax liability during the quarter is less than $2,500.

Employers must then file a return reporting and reconciling amounts withheld, via Form 941 (Employer's Quarterly Federal Tax Return). The due dates for Form 941 are as follows:

For The Quarter	Due Date
January, February, March	April 30
April, May, June	Jul 31
July, August, September	Oct 31
October, November, December	Jan 31

If the taxes have been paid in full properly, an additional 10 days is allowed for you to file Form 941.

For more information, see IRS Publication 15, Circular E (Employer's Tax Guide) and Publication 15-A (Employer's Supplemental Tax Guide), at www.irs.gov, or call 1-800-829-4933 and receive free copies by mail.

Unemployment Taxes (FUTA)

The Federal Unemployment Tax Act (FUTA) allows federal and state governments to work together in offering unemployment taxes to displaced workers. Most employers will pay this tax at both the federal and state levels. Employers generally must pay unemployment taxes first at the state level, and these amounts are then credited to amounts due under FUTA.

FUTA is paid only by the employer, not the employee. The rate is 6.2 percent of the first $7,000 in wages (maximum, $434 per employee per year). These amounts are payable via Form 940 (Employer's Annual Federal Unemployment (FUTA) Tax Return), or the shorter and nicer Form 940-EZ, which most small businesses will prefer.

Football Beats Payroll Taxes

Filing and paying payroll is easy for some, but the special knowledge required is usually acquired slowly over time.

One Saturday I decided, enough of paying outsiders to do this—I will just learn it myself. Even though the taxes were due on Monday, I figured that with my amazing accounting and financial skills, everything would soon be under control.

I began by spreading out several federal and state forms, letters, and publications on the kitchen table. Soon I was moving along, but things got thick real fast. The afternoon wore on. I was not making good progress. A headache was underway.

I read just about all of the materials and still couldn't answer the question, "So where do I begin?" much less "What must be finished by Monday?"

I reread some of the materials, but my understanding of payroll taxes was not coming into focus. The headache pounded on, and I wanted to do something else.

Then I had a great idea: I would call back my accountant to finish the returns due on Monday, watch what she did, and with this extra knowledge, I would know enough for the future. In the meantime, a football game was on TV.

Fortunately, I reached her on time and everything was completed. But with the headache gone and the filing crisis in the past, I never took much interest in doing payroll taxes again.

Form 940, along with the payment, is due as follows:

For The Quarter	Due Date
January, February, March	April 30
April, May, June	Jul 31
July, August, September	Oct 31
October, November, December	Jan 31

If the taxes have been paid in full properly, an additional 10 days is allowed for you to file Form 940.

State unemployment tax programs vary, but the tax rate is often related to your hiring-and-firing record. If an employer lays off employees frequently, the unemployment tax rate will be higher.

Independent Contractors, Form 1099 MISC

Taxes are not withheld on amounts paid to independent contractors; however, if more than $600 per year is paid to any one person, the small business must report this to the IRS via Form 1099-MISC (Miscellaneous Income). To accomplish this, ask for the Social Security number (or EIN) of the contractor as soon as the relationship begins, and ask the independent contractor to provide a completed Form W-9 (Request For Taxpayer Identification Number and Certification).

If this is not completed, employers must withhold 30 percent of payments due to the contractor as backup withholding.

Any and all amounts crossing the table from employer to contractor are reported on Form 1099-MISC, regardless of whether it is for labor, services, materials, or expense reimbursements. It is then the independent contractor's responsibility to report the details to the IRS, usually via their Schedule C (Profit or Loss From Business).

Small business owners should not be capricious in classifying persons as independent contractors as opposed to employees. The IRS has long been aware of abuses in this area. See Chapter 6 for rules and a complete discussion of this issue.

Penalties and Paying Late

All of this is immensely complex, but if your small business screws up in some way, the IRS and it's state-level cohorts are not upset, since your business will get hammered with large and immediate penalties, fees, and interest for items such as:

- Failure to pay or make a deposit on time. The penalty for paying late is usually 0.5 percent per month. Interest is charged on penalties and unpaid interest.

- Failure to file a return on time. The penalty for filing late is usually 5 percent per month.

- Bounced check.

- Failure to file an information return.

- Failure to provide employees or independent contractors with a copy of their W-2's or 1099s on time.

- Failure to provide certain information on an information return, such as taxpayer ID numbers.

If your small business is in trouble, don't even think of slow-paying on payroll taxes. This is a great way to get into big trouble, and payroll tax liabilities survive bankruptcy anyway.

Payroll Taxes: Getting It All Done Accurately and On-Time

Paying and reporting federal and state payroll taxes accurately and on time is not easy or pleasant. Small business owners should consider the following ways of ensuring that these important tasks are handled well.

Do It Yourself

For most small businesses, this is the least desirable option. For beginners, meeting payroll tax responsibilities is a tedious, time-consuming and error-prone undertaking. Most important, it ties up the small business owner and precludes him from doing more important tasks, such as new business development or recruiting.

A partial solution may be to consider a number of new electronic filing and payment systems. Over six million small businesses are now using systems such as Creative Solutions (www.creativesolutions.thomson.com), File Your Taxes, (www.FileYourTaxes.com), Lewis Software Associates (www.lswonline.com), LTtax (www.payrolltax.com), and others.

Doing payroll taxes in-house should probably be considered only if the small business owner has already mastered this area and has sufficient free time to keep on top of everything.

Accountant or CPA

Asking your CPA to make sure that payroll tasks are handled well is a great alternative, because most already undertake this responsibility for other clients and can accomplish it with minimal involvement of the small business owner. There are additional benefits as well, because the CPA probably is concerned with other corporate matters such as income taxes, and all of this can be done together.

On the downside, there are often minor logistical problems such as getting payroll information to outside accountants and getting back the completed returns for signature and mailing. These are nothing a courier can't handle. Also, using a CPA will likely cost more than other alternatives, although CPAs can often assign lower-paid assistants to do the work. Finally, CPAs are not perfect; they must sometimes be reminded that due dates are coming up and the work must be completed a few days in advance, so that everything can be returned, reviewed, printed, signed, paid, and mailed on time.

Automated Payroll Tax Services

Many banks and specialty companies such as ADP (www.adp.com), Paychex (www.paychex.com), and SurePayroll (www.SurePayroll.com) offer automated payroll tax payment and reporting services to small businesses. Each pay period, hours are reported to these firms by telephone, fax, e-mail, or through the Internet. The service provider then prints payroll checks and withholds the proper amounts of local, state, and federal payroll taxes from both the employer and employee, out of the small business's bank account.

The employer is then in a good position to prepare, sign, and file the various quarterly and annual tax returns. Outsourcing these headaches may be quite valuable to many small businesses.

Fees amount to about $50 per pay period for 20 or fewer employees.

If standing in line at the bank is not enjoyable, and if your time is worth something, these services are a great deal.

Many firms in this industry also offer related services such as retirement plans (previously discussed), HR management, benefit administration, workers' comp, Section 125 Flexible Spending Accounts (already described), plan administration, customized employee handbooks, and more.

Quickbooks and the Accounting System

Many small businesses use Quickbooks or similar PC-based accounting software. For a fee of about $200 per year, users subscribe to payroll tax tables that make sure the program is loaded with the latest tax rates.

When it's time to do payroll, the software calculates all relevant taxes, deducts employee and employer portions, and prints payroll checks and pay stubs. And when it's time to file reports, the software fills out state and federal tax forms.

For an additional fee, Quickbooks offers an add-on Internet-based service that allows users to e-file and e-pay Forms 940, 941, and 941 Schedule B.

This option doesn't cost as much as other alternatives, but the small business owner must stay aware of due dates and deposit dates to avoid fees, penalties, and interest. Further, a working knowledge of payroll taxes in general is required so that returns may be reviewed for obvious errors.

Other Small Business Taxes

Several other taxes may be overlooked by small business owners, but this doesn't mean they go away—local governments sometimes take years to figure out that a company is operating within their hunting grounds and then demand payment for back taxes, penalties, and interest. Some small business owners use alternate addresses and other means to circumvent these liabilities. Here we discuss the real-world pros and cons of these devices.

Business Licenses and Business Tax

Many cities require that any private business operating within the locale obtain a Business License or Tax Registration Certificate for the privilege of conducting business within the taxing jurisdiction. Even if there are no offices in a particular location, a license or certificate is often needed if the firm conducts business transactions. Many cities require each location to have a separate business permit, and each business activity must also obtain its own permit. If your firm provides temp help in medical, clerical, and technology services out of offices in the north, south, east, and west sections of the city, then 12 (3 × 4) permits may be needed.

Rates are often structured as a minimum fee, or as a percentage of gross receipts, whichever is greater. "Gross receipts" means that the city gets a piece of the action (say, 1 percent of revenues), regardless of whether the small business sells products or services. Unlike sales taxes, however, these taxes are not normally passed on to the buyer.

Cities regularly check building directories and use other means to find small businesses that conduct business but do not pay taxes within their domain, so check in advance to learn your specific situation.

Taxes at the city level may well affect relocation decisions, so be sure to include this when considering a move or expansion.

Special Permits

Permits may be required for some businesses such as restaurants, health and beauty parlors, and massage parlors.

Police and fire permits may be required also, and to obtain these, small businesses must often pass an inspection to ensure that the premises are safe, contain certain equipment, and have exit policies.

Special permits may also be needed by small businesses that do not have a permanent location in a particular city, but sell on the street or on public property during various events.

Professions and Occupations Tax

Some cities have a Professions and Occupations Tax as a kind of catch-all revenue source. Indeed, one city defines this as "all other business activities not specifically taxed by other sections," so it's hard to get around this one.

Check with colleagues and with your CPA to learn about this tax and to see if it is actually paid by other small businesses. In some cities, large businesses must do it right, but most small businesses either do not pay the tax at all or else grossly underreport their tax liability.

Excise Taxes

Excise taxes are paid when specific goods are purchased, or upon certain activities. In contrast to sales taxes, excise taxes are often included in the price of the product. There are also excise taxes on activities, such as on wagering, or on highway usage by trucks.

A small business may be liable for collecting excise taxes on alcoholic beverages, cigarette and tobacco products, gambling, gasoline, tires, energy resources, activities associated with waste management or hazardous substances, recycling fees, e-waste recycling fees (now in California), and even fishing tackle boxes.

Other Local Taxes

Local authorities have created too many taxes, fees, surcharges, and special charges to be listed in any book, which is why each small business owner must check with a CPA, vendors, associates in the industry, and local government Websites (some of which are quite helpful) to learn the total tax picture.

For example, unforeseen local taxes may include any number of items such as disposal fees, environmental fees, facility fees, generator fees, hazardous substance taxes, occupational lead-poisoning prevention fees, and even ballast-waste water-management fees.

■

As noted in the beginning, taxes are the single largest expense for most small businesses. There are many different types of taxes, and compliance, reporting, and payment is often complex. Entrepreneurs may prefer to spend time in other areas such as new product development or generating new revenues, but an understanding of the tax picture is an important and productive investment of time, too.

Chapter 8

Getting Professional Help

Small business owners are often victims of the saying, "You can do anything, but you can't do everything." Many attempt to keep their sales and operations running at full throttle but inevitably run into legal problems, accounting and tax concerns, the temptation to become self-styled computer gurus, or to otherwise wear the hats of diverse professionals. Often, the small business owner does not seek outside help at all. Many avoid professionals to save money; they may find "professional types" intimidating; or they just don't understand that there are only 24 hours in a day. This chapter takes away some of the mystery in working with outside professionals.

Attorneys

Attorneys are perhaps the most maligned professionals and the most intimidating to small business owners. We need to know how they work and when to use them. It's valuable to have a trusted business and contracts counselor ready to go when potential legal issues arise.

Generally, attorneys are needed in three types of situations. These occur when your small business is:

- **The Defendant.** This means your small business has received a demand letter from the legal counsel of another party, or you're being sued. Usually, this involves disputes over unpaid bills, but it may also involve breach of contract, ex-employee complaints, or other matters.

- **The Plaintiff.** Here, you are unable to get unreasonable parties to listen to a problem and satisfactorily respond, and the legal system is needed to force them to address the matter. This usually involves clients who don't take your bills seriously, but it may also involve temperamental vendors, treasonous ex-employees, or theft of company property.

- **In Need of Information.** Hard information is needed to avoid making a mistake. For example, you are entering a new business area and need an attorney to draft new sales agreements, or help is needed in negotiating a lease for new premises, including zoning concerns.

It's better to get legal counsel involved sooner rather than later. Many small business owners wait too long before seeking legal advice and paint themselves into a corner by saying or writing too much to the other side.

Here are some other common areas of concern where legal help is frequently needed:

- Should we set up a corporation or L.L.C.? We need the company to be properly registered with the right legal documents.

- An agreement just arrived from a new big-time customer, but the terms are unreasonable—so we need a legal pro to explain our position to the client's legal counsel.

- An ex-employee or competitor is saying bad things about our services. Can we stop them?

- I delivered my product or service, but now a client says it's not right and won't pay for it. We can't take it back, and we must get paid. We need help in getting the customer to take this seriously.

- Is the proposed lease on our new warehouse reasonable? How do we get the landlord to make some changes?

- An unscrupulous attorney has filed a lawsuit against us. Should we fight or give in to extortion?

- We've invested a lot in a new product. How do we get patent and trademark protection?

- A factory across town is selling us a used piece of machinery. We need a solid purchase agreement to make sure there are no liens attached and that the title transfers properly.

- How do we set up retirement accounts, trusts, other businesses, officer loans, and fund transfers to minimize taxes among the owners?

- We're buying land to build a new outlet. Help is needed in getting the proper zoning, permits, insurance, bank loans, and sales agreements.

- We want to get out of an agreement, but the other party says no. Can we terminate early?

- We are getting into a new business area and need new contacts.

- The state passed a new law. Does it affect our small business, and how do we avoid problems?

It's only a matter of time until an attorney is needed. Although the legal profession has been much maligned in recent years, most attorneys are hardworking, honest, and sincerely want to provide value to help your small business grow. It's best to get aligned with the right person now.

Beyond offering legal expertise, attorneys can get into the middle of tangled and emotional disputes and sort out the issues and negotiate problems in a detached, rational manner. This is often of great benefit to small business owners (who are normally very emotionally involved). In many cases, attorneys may report the facts back to their respective clients, and when both sides understand their positions from a legal counselor, things fall into place very quickly.

Finding the right business legal counsel is not difficult. Begin by asking your CPA and colleagues, or a local chamber of commerce, or just do a Google or Yahoo search for something like "Sacramento business attorney," "Hartford business litigation," or "debt collection lawyer Pittsburgh." Call around to see who seems to be the best fit. Explain that you've got a particular issue today but are really looking for a long-term relationship. Then consider criteria such as:

- Who returns your call, and how quickly?

- Is there a particular area of expertise? A debt collection attorney, for example, may not be the best at patent issues. On the other hand, your particular situation may be straightforward and not require lengthy experience, and just about any competent attorney may work out fine.

- How many years of experience does this particular attorney have? Does the attorney have partners with more or less experience?

- Does the attorney understand the nuances of your situation, or are you somehow not really getting through? Invoking small details at the right time often makes all the difference in legal matters.

- How big is the law firm? (Most small businesses fit best with smaller law firms.)

- Does the firm have paralegals or help available at lower billing rates for legal research, routine filings, and clerical tasks?

- Are the rates affordable? Hourly rates range from about $100 to $400 per hour, depending upon the location, required expertise, and size and prestige of the law firm. Of course, price-shopping may not be a great idea when shopping for an attorney. Higher-voltage attorneys can often get things done more quickly and less expensively.

- Are you comfortable in speaking with this attorney, or do the communications seem hurried and difficult to follow? (If this is experienced in the "selling" stage of the relationship, imagine what will happen later.)

- Are references available? Does the attorney have a long record of working for other local small businesses, especially in your industry? (Of course, conflict-of-interest rules would prohibit this firm from working with a small business if the firm has represented an adversary, so get this out of the way early by asking.)

If things don't work out, it's no big deal to change attorneys. Further, it's perfectly acceptable to switch attorneys when different issues arise.

Attorneys are licensed and regulated at the state level, so law firms may offer different billing arrangements depending upon the situation and business considerations. These may include:

- **Hourly Rates.** Expect to sign a retainer agreement and put up about $1,000 as a retainer fee. When this is burned off, expect to write another check. Most small business representation is accomplished with hourly-rate agreements. Out-of-pocket expenses are also billed to the client.

- **Flat Fee.** Many lawyers are able to estimate quite accurately the time requirements for particular situations, and may therefore quote a flat fee to remove uncertainty. For example, an appeal of a debt collection judgment may cost $2,000, or incorporating a new small business may cost $1,500.

- **Contingency.** Some law firms may agree to a contingency arrangement, where they "work on spec" (speculation) and receive 25 percent to 40 percent of the judgment amount—if they win and the judgment is actually collected (many times, the judgment is not paid). This arrangement is most often seen in longer, more complex matters (such as class-action lawsuits). Most law firms do not favor this form of compensation.

In all cases, an officer of the small business must sign a retainer agreement, where the law firm is assigned the right to represent the firm in this matter, and where the client agrees to pay for services including an up-front retainer.

Go to www.TheSmallBusinessOwnersManual.com. to see a sample retainer agreement.

Here are some common questions and fallacies about working with the legal system and attorneys:

- "Attorneys mostly work on retainers, so I don't have to front any money." Wrong. Most of the time, you pay a retainer fee of $500 to $2,000 and your legal counselor works by the hour. Contingency deals are not popular for smaller matters, and besides, if you believe in what you're doing, why share it with an attorney?

- "My problem is complex, and I need a great attorney." Actually, most matters are very routine, and just about any attorney who understands commercial law can handle the matter.

- "It's rude to ask about fees." Most attorneys understand that money is important. It's perfectly reasonable to ask, "What is your hourly rate?" "Can we use an associate at a lower rate for research and other work?" and "How much do you think this will cost, and how long will it take?" Most attorneys are ethical and are conscientious about the rates they charge for their work, so they will not steer clients into costly legal battles.

- "Can I recover my legal fees?" Maybe. Ask your attorney up front if the court may award legal and collections fees as part of the judgment. Remember, getting the judgment is only half the battle. After this comes the battle to collect, and the court will not help much in this effort. Also, ask about the chances of losing—and paying the legal bills of the other side.

- "Attorneys are no smarter than I am." Most attorneys are actually very intelligent. Law schools do a good job of ensuring that only those who are intelligent and committed end up practicing law.

- "Justice is swift." In civil matters especially, expect that most disagreements will grind on for a long time. It will sometimes take years for both sides to answer questions, gather and present information, and sort through the legal issues. To you, the answer is immediate and crystal clear, but it still needs to be understood, processed, and digested by a dispassionate and meticulous legal system. Don't expect anything fast. Further, if a judgment is awarded, many more fees may be incurred, forcing the other side to pay—and there is a good chance of never collecting. That is why in many situations, legal remedies don't make sense: Why spend $5,000 in legal fees over two years to collect $3,000? When the decision is made to "go-legal," pace for the long run. Having said all of this, stubborn adversaries sometimes settle quickly when both sides are faced with legal fees.

- "There is little I can do because my problem is with a defendant who is far away." If a problem is in another state or even in another country, call around or use the Internet to find an attorney with an office down the street from the bad guy. Many problems between small businesses occur when one party thinks that the other party cannot enforce the agreement. Merely receiving a call or letter from a local (local to an adversary) attorney may bring quick results.

- "I can't afford a long legal battle." Sometimes, a scary letter from an attorney is enough to get the other side to see things your way. This provides notice to the bad guys that they may be able to fool around with your small business, but they can't ignore the legal system.

- "I don't want to appear in court and testify." Actually, most matters never get to trial. Attorneys from both sides will sort out the issues, tell everyone the strengths and weaknesses of their arguments, and offer a deal reflecting each side's chances of winning in court. There is nothing to force stubborn clients to accept an out-of-court settlement, but they usually do, once tempers cool off and the prospect of increasing legal bills becomes paramount.

Joe's Euro-Customer Says "Whoa" to the Deal

My small business was exporting a large piece of equipment to a small company in Geneva, which had sold the same equipment to a large company in Paris. Once everyone was connected, we signed the documents and my company commenced spending a large amount of money to buy extra parts and customize the machine. This investment was for a very special configuration, and everything would be lost if the deal fell apart. We finished in plenty of time and began planning the shipment.

I called the Geneva company to work out shipping details and left a message for the owner to call me. He did not respond. Two days later, I called again. I called again the next day. No return calls.

After some time, we finally connected. He told me he was sorry, but he no longer needed the equipment. He said his customer had canceled the deal, and there was nothing he could do. I was not sure if this was true, or if he had merely found a better price from another seller. When I began asking questions, he told me he could no longer talk, because it was time to go and attend to his horses.

Over the next few days, I called a few more times, but his secretary continually told me that the company owner would not talk to me because he was with his horses. I realized that since I was in far-away California, the large amount of time and money I had put into this deal did not bother him a lot. So I took another route.

The next call regarding this matter was not from Los Angeles to Geneva, but from a Swiss attorney specializing in small business matters, with offices very close to my horse-loving customer. The attorney quickly connected with my customer and explained in the local language that the agreement was enforceable, and that my company would sue if he did not perform.

My Swiss adversary suddenly realized this was a serious matter. He could hang up the telephone on me, but now he was being forced into a local court, where he had no defense. Maybe he feared that he would lose his horses.

It took just this one telephone call to get things moving again. Suddenly, the deal came to life and the big company in Paris wanted the equipment again after all. We then shipped our machine, and it was received and installed without incident. Thanks to my new attorney-friend in Switzerland, we worked out special payment arrangements from the customer to make sure the money went into an escrow account before shipping, because we now had special concerns about the intentions of my horse-loving customer in Europe.

Legal problems are all too common today, and since small businesses typically work with many customers and vendors, it's only a matter of time before an attorney is needed. Begin looking for the right legal counsel to help your small business navigate through the uncertainties that will lie ahead.

Accounting and Certified Public Accountants (CPAs)

Most entrepreneurs will have a continuing need for professional accounting services, even those with a good deal of expertise in the profession. Certified Public Accountants (CPAs) offer many types of plans to meet the specific needs of small businesses.

The title "CPA" means that the person you are dealing with is a professional who has studied accounting theory and has passed a nationally standardized two-day exam. In most states, the designation also means that this professional has passed a certain number of university-level accounting and finance courses and has previous work experience in public accounting (perhaps two years' minimum). Thus, we are assured that the professional is indeed competent to undertake the work and responsibilities needed by your small business. Referring banks, clients, vendors, and taxing authorities to your CPA assures them that the information about your small business is correct and credible.

Many small businesses use their own PC-based accounting programs, which offer immense in-house capabilities when compared with the ledger-based systems of the early 1980s or even software available only a few years ago. Small businesses are encouraged to use this technology to keep their own set of books with up-to-the minute information. Nevertheless, outside expertise will still be needed as outlined later. Although hardworking, earnest, but inexperienced persons involved with a small business may work mightily at learning and applying Quickbooks, Best Software's Peachtree, or Microsoft's Great Plains, there is only so much a non-accountant can do.

Here are the areas in which professional accounting expertise offers great value to the small business owner.

Bookkeeping and Records

A good CPA should set up the initial chart of accounts and make a number of entries into the books so that beginning balances are set to the correct amounts, and so that future entries are merely repetitions of earlier transactions. That way, less experienced accounting, bookkeeping, and even clerical staff may handle routine tasks and daily entries. At year-end, CPAs make certain non-routine entries for depreciation, amortization, taxes, changes in officer-loan and equity accounts, and so on.

Further, state and local taxing authorities (and other agencies such as CIS) require that employee, sales, and other records are kept for varying lengths of time. The CPA will maintain many of these archives and advise as to which information should be stored at the office, and when it should be destroyed.

It's a bit less expensive and easier to have a CPA or subordinates work in their own offices and make entries into the books physically located on a PC at your office, thanks to technologies such as CD burners, Symantec's pcAnywhere, and Citrix Online's GoToMyPC.com. The latter two options allow distant users to log in to the PCs or the network at your location and enter transactions directly into the accounting system.

A CPA should be involved in closing the books at year-end, in preparing financial statements, and in special ad hoc projects, but the day-to-day tasks should be handled by an in-house accounting staff. This may include a full complement of clerical, bookkeeping, accounting, and financial experts, or perhaps just a spouse. Distributing the work in this manner will keep accounting expenses low and allow critical information (such as cash balances) to be readily available when needed. Even when work must be performed by a CPA, most should be accomplished by lower-paid bookkeepers and accountants; the CPA should begin billing only when CPA-level skills are truly needed.

Tax Planning and Preparing Returns

The CPA should be involved with all taxes associated with the small business, including corporate income taxes, payroll taxes, sales and use taxes, other taxes (excise, professions, etc.) and personal income tax returns. It is not normally productive for the small business to do much of this in-house. The CPA already knows what's going on since he or she is looking at the books and making periodic entries anyway (as already discussed), and so they are in a perfect position to advise on how to minimize and defer taxes. To avoid problems, don't assume the CPA understands everything. Discuss exactly what is expected and make sure a list is in place (something like the following):

> The following applies to federal, state, and local taxes of concern to our small business.
>
> ■ Tell us when various information and reports are needed.
>
> ■ Prepare monthly sales tax returns and send them to our office for signature and payment.
>
> ■ Prepare monthly payroll tax returns and tell us when to make deposits; send us completed Form 8109 payment coupons and state forms.
>
> ■ Do all monthly, quarterly, and annual payroll tax returns.

- Tell us when to send in estimated income tax payments.

- Complete the annual corporate income tax returns.

- When information or action is needed, please give us three days' notice so that we will have time to react (for example, sign a return and print the check). Do not expect us to drop everything and act at the last minute!

- When new employees are hired, instruct them as to how to complete forms W-4, I-9, and anything else that may be required. Keep employee files with these records. Also, issue employee handbooks and keep a journal of who has received them, and when.

- Handle all correspondence and communications with taxing authorities.

CPAs are widely assumed to be well-organized and on top of things, but this is often not true. An informal understanding such as the one already discussed will avoid the common problem whereby a tax payment is missed, a large penalty is incurred, or both parties were waiting for the other party to act.

Business Consulting

Since the CPA is involved in every part of your small business—and others— it often makes sense to get advice on business matters such as how to obtain financing for a special need, the best way to receive and account for credit card payments, how to commence operations in a different state, and a wide range of other concerns.

Auditing

Normally, the financial statements prepared by your CPA are "CPA Reviewed," and not audited. This means the CPA has checked that the numbers are in the right accounts (according to what you have communicated) and that they balance, but there is no auditing to assure that what you have said is correct. For example, certain year-end deposits may be classified as additional sales, when in fact they are really draw repayments from the small business owner. Some lending institutions may require "CPA- audited statements," and in that case, a sampling of deposits to the account would be traced, examined, and corrected. Results from the sampling are extrapolated to the rest of your reporting. Therefore, if 10 percent of the deposit samplings are actually draw repayments, then 10 percent of the total deposits would be reclassified, and sales would decrease by this amount. Auditing services are normally managed by the CPA but performed by less-experienced (and less-expensive) staff.

There are many other types of financial, operational, and compliance audits where a CPA may be involved. These could include situations where the IRS arrives with its own auditors to check the books (usually not a good day), efforts you direct to make sure internal policies and records are being kept properly, and client or vendor audits in accordance with agreements ("We agree to pay subcontractors in a timely manner at certain rates"). As the small business grows, it's best to let outside professionals handle these tasks, and especially a capable and trusted CPA.

Finding a CPA that is right for your small business is not especially difficult and is similar to looking for an attorney, as already described. Hopefully, you will work with your CPA more than with your attorney, which is all the more reason to look carefully.

Joe's Rigorous Search for a CPA

My business was taking off, I hired my first employees, and tax time was approaching. It was time to develop a long-term relationship with a CPA, but I knew no one.

I figured that my business was not that complicated, and I just needed help with taxes, as do millions of other small businesses.

One of my most important criteria then was location. I had been working with another CPA in a different business undertaking, but this often required a lot of driving for our monthly meetings.

I began right in my own office building. I noticed that there were several CPAs on the same floor, and it was helpful that I could walk right in and see everything in operation during the day.

For my first visit, I decided to walk in unannounced and talk with the CPA firm closest to my office, about 10 yards away. I came away certain that they could do the job, but there seemed to be too many people churning out the numbers, and I felt it would be a bit impersonal.

My next visit was a bit further away—about 15 yards. Larry, the CPA, was busy when I walked in without an appointment, but he made time for me anyway and we talked. He was gregarious, decorated his office with model trains, and told me he didn't like taxes very much. He was huge—over 300 pounds—and walked with a cane. He made jokes about our pompous landlord. I liked this guy.

He had one or two very experienced accounting people to help out, and I felt this was about right for my situation.

I decided to give it a try.

Ten years later, through many ups and downs, we are still working together. And I still do like this guy.

To begin, ask for referrals from business colleagues or your attorney, or check with the local chamber of commerce. You can also do a search on Google, Yahoo, or another favorite site, using keywords such as "San Jose CPA" or "CPA Memphis" Then, come up with a list of criteria, which may include:

- Who returns your call, and how quickly?

- Is there a particular area of expertise? (Chances are, just about any CPA can handle the needs of your small business, unless special expertise in e-commerce or another area is needed.)

- How big is the CPA firm? (Most small businesses fit best with smaller firms.)

- Does the CPA firm have help available at lower billing rates?

- Are the rates affordable? Hourly rates range from about $75 to $300 per hour. Ask for an estimate of monthly fees. Most CPAs will be able to provide this information by asking how many checks and deposits are made per month, and the number of employees.

- Are you comfortable in speaking with this CPA, or do the communications seem hurried and difficult to follow?

Next, ask for references from other small businesses, and call to confirm that your evaluations are correct.

Finally, visit the office and meet everyone who will be involved with your company to verify that you'll be comfortable in working with your new CPA for a long time.

Many small business owners are confused in the beginning about using different types of accounting help, and who does what. So here is what you need to know and how everyone should be managed:

- **CPA (Certified Public Accountant).** As already discussed, the good news is that the CPA can do everything, including setting up a system, entering data, producing statements, and getting out the taxes—but CPAs are relatively expensive ($75 to $300 per hour). Many CPAs work with lower-level assistants who help with the grunt work (such as data entry or reconciliations) at lower rates. It's normally a good idea for every small business owner to watch the books closely and do as much as possible in-house, but business owners should make sure that the CPA handles complex and special areas such as payroll taxes, sales taxes, income (state and federal) taxes, and annual statements (often required by banks). When annual statements and tax returns are finished, spend a few extra minutes and get the most out of your CPA by asking for an explanation of the statements and highlight areas of special success or concern.

Joe's Bookkeeper Studies Accounting, Check-Printing Chemistry, and Fraud

My service business was growing rapidly, and I needed to hire a full-time bookkeeper. I met Babs through a help-wanted ad, and after the normal screening process, including a credit and criminal background check, she was hired.

Babs lacked some skills, but pulled herself up by the bootstraps, taking courses at a local college. She learned a great deal at the office, too, and I took pride in her rapid advancement.

Two years went by. She continued to improve and soon knew just about everything. I kept careful watch on the accounting system anyway. Unfortunately, Babs had a special fascination with white-collar crime and thought long and hard during the day about holes in our accounting system. She soon found one.

Our normal procedure was that I authorized payments to vendors, and then issued only the right number of checks to her for printing. Babs printed the checks, gave them to me for signing, and then I gave them back to her to send out.

But Babs changed the system slightly. She found that she could supplement her income by using an increasingly popular chemical to wash the laser-printer toner (ink) off the check, replacing the payee name with hers, and then depositing checks to her bank account.

In a few days, the program made her a valued customer at a local bank. But angry vendors began calling for their overdue payments. We traced the letters and found that Babs had never sent them. It didn't take long to figure out everything from there.

The local police were disinterested in the case, even after my suggestion that—because I knew the crime, the bad guy (girl), her address, and exactly what happened—they could look good by quickly solving the case and impress their boss. After two months, they finally arrested her, after I complained to higher-ups.

The bank was concerned at first, but their major priority was to determine if they were at fault. When they determined that a fraud had indeed occurred but there was no bank liability, they lost interest in helping. In fact, I needed to get an attorney to force them to provide information to the police. The bank had no interest in helping my small business or the police, but were happy to charge fees when forced to comply.

Earlier, I sometimes wondered if I spent too much time looking at all the numbers in the accounting system. Babs taught me a lesson here about trusting accountants, printing chemistry, and fraud.

- **Accountant.** The capabilities of and pricing for an accountant lies between those of a CPA and a bookkeeper. You may want either an accountant or a bookkeeper to enter transaction information into your books. Accountants are supposed to understand accounting theory and thus make decisions on how to handle irregular transactions. However, accountants are not licensed, nor are they even required to take a minimum number of accounting courses. When reviewing resumes, remember that anyone with experience can call himself an accountant. The person selected should convince you of their ability to take on extra responsibilities and handle more complex situations.

- **Bookkeeper.** A bookkeeper enters information into a preexisting system, and does not handle irregular transactions. Bookkeepers are most needed in stable situations, where the same types of transactions are entered in large quantities every week, and only the numbers change. Bookkeepers should make entries only as directed by accountants or CPAs. Finally, *bookkeeper* is the only word I know of in the English language where there are three sets of repeating letters in a row.

- **Data Entry Clerks.** Data entry clerks are not expected to know anything about accounting. They receive low pay and simply enter numbers from various media (for example, time cards or expense reports) into spreadsheets or accounting programs.

- **You.** You must supervise everything. Never live in bliss, assuming that everyone is doing the right thing. New issues requiring attention arise frequently, and employees are both encouraged and impressed when they see the small business owner taking an interest in their work. Perhaps "attention" is the most important word here. Anyone associated with the accounting system must see that you know what is going on, or bad things will eventually happen. Don't become a full-time accountant, but spend at least some time every day looking at different areas of the system to remain up-to-date on what is happening, to appear vigilant, and to make sure that no one is tempted to take liberties.

Updated rates for different types of accounting expertise can be seen at www.tsbom.com.

Computer Expertise

Information Technology (IT) is at the core of just about all businesses these days, but as they say, "…IT happens;" and it's only a matter of time before something breaks. The immediate problem is not the device itself, but the lost productivity of employees.

When it comes to computers, small business owners usually fall into two groups: those who have no interest, and those who fancy themselves as semiprofessional computer technicians. Inevitably, however, outside IT expertise will be needed as the business grows, and so we discuss here when to do it yourself and when to call in a pro. We focus on what constitutes the best use of the entrepreneur's time, and when the risks of doing it yourself outweigh the cost savings.

All small businesses should have some in-house capabilities to fix common problems, such as de-installing and reinstalling programs, attaching and detaching various cables, cleaning printers (the cause of many outages), and changing toner cartridges. It's important to fix even the smallest IT problems immediately and competently to stop related problems from occurring, for employee morale, and to maximize productivity.

Beyond this, it's great to jump in and fix a problem if you've got technical aptitude, but this must be tempered by the realization that it is indeed expensive for a small business owner to spend four hours fixing a problem that could be fixed in one hour—the right way—by an experienced IT technician.

Therefore, all small businesses should be able to handle common problems in-house, but also have an ongoing relationship with a capable IT computer maintenance firm that knows your machines, peripherals, and overall structure. Call for professional help after asking yourself the following questions:

- Is this problem really worth my time?
- Is this a one-time fix, or will this problem likely recur?
- Do I really want to learn how to fix this problem, or am I doing this to escape from more important but unpleasant work?

Shopping for an IT pro is a bit different than finding a good attorney and CPA (as already discussed). That is because attorneys and CPAs must hold university degrees, pass professional examinations, and gain licensing to practice, but there is no such requirement among computer technicians. Although many of these experts have gained a Microsoft Certified Systems Engineer (MCSE) or similar certification, many practicing computer maintenance contractors have not. There is no stopping these "learn on the fly when I'm not serving fries" types from marketing themselves to your small business as the expert who can fix anything in just a few minutes. Just to make things a bit more complicated, there are actually many non-MCSE (or similar certification) experts offering their services who are actually quite competent.

With all this in mind, here are some points to remember when evaluating who should be called when technical help is needed:

- Who returns your call, and how quickly? This will help determine how quickly the technician can be on-site to fix your equipment. Remember, the most expensive part of IT downtime is lost employee productivity.

- What response times are promised? Within four business hours or "it depends what else is going on"? Most companies specializing in this area will have backup experts to send in quickly when needed. Also ask if maintenance can be accomplished before or after regular business hours (which further reduces intrusions on regular operations).

- Is there a particular area of expertise? Explain your operating system(s), major installed programs, antivirus protection, backup systems, and network setup. Note that even among MCSEs, one certification may be more or less valuable for your situation. For example, a certification gained when WIN 98 was king will be of less help if the company now runs WIN XP, or in a Novell networking environment.

- How many years of experience does this particular IT expert have? Can other expertise be called in when needed? (For example, if your small business runs routers and switches beyond the expertise of a particular computer repair technician, ask for the resume of a colleague who handles networking.)

- How big is the computer maintenance company? Many computer pros work solo as freelancers or contractors—but can you afford waiting for days until bigger clients are serviced and your problem is finally resolved?

- The latest trend in small business systems maintenance is to resolve problems via remote connections. Many issues can be repaired in that way in just a few minutes, so you needn't wait hours or days for an on-site visit. Can your system be maintained in this way? What happens if a critical piece of equipment needed for remote maintenance (for example, a router) goes down?

- When easy-to-fix problems occur, will the technician explain how you may fix them in the future, or does this generate a surly response?

- What are the rates for on-site visits and remote maintenance, during regular business hours, off-hours, and for emergency response? Hourly rates range from about $55 to $200 per hour. As always, remember that you often get what you pay for.

- Are references available? Hopefully, the references can affirm the fast response times, reasonable rates, and competency of your chosen computer maintenance vendor.

Beyond this, a few tips are offered here that will stop about 80 percent of computer-related problems from ever occurring:

- Make sure that every machine is protected against viruses, trashware, spyware, and Internet pop-up ads (as discussed in Chapter 14).

- Further, communicate to all employees what they should and should not do to minimize the chances of infection. For example, never open e-mail attachments without scanning first for viruses. Without good protection, even new Internet-attached machines will experience problems very quickly.

- Communicate to all employees that programs, additional software, or peripheral devices cannot be installed on any machine without the explicit permission of an IT professional. Seemingly innocent "updates" are often the cause of serious problems.

- Many problems can be fixed simply by rebooting the machine. Help should not be sought unless the problem recurs consistently after rebooting. All machines should be rebooted at the end of each day, so that they will be ready for a fresh start the next day.

- When Internet connections are lost, the problem can often be fixed by unplugging all DSL modems, switches, and routers, waiting ten seconds, and then restarting.

- Don't be in a big hurry to install the latest drivers and software updates. Remember the old adages, "If it ain't broke, don't fix it" and "Never install any version of software ending in point zero."

If an employee or a nephew is good at computer maintenance, think twice about asking them to fix your machines. This exposes your IT systems to further accidental or intentional damage, and compromises confidential information. While firing a computer maintenance firm is easy, things are a bit more complicated when the relationship is not simply business-to-business.

Links to firms offering business computer services on a national level can be seen at www.TheSmallBusinessOwnersManual.com.

Finally, as the small business grows beyond about 15 machines, working with a computer maintenance company will likely become uneconomical, since a full-time systems administrator will do a faster, less expensive, and better job for your small business.

Chapter 9

Business Insurance

Insurance stands right up there with taxes as one of the least exciting aspects of running a small business. The annual insurance review is often considered a chore leading to a large purchase that will never be used. Most small business owners understand what they are buying when the policies are up for renewal, but then quickly forget the details. There is a very short "half-life" for retention of insurance information. Still, any ongoing company needs various types of insurance to protect itself and to meet its obligations to others. Also, small business owners must know enough about insurance to understand when it is acceptable and prudent to demand that vendors, customers, and other business partners provide insurance protection to your small business. Note also that some types of insurance allow tax-free transfer and provision of benefits to small business owners and employees. Finally, one of the major benefits of business insurance is that arcane and complex business-busting problems are effectively outsourced to the insurance company.

Insurers receive their fair share of negative attention these days, but it's great when the problems discussed in this chapter are negotiated on your behalf by teams of professionals (insurance adjusters, attorneys, and others), rather than the stretched-thin staff of your small business. This chapter provides a summary of the most common small business insurance concerns. Although this advice will generally be useful to just about all small businesses, insurance regulation and offerings vary significantly from state to state, so be sure to talk everything over with a local agent.

Business Insurance Agents

Most business insurance packages are all but indecipherable to those outside the insurance priesthood, given that clients must wade though the thick legal mumbo-jumbo in policies, riders, amendments, exceptions, declarations, supplementary declarations, notices, and more. But that's not so much of a problem if the agent representing the products really understands business insurance, and your industry in particular.

Insurance agents must be licensed in the state where they practice, and insurance companies are rather selective about who may represent their coverages. The majority of agents do understand their products quite well and work hard to uphold industry standards of honesty and integrity. Most insurance professionals are concerned about doing a good job because they are capable people, but also to keep their licenses in good standing and to retain the right to sell various products. This provides great assurances to small business owners and makes the buying process a lot easier; but as with everything, some are better than others. It's therefore important to find an insurance sales agent who knows the products relevant to your industry, can comfortably explain them to you, and ensure that your small business has adequate but not excessive or duplicate, coverages.

To shop for an insurance agent, speak with industry colleagues for recommendations, check the Website of a local chamber of commerce, or ask your CPA or attorney. Another productive source is your favorite Internet search engine. Enter keywords such as "Philadelphia business insurance" and then examine the interesting links.

When it's time to go shopping for insurance, tell the agent your situation and concerns, and also provide the documents indicating that your small business agrees to maintain certain levels of insurance coverages. For example, building landlords usually demand that business tenants insure their premises (more on this later). Other examples include covenants with banks, customers, and perhaps officers and directors. With this knowledge, an informed agent is also in a position to recommend commonly used insurance policies for firms in your industry, and tell you when your small business should be named as an additional-insured under the policies of customers or vendors.

A good agent can explain what is needed, as well as the risks, costs, and coverages, and then show it to you in writing, when all the paperwork arrives. This can save a lot of time that you can use more productively.

Finally, it never hurts to show your current policies to a competitive agent two or three months before renewal time to check on the current market.

Business Insurance Types
Workers' Compensation

"Workers' Comp" is required in most states, and this protects the workers in your business from injuries on the job. It does not cover injuries or illnesses that occur outside of work; General medical insurance coverage is often offered for this purpose (discussed later). Obviously, the source of a problem can be unclear, and when an employee with a medical issue asks for help, it's great if the employer can come through, regardless of the cause.

Workers' Comp rates are based on several factors, but primarily on the following:

- The number of workers

- Total compensation paid by the company (including just about any-thing imaginable, including wages, bonuses, commissions, overtime, sick pay, vacation pay, tool allowances, contributions to retirement accounts, profit-sharing, housing, meals and more)

- The type of business (most important). For example, companies that repair high-voltage transmission-line towers pay higher rates than companies in the stamp collecting business. Workers' Comp can usu-ally be purchased in a package of other policies acquired from a gen-eral insurance provider, but in some cases, Workers' Comp is acquired directly from the state.

    If independent contractors or subcontractors are used, be careful. Most state laws hold that a contractor (in this case, your small busi-ness) is responsible for injuries to employees of subcontractors, in the absence of other insurance. The exposure here occurs if the sub-contractor does not have insurance, has inadequate insurance, or the injured worker's attorney figures that it costs nothing extra to name your small business in a lawsuit against others. Also note that inde-pendent contractors without employees, whose duties closely resemble those of an employee, may be considered an employee for insurance purposes. Be prepared to ask subcontractors for proof of insurance. If this can't be provided, pay the Workers' Comp premium for the extra workers and charge the subcontractor. Don't rely on language in agreements that appear to pass insurance obligations off to others.

What about you? Executive officers in most states are considered employees of their corporation and are therefore covered for injuries; however, they are also included in calculating premiums.

Beyond this, the Occupational Safety and Health Act of 1970 and related state plans require employers to provide employees with a safe and healthy work-place. Enforcement of these regulations may include both civil and criminal pen-alties for non-compliance.

Workers' Comp is no substitute for medical insurance, because it only cov-ers problems occurring on the job, and even then, the claim must be legitimate. Some states, such as California, have suffered for years under a system where employers pay high Workers' Comp rates but injured employees don't receive much compensation. The reason: The system pays out millions in claims for administration of the program, for fake injuries, and for fake-injury attorneys. It's a bad system, but small businesses have no choice about buying Workers' Comp insurance.

Coverage is usually expressed as a number, such as "100/500/100." This means the policy pays:

Bodily Injury by Accident: $100,000 maximum for each accident.

Bodily Injury by Disease: a $500,000 policy limit.

Bodily Injury by Disease: $100,000 for each employee.

Think about your situation and make sure there is enough coverage under likely scenarios. Remember that if an on-the-job accident occurs and the Workers' Comp policy pays out to the limit, your small business will likely still be liable for any deficiencies. This type of financial injury may be fatal to many small businesses.

Property

Property insurance covers business assets, and not real property. These assets may include equipment, tools, machines, furniture, fixtures, computers and office equipment, and related property used to produce income. Besides

The Earthquake Hits Home

On January 17, 1994, the wild shaking of the Northridge earthquake awakened everyone in Los Angeles. Me included. I soon began walking to my office about a mile away, and I passed a 10-floor office building that now had a few large cracks running from the fourth floor to the top. "Not too bad," I thought, but suddenly the police and a truckload of National Guard troops arrived and surrounded the building. No one was allowed in. Not even the dozens of small business owners who operated out of the building. (As you might imagine in Los Angeles, marriage counselors, psychologists, and psychiatrists largely occupied the building.)

Over the next few days, city authorities decided the structural integrity of the building was unknown, and no one was sure if it would remain standing. Troops stood watch around the building as crowds were kept away. This included many small business owners who begged to go into the building to quickly grab important records or property and cash. But no one was allowed to enter.

Finally, a large crane with a wrecking ball arrived. The crane began knocking down the building, starting from the upper floors, as a large crowd watched the depressing sight. Now and then, someone would yell as the wrecking ball hit his office and computers, furniture, and file cases fell to the ground. Confidential papers floated through the air for blocks around. Some of the property seemed recoverable, but no one was allowed even to sort through the remains of the destroyed building.

The earthquake resulted in a total loss for all business owners in the building. Those with adequate insurance at least gained financial reimbursement for their lost offices, property, records, and valuables.

tangible fixed assets, property insurance may cover inventory, accounts receivable, cash, and even business income. Make sure that if there is a fire, major theft, or other peril and everything is lost, the business will receive enough insurance proceeds to restore everything. To accomplish this, get a list of all assets (probably from your balance sheet), and then think about where your property is—and goes—and ask the insurance sales agent to make sure there is adequate coverage. For example, special riders may be needed for trade shows, inventory in transit, vehicles parked off-site overnight, or equipment moved around to customer premises. Also, be sure to know if the coverage causes problems most likely to occur where the property is located. If a warehouse is located along a river, for example, don't assume there is protection against losses from floods. Ask—and have an insurance company representative actually show you in the policy where it says so in writing.

General Liability

If your small business rents its premises, just about all lease agreements require that the lessee (that's you) pay for General Liability Insurance. Here is typical language found in a lease:

> Lessee shall, at Lessee's expense, obtain and keep in force during the term of this lease a policy of comprehensive public liability and property insurance insuring Lessor and Lessee against any liability arising out of the ownership, use, occupancy or maintenance of the Premises and all areas appurtenant thereto. The limit of said insurance shall not, however, limit the liability of the Lessee hereunder. Insurance provided hereunder shall be in companies rated A+, AAA or better in "Best's Insurance Guide." Such insurance shall be a combined single limit in an amount not less than $1,000,000.

In this situation, the landlord requires $1,00,000 in coverage per incident from a quality company that is sure to pay if a problem occurs. Note that the small business remains liable for losses not paid by the insurance company.

In most cases, the lessor (landlord) asks to be named as "additional insured," so that if something terrible happens, the insurance company may pay the landlord directly. Insurance companies are then happy to provide a certificate of insurance to the additional party to affirm this understanding.

Examples of terrible things might include a forklift that accidentally punches a hole through a wall and into an adjacent business, or an electrical problem that burns down your office and the entire building at night.

General Liability Insurance is often purchased in minimal amounts by small business owners, but then results in inadequate payouts when problems occur. For just a few dollars more, problems resulting in bankruptcy can be avoided, so perhaps this is not the best place to skimp when purchasing insurance coverages.

General Medical

In contrast to Workers' Comp, General Medical protects employees from illnesses and accidents that are unrelated to work. Although employer-paid medical insurance is not required, IRS regulations hold that this expense is deductible only if everyone gets the same deal. If medical insurance is offered to one person in the firm (such as yourself), everyone else must received coverage under the same plan.

Employers often pay for the medical insurance of their employees, because it makes employees feel secure, creates a sense of gratitude, and assures employers that workers will not suffer financial problems and remain off the job for lack of good medical care. This is especially important in these tumultuous times for the medical services industry, as employees rightfully fear living without general medical insurance.

Employers can buy insurance coverage for a relatively low cost, as compared to the employee. (Yes, medical insurance is expensive from any perspective, but it's cheaper if purchased by the employer.) On top of everything, employees may have a hard time finding coverage on their own, and the expense of this insurance is rarely tax-deductible by workers. If the employer pays for medical insurance, this important form of compensation basically passes to the employee free of taxes. (See the Medical Expenses and Insurance section of Chapter 7, and the IRS Section 125 Plans section at the end of this chapter.)

Under most plans, the employer pays a percentage of the premium, and employees have the option of buying in or not. For example, your small business may agree to pay 80 percent of the cost of employee insurance, and 50 percent for their dependents. The employer then deducts the employee contribution from paychecks. Other employees may say, "No thank you, my spouse has a better deal." In that case, get a written statement from the employee affirming this decision.

Employers are not supposed to notice that the cost of medical insurance varies greatly depending upon who is hired. But some do. For example, the cost of insuring a healthy male in his fifties with a wife and two children (that is, employee and three dependents) may be eight times the cost of a single male in his twenties. To learn the cost of adding someone to the company policy, call the insurance provider and provide the name, age, and gender of the prospective employee, the number of new dependents, and indicate whether there are any preexisting medical conditions that will become the responsibility of the new insurance carrier.

Most employer-sponsored medical insurance plans require a certain buy-in percentage, meaning that the small business must recruit a certain portion of the total employees into the plan. For example, many medical insurance plans require that over 70 percent of eligible employees agree to participate. Related to this, the employer must state in advance what percentage of the plan is paid for by the employer. In addition, the employer must require that all employees wait for a stated period of zero to 90 days after hiring before coverage commences. Again, consistency is important here; everyone must get the same deal.

Medical insurance policies vary enormously in their coverage. At a minimum, the medical policy may pay a small percentage of only the most urgent problems, or the sky may be the limit. Here are the three major cost determinants of medical insurance plans:

1. **Types of Medical Services Included.** Coverage for many products and services may be offered, including medical and health care treatment, maternity care, orthopedic care, pharmaceuticals, dental care, vision care, psychiatric counseling, chiropractic care, alternative medical coverage, and add-ons such as supplementary accident insurance or dependent life insurance.

2. **Type of Plan.** Another way to improve the deal and run up the cost is to dump less-expensive Health Maintenance Organization (HMO) plans and buy into Point of Service (POS) or Preferred Provider Organization (PPO) plans. HMO plans are out of favor with doctors because reimbursements are low, and employees don't like the red tape required to receive treatment. POS and PPO plans allow employees greater flexibility in receiving care from different doctors, in or out of the provider's coverage area. There are also many hybrid plans, and they are all expensive.

3. **Financial Factors.** The third major set of determinants involve how much employees may pay to medical care providers. This primarily involves the "co-pay" (the employees' portion of a doctor's office visit, for example, $15 per visit); the deductible ("employees pay for 20 percent of costs after paying 100 percent of the first $1,000"), coinsurance, which is the percentage of covered expenses for which employees are responsible, and the maximum benefit. As employees pay more to care providers, the overall cost of the medical insurance goes down.

Other business-specific factors that determine overall cost and eligibility are:

- **Number of Employees in the Firm.** The smallest plans require a minimum of two employees. Usually, husband-wife teams count as only one employee. Note that if there is only one other full-time employee and he or she resigns, general medical insurance coverage will normally be terminated.

- **Pregnancies.** When a small business applies for medical insurance, the number of pregnancies usually must be reported to the new insurance company.

- **Industry.** Under which SIC codes is the business classified? Again, high-voltage transmission-line workers may pay higher rates than stamp collecting firms. See www.TheSmallBusinessOwnersManual.com for a list of SIC codes.

All this may become a bit complex, so a good insurance sales agent may really provide an important service here. The agent should know the pros and cons of the different plans in the context of the needs of your small business, and reduce the zillions of options down to just a few. It is certainly feasible to ask representatives of the insurance providers very specific questions about different plans under consideration, but only the agent can effectively compare plans across different medical insurance companies.

COBRA (Medical Insurance) Must Be Offered to Departing Employees

COBRA, the Consolidated Omnibus Budget Reconciliation Act, was passed by Congress in 1986. The law allows certain former employees, retirees, spouses, and dependent children the right to temporary continuation of medical insurance coverage under the plan and at the group rates paid by your small business, plus 1 percent. The ex-employee must pay either the small business or the insurance company to exercise this option.

At first, this may sound like a good deal to ex-employees, but many then realize that COBRA is more expensive than anticipated because your small business formerly paid a part of the premium but is not required to subsidize the expense after employment ends. COBRA is ordinarily less expensive, though, than individual health coverage.

COBRA coverage will likely be snapped up by healthy people who simply need temporary health insurance, and by those who are pregnant, over 50, in poor health, or attached to a specific doctor.

COBRA coverage need not be offered in firms with less than 20 employees, or if the ex-employee was canned with cause, such as for gross misconduct. The law sets no minimum types or levels of benefits. It does, however, require that these plans have rules outlining how workers become entitled to the COBRA program.

Small businesses must offer COBRA medical insurance coverage to all ex-employees within 44 days of termination, but many forget. In that case, ex-employees may get the attention of a government investigator, or sue your company in federal court. But this will only be a problem if serious medical problems have occurred. Otherwise, negligent employers must pay $110 per day to the ex-employee.

Following notice, ex-employees have 60 days to accept COBRA coverage, and then 45 days to make the first payment. If employees stop paying after the program is underway, they have effectively canceled COBRA medical insurance coverage. Your small business is not obligated to pay the medical insurance premiums and then beat on the ex-employee to get back the money. After 18 months, continuation under the COBRA ends.

Also, note that many large medical insurance providers will directly contact the ex-employee, go over all of this information, collect payments, administer the plan, and otherwise relieve your company of much work. Additionally, the Group Administrative Manual printed by the insurer tells the small business how to further manage the COBRA program.

Small businesses should be aware of their requirements under COBRA, but they may be indifferent as to choices made by the ex-employee because this will result in no additional revenues or expense to the company.

Directors and Officers (D and O)

D and O protects small business owners and other insured officers and directors against lawsuits where someone is trying to get past the business and into personal assets. This may include customers claiming injury from your products or services, vendors or creditors trying to collect in bad times, or a competitor who claims damages for an unlawful action committed by your company.

D and O is generally not associated with problems arising out of alleged sexual harassment, discrimination, or other employment-related areas. For this, Employment Practices Liability Insurance (to be discussed) is needed.

This special protection is most valued by directors and officers who already have great personal wealth. Outside directors may also demand it to protect themselves from lawsuits, because the compensation received from your firm is negligible. D and O is not frequently purchased by small businesses but should be considered if large amounts of wealth have been transferred from the small business into the personal accounts of officers and directors, or if the integrity of the corporation was not well-respected and the corporate veil may be pierced with relative ease.

Employment Practices Liability

Everyone these days has heard horror stories about entire businesses being lost when an unhappy (current or former) employee teams up with an aggressive plaintiff's attorney. Any business with employees is exposed to lawsuits arising out of harassment (sexual and otherwise), discrimination, disabilities, unlawful hiring practices, wrongful termination, and more. This special insurance covers not only the small business owner but also others in the company, even if they are clearly guilty.

Perhaps the most chilling threat arises when, unknown to the small business owner, two employees are having personal issues and decide to sue. For example, a manager may be pressuring a subordinate quietly for sexual favors. In that case, the bad news is that the small business can be sued and found liable—the good news is that the company is defended in court and covered for losses and damages with Employment Practices Liability insurance. The company is insured whether found innocent or guilty (except of course for criminal acts). Another example is when an employer forgets to add a new employee to the General Medical Insurance plan and a major medical problem arises. Or perhaps a manager is fired in violation of her employment agreement.

This is one area where some attorneys have given a bad name to their profession. Some law firms take on dubious complaints on behalf of employees, and basically shake down the employer, saying, "Look, it's going to cost $100,000 to defend against this frivolous claim, and there is a chance of losing $250,000, or we can settle now for $150,000." Many small businesses will be damaged seriously by this exploitation of the legal system, so this is one situation where a small business owner may be angry for being the victim in a legal extortion scam, but thankful that Employment Practices Liability insurance pays for everything and makes the headache go away.

Few firms actually purchase this special coverage, which in most cases means they are one shake-down away from bankruptcy.

Errors and Omissions

E and O is an especially important special coverage for those who provide services (as opposed to products), such as computer programmers and IT consultants. This basically provides protection for cases where your small business causes damages to others.

For example, perhaps a Web-design firm builds a site for a private religious high school that accidentally links to a lingerie seller. The parents sue the school, and the school wants your small business to pay. But E and O insurance offers protection here. Another example is if an employee experiences medical problems, and then we find out that medical insurance was never acquired for this person.

E and O claims greatly outnumber claims under Directors and Officers insurance and Employment Practices Liability. Many large clients demand E and O from their small business vendors, but it might be a good idea, even if it's not required. Consider demanding proof of E and O insurance from certain vendors who work for you.

Product Liability

In today's litigation-happy environment, many lawsuits are based on claims that manufacturers, importers, distributors, and sellers of products are liable for the damages and injuries caused by just about any product. If your small business is somewhere along the chain of suppliers providing a product subject to such a lawsuit, it costs the plaintiff just a few dollars more to name your firm as a codefendant.

Product Liability coverage is often added to General Liability policies, but don't assume that your firm is insured for exposures in this area. Firms desiring increased and special protection may purchase additional Product Liability amounts. This may be especially relevant with older small businesses that have sold larger numbers of products, and perhaps in times when regulations were more relaxed.

Cessna Carpet-Bombed by Product Liability Lawsuits

Perhaps the best-known horror story in this area involves Cessna Aircraft, long venerated for supplying smaller airplanes to the civil aviation marketplace. FAA regulations changed over the decades, but Cessna could not retrofit its 100,000 previously sold aircraft with modern safety features.

Accidents happen in aviation, where something as simple as running out of gas can be fatal. Product Liability lawsuits against Cessna increased dramatically; and the company often needed to defend products built 20, 30, or 40 years ago against current regulations. Eventually, about 50 percent of the price of a new Cessna aircraft was attributed to Product Liability insurance, and in the late 1980s, the company ceased production of single-engine aircraft entirely because of this problem.

For many years, it seemed that this respected American icon had been knocked out of the skies for good. Finally, the regulatory environment changed for small aircraft makers and after a hiatus of well over a decade, Cessna took off again with new models.

Note that these policies do not include problems covered by Workers' Comp or Contractual Liability insurance, and exclude damage to work, intentional damages and injuries, liabilities from contracts, and recalls.

Operations in Progress and Completed Operations

Small businesses providing services must be concerned with coverage for operations in progress as well as for completed projects.

The operations-in-progress exposure arises from claims associated with projects currently being performed by a services contractor, where property damage or bodily injury allegedly occurs.

An easy example involves a plumbing contractor. Wenches-with-Wrenches Plumbing, Inc., is installing copper pipe in an older building, and a major leak and subsequent water damage occur at night resulting from a mistake WWW made while working earlier in the day. This is probably covered under the General Liability policy, but make sure. Perhaps a special add-on is needed for your industry. Ask the insurance agent how this ties in with your Workers' Compensation policy.

Later, WWW completes the project. This is usually defined as when the small business contractor has completed all contracted work, or when the work associated with the damage or injury has been put to its intended use by parties not associated with the small business subcontractor.

If the exact same problem occurs, "operations-in-progress" will no longer pay, and the issue falls under "completed operations" insurance. WWW may or may not be insured, so it is important to ask to see it in writing when the policies arrive.

Note that WWW is responsible for all losses, regardless of whether the insurance company pays up. Many contractors and firms in the service industry are required to carry these forms of insurance, so skimping here may put your small business in default of a contract. As the small business grows and time passes, this loss exposure increases because so many older projects quietly age and come to the attention of plaintiffs with a keen interest in suing your small business and winning the legal lotto.

Business Interruption

Disability insurance covers lost personal income, but what about the income of your small business? Businesses may be put out of action by all sorts of causes—from fires and floods, to the business shutdown of a big customer due to terrorist threats, to a runaway truck that crashes into a retail storefront.

This coverage may mean the difference between solvency and bankruptcy, because the carrier would pay all the regular bills and expenses until your small business is restored (although Business Interruption Insurance does not pay for losses or damages). Business Interruption coverage may be included in the General Liability policy, but speak with the agent to ensure that the amount is sufficient for normal monthly income and expenses.

Not surprisingly, the definition of "Business Interruption" varies, so make sure this coverage fits the situation of your small business. Note also that terrorist threats are increasingly not covered by conventional policies, but may be purchased as an add-on.

Short- and Long-Term Disability

Disability insurance is usually considered a way to protect income—not cover medical expenses or losses—if the insured is unable to work. Short-Term Disability is for a limited period of time, say two years. After these benefits are exhausted, Long-Term Disability Insurance may be purchased, which usually covers the worker until retirement, or age 65.

Short-Term Disability is often designed to cover the waiting period before Long-Term Disability benefits begin. In most states, employers are required to purchase Short-Term Disability Insurance, and this is paid for through deductions from employee paychecks. In some states, this insurance is not required for the small business owner; however, it should be purchased because real medical problems may occur and the benefits from state-sponsored plans are reasonable (but not large), considering their price as compared with private Short-Term Disability Insurance.

Note that the benefits here are offered on an after-tax basis, meaning that they are effectively not subject to payroll taxes. As might be expected, older workers will pay higher rates than younger ones.

Disability Insurance policies are important to the small business owner, and they also appeal to employees, helping to build morale and loyalty. All will sleep better at night knowing that help in the form of cash will be coming if a work-stopping medical problem occurs.

To decide how much coverage to buy, consider the level of income needed to maintain present lifestyles, including rent or mortgage payments, food, automobiles, other loans, and other monthly expenses. The policies normally range from 60 percent to 70 percent of pretax income and may be critical because related benefits from Social Security will not come close to covering these expenses. State-sponsored plans are usually meager, so if this is not enough, consider purchasing additional insurance from a private carrier.

Disability Insurance policies come with an elimination period, which is similar to the deductible amount on other types of insurance policies. Typically, this is 90 days, which means that workers (and you) must have the financial resources to pay bills until these benefits kick in. As the elimination period increases, the price of the insurance decreases, because many medical problems are well under control by this time.

What, exactly, is a disability? Understand this well, since the description varies among carriers and policies. There are two general definitions. "Own occupation" means that a worker cannot perform activities required for a particular occupation. This is more restrictive, but cheaper, than "any occupation." If the latter definition is used, an insured will receive benefits only if no income-producing activities at all can be performed.

There are many other bells and whistles that may be considered with both Short- and Long-Term Disability Insurance, but one of the most important is whether the policy is guaranteed to be renewable. This will be especially important to older workers. Renewals are not guaranteed unless premiums are paid and "Non Can" (Non-Cancellation option) is purchased.

Disability Insurance may not normally be offered to workers or small business owners who are already disabled, have an existing medical problem, are pregnant, or earn less than $18,000 per year. In that case, life insurance may be the best answer.

Both Short- and Long-Term Disability Insurance may be offered through conventional medical insurance carriers and companies offering payroll services. To find a carrier, apply, and get a quote, type "Disability Insurance" into your favorite search engine. The best source,however, is probably your insurance sales agent, who is uniquely positioned to make sure the Disability policies tie in with other forms of insurance paid by your small business.

"Key Man" or Life Insurance

Various forms of term and whole-life insurance (sometimes called "Key Man Insurance") are sometimes purchased by the owners of small businesses, where one partner is compensated for the loss of another. A common example is when business co-owners buy coverage such that if one dies, the others receive a payout. The thinking here is that in many small businesses, each person is critical, and the business is not viable unless all are hard at work in their particular areas of expertise. The surviving owners receive a payout to purchase the interests of the deceased partner from the estate. Then, the company may be continued without distractions, or it may be sold.

Once again, your business insurance sales agent is well-positioned to recommend what is best here and to make sure that all serious risks are addressed without purchasing duplicate or unnecessary coverages.

Insurance, Tax Advantages, and Cafeteria (IRS Section 125) Plans

Insurance often provides a tax-free way to transfer benefits and constructive income to the small business owner and employees. This is accomplished, for example, when General Medical Insurance is paid for by the small business. Employees receive this benefit free of payroll taxes.

Small business owners interested in using this allowance should investigate IRS Code Section 125, which allows employers to pay for benefits offered to employees, without reporting this as additional taxable compensation. Health care, vision and dental care, group-term life insurance, disability, adoption assistance, flexible spending accounts to employees, and dependent care assistance programs all may qualify as allowable under Section 125.

In return for these tax-free benefits, employees often agree to salary reduction agreements and then also contribute a portion of future salaries on a pretax basis to pay for the qualified benefits.

One indirect benefit is that Workers' Comp insurance rates decline, because payroll decreases.

See Chapter 7 for more information on minimizing taxes, and learn more about Section 125 Cafeteria Plans in IRS Publication 15-B (Employer's Guide To Tax Benefits) at www.irs.gov.

■

Honesty and accuracy are important in applying for all types of insurance. It may be tempting to tell the insurer that a fire alarm and suppression system is installed in your building because the rates will be less expensive; but at the end of the day, most small business owners need to know that they are really insured. Otherwise, when a real problem occurs, the insurer may declare the policy null and void because the application was not correct.

It is clear that business insurance is a complicated undertaking, so many growing businesses retain professional insurance advisors to manage and coordinate all types of coverages. These consultants do not sell policies but make sure that the small business has sufficient insurance to meet all contractual and regulatory requirements, check for duplicate coverages, shop for the best rates, negotiate payouts, and keep watch over changes and their effects inside and outside of the business. Business insurance advisors are difficult to locate on the Internet, but several are listed at www.TheSmallBusinessOwnersManual.com.

There are many other types of insurance that may be relevant to your small business, so ask your business insurance sales agent as well as industry colleagues to make sure that your total insurance coverages are similar to others in the industry and to help you sleep well at night.

Chapter 10

Finding and Leasing a Business Location

This chapter is concerned with finding the right location for your small business and then negotiating a good deal to lease the new premises. It's usually a good idea to lease rather than buy, especially in the beginning, because needs may change dramatically in the first few years of operations, and leasing offers greater flexibility.

Using an Agent

There are many factors to consider in locating a property and negotiating a deal. For most small business owners, this activity is rarely necessary, so working with a professional real estate leasing agent who knows the geographical area, market prices and trends, local customs, industry players, and normal lease terms and conditions is highly recommended. Leasing agents also have access to data on local demographics and average leasing rates. Further, while it's possible to find a good location just by driving around, most leasing agents have access to virtually all available properties through on-line industry databases (with the exception of certain privately owned commercial developments that prefer the "do-it-yourself" approach, and smaller sublease deals).

Most agents are paid through commissions and fees by the landlord after a deal is signed. While some argue that leasing prices are then marked up accordingly for the new lessee, the counterargument is that landlords cannot get away with charging more than the market rates. Many consider that the agent is merely getting paid the same amount the landlord would have spent on selling expenses, so there is no need to increase prices for the new lessee.

Be aware that compensation to the leasing agent is a function of square footage, term, and price per square foot of the new premises. An upscale boots merchant looking for a seven-year lease on a 3,000-square-foot retail site will likely get much more attention than a parts distributor shopping for a three-year lease on a 2,000-square-foot warehouse.

In most cases, commercial leasing agents must be licensed at the state level as real estate brokers, and so a certain level of ethics and professionalism can be expected.

Finding a good leasing agent is not difficult. The best way to do this is to drive around an interesting area and look for "Now Leasing" notices on a few promising locations. Then call the agent shown on the notice, who will likely be an expert on that particular neighborhood, and he or she will be able to advise you on all kinds of arcane local deals and details that would be impossible to know otherwise. Another way to find an agent is simply to adapt some of the same techniques used to find an attorney or CPA (as described in Chapter 8).

Locating and leasing the right premises has significant long-term implications on the operations and success of any small business, and so a commercial leasing agent is highly recommended.

Determining the Best Location

The right location is of critical importance to some but not all small businesses. Restaurants and retailers, for example, depend upon shoppers and foot traffic; and the most important factor for an aluminum anodizing firm is fast access to chemical suppliers. A doctor may prefer to operate in a building geared to the medical profession near a prestigious hospital. But many service-oriented or professional services firms may be more relaxed about location and concerned about price and other factors. In e-commerce, successful firms are springing up all over in very remote places.

Considering the following questions will help narrow-down the choice of locations:

- What is the lease budget?
- What type of location is best?
- Does the location have the facilities and features needed by your operations?
- Is the location properly zoned?

What Is the Lease Budget?

A quick way to narrow down locations is first to consider the budget. Hopefully, some research was completed on the type of facility needed and associated leasing rates when the business plan was developed, as described in Chapter 2. If new research brings in numbers that upset the financial models in the business plan, this is cause for concern; perhaps the best move is to go back to the beginning and reconsider everything.

Landlords will be looking for a lease term of at least two years, and preferably five or more. The good news is that rental expenses will be quite predictable once the lease is signed; the bad news is that signing a long-term lease before sales revenues are pouring in is scary. Running a small business, however, is not for the feint of heart anyway, so perhaps this is one of those times when conviction is needed.

What Type of Location Is Best?

If location is important, then your best thinking is required because this decision may easily make or break the business. Shopper psychology plays a huge role in whether things will work or not, and the most innocuous and seemingly unimportant factor may have a major impact on revenues in the first year or two of business. After this, chances are that shoppers will be accustomed to the location and keep returning.

If location can affect revenues, tell the leasing agent to narrow the search by considering the following factors:

- **Parking.** Few shoppers like to pay for parking. The best location can be a dud if customers don't see a quick and free place to cool their wheels.

The Cute Little Restaurant Where Joe Eats Every Five Years

Near my office is a chic neighborhood with lots of cute boutiques and attractive, high-priced stores selling jewelry, women's shoes, antiques, and exorbitantly priced items to furnish and decorate the home. A perfect place for restaurants, and indeed, many are mixed in among the other stores, which run along a colorfully lit and well-landscaped road that slowly turns from north to west.

Cars arriving from the north first see a cute restaurant with inviting frontage including outdoor seating, allowing diners to view other shoppers and stores. It seems an irresistible place to stop and enjoy a leisurely meal; the perfect location.

Nevertheless, almost a dozen restaurants have opened and closed here over the past 20 years, all of them cute and inviting, but none successful. Every five years or so, I stop in, enjoy a pleasant meal, and remind myself to stop back soon. But I don't.

The problem is very subtle, obviously overlooked by every new tenant, but boils down to uncomfortable parking. Arriving visitors cannot see the parking entrance until they have passed the restaurant. The next free parking area is a few hundred yards down the street, but hungry shoppers parking here are usually diverted by other attractions and never quite make it back.

The restaurants come and go as each small business owner makes the same mistake, and each loses a huge amount of money as he continually invests in the cute little restaurant at the corner of the road.

- **Proximity to Other Businesses.** Sometimes, seemingly competitive businesses may complement each other and create a critical mass that attracts more shoppers than each could do individually. Further, many small businesses prefer to be near anchor tenants or big-box retailers who advertise heavily and attract huge amounts of traffic all by themselves. Think this out carefully. It's possible, for example, that everyone will do better if your leather shop opens in an area with many successful fashion boutiques, even if one already sells leather goods. On the other hand, both may fail. This is where a critical market analysis—and a little luck—can make all the difference.

- **Price Points.** Shoppers often expect to find certain types of pricing in different areas, and surprising them is usually not a good idea. Discount goods, for example, will probably not sell well in an upscale area, and the store will certainly not be popular with nearby merchants. The reverse is also true.

The perfect location does not exist, but analyze each site up and down and left and right to see which is best. Even then it's possible that none will really work out.

Many books and university courses are designed around this very subject, but none can substitute for your best efforts to understand the neighborhood and the shoppers in a potential new location.

Checklist of Needed Facilities and Features

In addition to price and location, it's important to list operations that will be conducted at the new location, and the required supporting facilities. If a desirable location lacks certain requirements, this can be mitigated to some extent by leasehold improvements, especially if paid for by the landlord (more on this later). If major improvements or changes are needed, chances are that the deal will not make sense because the landlord will need to pass on the costs to the new tenant. Another nearby location may already have these improvements with no extra markup. Further, landlords may seem nice during the negotiating stage of the relationship, but asking for anything not explicitly agreed upon in the lease after it is signed will likely turn out to be an unpleasant and expensive experience. Of course, each small business must develop its own list of special needs, but the following sections discuss common concerns.

Electrical

If your firm uses three-phase machinery, 220-volt equipment, or just uses a lot of electricity, make sure the building can handle your needs. Remember that as more electricity is used, more heat is generated, creating the need for additional cooling systems, which use even more electricity. Adding more amperage can be very expensive. Finally, many businesses these days run servers or other machines where power surges or downtime due to electrical outages is unacceptable, so find out from the local utility company if this kind of problem is common. Either way, industrial-strength power-surge equipment and backup power supplies may be a good idea to protect computers and other equipment.

Elevator Hours

Will the elevator work when needed to move people, equipment, inventory, or supplies to your floor? In some modern buildings, elevators are restricted during off-hours, but using them for supply purposes is also not allowed during business hours.

Fire and Safety

Just because a building is for lease doesn't mean that it's in conformance with local fire, building, and safety codes. You could be responsible for this. Check with the fire department and other agencies to make sure expensive penalties, inspection fees, and construction will not be incurred.

Hazardous Substances

All kinds of substances may be considered hazardous, from medical supplies to photographic chemicals to the small amounts of various substances found in inventory samples. Most building leases explicitly disallow hazardous substances, so a small business is automatically in default and at the whim of the landlord from day one unless this is disclosed and agreed upon up front.

Hours

A 24/7 work week may be your normal schedule, but perhaps this is not allowed in the lease. Make sure the building's hours of operation are in accordance with business needs.

HVAC

Do the premises have sufficient heating, ventilating, and air-conditioning equipment? If not, someone must pay for it; and after the lease commences, it's unlikely the building owner will agree.

A common scenario occurs when one business moves into the premises occupied by a previous operation that had few workers or machines. The new user then notices that temperatures cannot be managed by the existing system, and then learns that the current equipment is inadequate. Even office workers and computers can knock an HVAC system off balance. Also, if your operations require more capacity than the existing system, make sure that the situation is discussed in the lease: Either the landlord pays for the new equipment, or the small business must have the right to install what is needed. Further, make sure the building has enough electrical and plumbing capacity to handle the additional HVAC load.

An engineer may be needed to advise on this, or ask local HVAC contractors for their recommendations.

Also, can the HVAC equipment be turned on and off during evenings and weekends? Many office buildings are turned off during this time, so working conditions may be uncomfortable.

Loading Dock

Can modern 53'-tractor-trailer combos dock at the new facility, or only smaller vehicles for local delivery? Is the loading dock the same height as incoming and outgoing vehicles? If it is shared, will there be congestion if other businesses need it at the same time?

Noise

Will your operations produce noise from machines, public address systems, music, or visitors? Make sure this is explicitly allowed in the lease, or get it changed to avoid problems, fines, and possible eviction later.

Number of Workers

How many employees are allowed to work in the new premises? Watch out for situations where the business plan calls for 20 employees in two years, but the lease only allows 10. Options to lease extra space often do not make sense when it's time to expand. This is a common occurrence and can be mitigated by short-term leases, or by leasing a second location for split operations (business office and warehouse) until everything is consolidated.

Parking

Parking is a major issue in many locations, and it is not something that can be fixed easily later. If the business plan calls for 20 employees but the office lease allows for 14 parking spaces, then what happens? Many locations simply do not have the extra spaces to sell, at any price. Further, zoning laws may prohibit the number of employee and customer parking spaces really needed for your small business to make it. If you sign a lease and there is insufficient parking, "Checkmate."

Plumbing

Restaurants, especially, must make sure that the plumbing system can handle the incoming and outgoing water needs for food preparation, dishwashers, and restrooms. And does the water heater have enough capacity?

Restrooms, Kitchens

If facilities are needed with running water or to serve food, get everything in writing up front. Once the lease is signed, it's a little late to ask for permission, and the answer will likely be "Yeah, but it's gonna cost ya."

Telecom

Can the proposed location handle the number of telephone lines needed by your small business? And what about T1 or DSL lines or a satellite antenna? There's a good chance the new premises will need to be rewired for telephone lines and Ethernet (for computer networks), so get a bid and make sure it's in the budget.

Satellite/Antennas

If an antenna or satellite dish is needed, get permission up front. Digging up the roof and running cables and electricity to install this equipment can be expensive, especially after the lease is signed and the landlord is approached, hat in hand, asking for permission. Building owners don't like anyone drilling holes in the roof.

Shipping

Are daily shipments (in and out) allowed? Some building leases allow only FedEx or UPS shipments, so if more is needed, this may be a problem. Other buildings don't allow small businesses that ship lots of equipment.

Signage, Advertising

If the small business expects to post signage anywhere on the new premises, get this included in the lease—and in great detail, including the size, lighting and electrical needs, colors, and height. After the lease is signed, it's going to cost plenty to say, "Oh by the way, can we post just a small sign outside?" The landlord doesn't mind at all. In fact, this will cause great happiness when a big fee is charged for this privilege. Building leases should also describe how the company name will be posted on the building directory, on doors, and on parking spaces.

Visitors

What does the lease say about visitors? The nature of some small businesses is that visitors equal revenues. Some locations are not designed for this type of traffic and frequent visitors are not welcomed.

Joe Is Upset as Stars Are Born

I once worked with a small business that leased offices in a building catering to professionals such as CPAs, psychologists, attorneys, and computer people. We all shared some common areas, such as reception and conference rooms. Most of the occupants had occasional visitors who went unnoticed, and life there was serene, even though the facilities were a bit cramped.

One day, we noticed movers setting up furniture in an unused office, including special lighting, cameras, and furniture such as richly upholstered chairs and couches.

Soon, two young ladies were busily rushing past us each morning, gulping down coffee as they ran into their offices. A few days later, we noticed that the reception room was now bulging with many and—different—types of visitors.

The reception room was constantly buzzing with excited talk and laughter as we came in and out. The visitors were of all ages, ethnic backgrounds, and appearances, but none seemed to have very much material wealth, judging by their scruffy appearance.

I finally asked, and found that this new operation was in the business of taking photographs of aspiring actors, actresses, and models. There is no shortage of these types in Los Angeles, and most are usually looking for work. The two young ladies advertised by handing out flyers on Hollywood Boulevard and other well-traveled places, and by tacking these to telephone poles. There are many such firms in the Los Angeles area, but this one had a special twist: If you were "accepted," work was guaranteed within 30 days. This generated an increasing number of excited new clients.

Soon we also noticed a number of heated arguments coming from the new offices. Some of the aspirants did not seem too happy. As it turns out, the guarantee of acting or modeling work did not turn out exactly as many had hoped. Also, a number of other building tenants with more staid clientele were complaining.

One day, the offices were silent. Soon we noticed that they had been vacated. We asked the building owner, who informed us that the new business had not been completely honest with the landlord about the type and number of clients, and were quickly and quietly evicted from the building.

Zoning Rules

The planned facilities must adhere to local zoning rules. Even the perfect location may be trumped if zoning laws come into play. In fact, zoning laws are so important that we devote the next section to these considerations.

In general, don't assume anything, but make lots of calls and perhaps get it in writing to make sure that what you need will be available. But do assume that unless something is explicitly discussed in the lease, it's not allowed, and getting permission after the lease is signed will be expensive.

For Each Special Facility and Feature Needed...

1.   Is it technically possible?

2.   Does the landlord agree to this in writing in the lease?

3.   Is it in accordance with local planning and zoning laws?

Is the Location Properly Zoned?

Zoning laws (also referred to as land-use regulations or local ordinances) control certain activities in specified areas. For example, liquor stores are frequently prohibited from opening within a certain distance of schools. But many other situations are not quite as obvious.

As shopping for new premises advances and one starts to look appealing, check with the city planning or zoning board to make sure that your business activities are permissible. If the local zoning administrators object, there are avenues for appeal. However, if these seem too unlikely, expensive, or time-consuming, its time to move on to another location.

Even working from home may put a small business owner in violation of local CC&Rs (covenants, codes, and restrictions), zoning laws, or other regulations, although in many cases it's unlikely this can become a major problem.

If a conflict arises between the small business and the local government, the best move is to move on, since few small businesses have the time and resources to slug it out with city attorneys. The only way forward is to make sure all bases are covered before signing the lease and beginning operations. Otherwise, in the worst case scenario, the new premises will need to be abandoned, but the small business is still liable for lease payments. If this is a possibility, consider requesting a contingency clause in the lease, allowing a bailout—without this being a cause of default—if zoning decisions do not rule in favor of this location.

It may be obvious by now that small business owners are usually not well equipped to analyze and negotiate commercial leases, ensuring that they are consistent with business needs and local laws. Because it needs to get done right, call in an attorney. We will discuss this further.

Zoning to Control Businesses

Local officials concerned with land-use typically zone different parts of the city for different purposes. Many areas are zoned for residential usage and developments only, with supporting retail needs nearby. Other areas may be for commercial, business, light industrial, heavy industrial, warehouse/distribution, manufacturing, shipping, agricultural, or other purposes.

This seems simple enough, but problems may arise when the activities of your small business fall between the cracks. For example, an engineering firm may design products but build a small number of prototypes using special metals for testing. Should the firm be classified as engineering or light manufacturing? And are hazardous substances being used, even if in microquantities?

Zoning to Control Activities

Zoning regulations are also concerned with specific activities, such as signage, hazardous wastes, parking, traffic, aesthetics, pollution (air, water, noise, and light) and more. Further, some districts allow only a designated number of competing firms in a particular area to limit competition and enhance chances of survival. For example, a business office development may limit the number of cleaners, restaurants, or printing companies.

In some cases, an activity may be allowed if the new tenant spends a lot of money to solve associated problems. For example, the city may say that a new warehouse is allowed if streets are widened and traffic lights installed to accommodate incremental traffic. Yes, the city is gouging the small business for problems they had anyway, but see if it makes sense.

As noted previously, don't assume that just because the landlord is asking you to sign the lease, everything has been investigated and found to be correct. Also, don't assume that a small business can walk away from the lease if there is a conflict; make sure everything is right in advance of signing.

Finally, remember that just because another tenant is overtly conducting certain activities doesn't mean it will be acceptable for other parties to do the same. "Grandfathered" tenants in certain areas are frequently granted exceptions to zoning rules, but newcomers are not. "I thought it was okay because the last tenant was allowed parking on the sidewalk" will likely fall on deaf ears.

Zoning laws are usually invoked not by prowling bureaucrats but by complaints from tax-paying neighbors. If a small business is in violation of a rule, the problem may be handled by making friends with neighbors and not putting the problem in the face of city officials. For example, some areas have meticulously detailed regulations regarding the size, placement, colors, and lighting of signs. If a sign is not in conformance, neighboring businesses are less likely to complain if the sign owner is otherwise active in looking out for the interests of the entire development.

Resolving Zoning Problems

When zoning problems are encountered, some actions may be taken if the new premises look especially promising. Keeping the time and budget in mind, there are additional options available to get things changed.

First, make friends; then request a change, exemption, or variance. Local government may actually appreciate your business, its potential to pay local taxes, and the prospect of a new small business hiring local workers who will pay even more taxes. In some areas, in fact, local government will go to great lengths and offer tax breaks, zoning changes, and other incentives to land new businesses. Learn about the local situation from a savvy attorney, business colleague, or city official, and make a zoning argument at the next appropriate planning meeting.

If at first you don't get what you want, consider appealing the adverse decision. An appeal is strengthened by petitions signed by local voters and by expert testimony regarding the prohibitive costs and adverse results on the local economy if the city does not reconsider its current rules. If there is opposition to plans, try to make friends and strike a deal with the bad guys before the hearing. Because you are the newcomer here, the battle is theirs to lose.

Finally, consider filing a lawsuit against local governing agencies.

A legal proceeding cannot be filed because of unhappiness with previous decisions. Instead, a legal argument must be developed. For example, perhaps state laws are being superceded by local laws, or maybe local officials are improperly interpreting existing regulations. Learn right up front how long this is going to take, how much it's going to cost, and the chances of winning (remembering that victory cannot be guaranteed, even if the city is dead wrong). Also, how long can the city hold up the new deal in appeals? To get a good fix on this, ask an experienced local attorney who knows both the system and local personalities. Chances are, a lawsuit won't make sense, and win or lose, the hapless small business will still be stuck with the legal bills.

When approval of the new premises is held up by zoning concerns, this is likely a bad omen; the best option is to move on to a more business-friendly locale.

Leases for Commercial Property

Signing a lease for commercial premises is a serious undertaking. This could be the largest financial commitment of a small business, and the fit between the location and needs can greatly affect ongoing happiness and success.

Unlike many consumer-oriented documents, commercial leases are nonstandard in form and are usually customized to the needs of a particular location. Further, the language heavily favors the landlord throughout. Remember that there are few laws protecting businesses from making dumb mistakes—if a lease is signed that heavily favors the landlord, you're probably stuck with it and will be forced to comply for the full term (it's uncommon to break a commercial lease without paying heavy penalties). On the other hand, remember that many of the terms and conditions are negotiable.

It is unlikely, however, that a small business owner who negotiates a commercial lease every few years or so will really understand all the implications of the document and be able to effectively negotiate changes. Before signing, find an attorney with local experience in commercial leasing, and get a review of the documents when the deal looks promising, still leaving plenty of time to work things out or find another location if the landlord is not reasonable enough.

Chances are, the legal counsel used by a small business for other legal matters will not be the best in this case, since industry-specific knowledge is important. The attorney should provide a written review of the lease, comments on whether it is reasonable (given local customs and practices), and notes on suggested changes. Finally, the attorney should negotiate changes because it's unlikely that you'll be as convincing as a good attorney in explaining to a savvy and market-aware landlord why changes should be made. Investment in a legal review of the lease is well worth the $1,000 to $2,000 expense.

Regardless of what the attorney negotiates, however, the following are the most common areas of concern when evaluating commercial leases.

Lease Agreement Terms and Conditions Checklist

☐ What is the base rent?

☐ Is this a gross lease, triple-net, or full-service lease? The determination is made by who pays for increases in expenses associated with the property, such as building maintenance, janitorial services, fees, repairs, property taxes, security, utilities (water, gas, electrical), and extra personnel hired by the landlord. In a gross lease, the landlord pays for these items; the tenant pays in a triple-net lease. Triple-net deals are typically for longer periods of time and may involve substantial tenant improvements (discussed later). Of course, the rent should be a bit lower in a triple-net situation, because the small business must still pay for the property expenses previously described. A full-service agreement is a triple-net lease and then some; for example, the building provides telephone answering services, furnished offices, copiers, and mail handling. Full-service deals may also be known as executive office suites.

☐ Related to the previous question, do you want to maintain restrooms, contract janitorial and security services, and pay separate utility bills? (This can amount to a lot of work, and landlords can often handle these potential headaches more efficiently.)

☐ What rent increases are allowable during the term, and what is the method of calculating the increases? Are rent increases capped or unlimited? Can rent increases start immediately, or after one year?

☐ What insurance is required by the landlord?

☐ Is there a "build-out allowance" or allowable "tenant improvements" (TIs), where the landlord will pay to construct additions such as walls, partitions, lighting, doors, windows, electrical and plumbing improvements, painting, carpeting, HVAC, etc.? And who owns them at the end of the lease? Build-outs are common in longer-term leases, since landlords have more time to recover their investments. Remember that most building managers are more agreeable to build-outs that can be used by future tenants rather than customized construction that will likely be ripped out at the end of the lease.

Finally, note that build-outs are often a thinly disguised financing method to help the new tenant move in quickly and easily. The landlord is not being nice by offering this, so expect the rent to increase commensurately. For example, if the build-outs cost $12,000 and the lease is for 60 months, then the rent includes $200 per month to repay the TIs (plus a little more for interest and margin). On the other hand, if TIs are not needed, ask for a discount.

☐ How many parking spaces come with the leased property? Are more available if needed?

☐ Is subleasing allowed? (This is a desirable right if moving on to bigger premises before the term is finished is a possibility.)

☐ What is the term of the lease?

☐ What are the options concerning renewal, expanding, and right of first refusal if a neighboring tenant moves out?

☐ What happens at the end if the small business must remain an extra month or two ("holdover rent")?

☐ What are the renewal options?

☐ Does the landlord have the right to move the small business to a different location (common in office leases where new tenants may want an entire floor)?

☐ What is the security deposit; when and how is it returned?

☐ Exactly what areas constitute "the premises," including the number of square feet? Does this include common areas and wall thickness? Does the landlord commit to the square footage, or is it an estimate? (In any case, it's always better to measure it yourself.)

☐ On moving in, who pays for changed locks, keys, marking the parking spaces, and directory signage?

☐ On moving out, who gets to keep improvements such as lighting, HVAC equipment, the security system, and electrical improvements? Don't assume that tenant improvements such as these may be uprooted and moved—if these extra items are needed, make sure this is allowed in the lease.

☐ Is each of the "Lease Facilities and Features Checklist" concerns described here successfully resolved and written into the lease?

☐ What are the events of default? (Bankruptcy is normal; being one day late on rent payment is not.)

☐ When disputes arise, are they handled in court, through mediation, or through arbitration?

☐ Are the premises in compliance with ADA (Americans with Disabilities Act), and if not, who pays for items such as building ramps and outfitting restrooms?

☐ Does the landlord agree not to lease nearby space to competitors? (This is relevant, for example, in a small shopping center where two office supply outlets would be ruinous.)

☐ Some landlords will allow a "bailout clause," where lower lease payments or even lease cancellation is allowed if revenues do not reach certain targeted amounts. Be careful though. In some cases, asking for this will simply scare the new landlord into thinking that the new small business could fail.

☐ Similar to a bailout clause, a co-tenancy clause allows the lessee to cancel the deal and move on if an anchor tenant ceases business at the same location (this is mostly relevant in retail shopping malls, where small businesses feed off the traffic attracted by big-name tenants).

Some of the items discussed previously are negotiable, and some are not. The landlord will have more or less interest depending upon whether space is tight in the area, the size of the deal, whether there seems to be a fit between you and the other property tenants, and the prestige of the new business. Regardless, it's a great idea to lay all of this out in a spreadsheet to evaluate the status of the many alternative premises under consideration.

There are a few options to be played out if fast growth is expected, along with the possibility of outgrowing the premises. One possibility is to sign a short-term lease with options on extra space; but the landlord will likely consider this as merely a short-term lease and will expect a higher rent. This may well be acceptable.

A second option is to insist on the right to sublease. Then, when it's time to move on to bigger premises, find another company to take over the lease for the remainder of the term. Make sure the sublease tenant is going to pay, however, because your small business is still on the hook for the rent and other expenses if problems occur.

A third and final option is simply to rent a second location, where each site specializes in certain functions. For example, location 1 is the business office, and location 2 is for manufacturing. Or location 1 is the restaurant, and location 2 becomes the warehouse.

More information on locating and leasing commercial space is available at The Society of Industrial and Office Realtors (www.sior.com).

Chapter 11

Finance, Banking, and Getting OPM
(Other People's Money)

This chapter deals with money: how to choose a bank, the most common sources of financing, and how to prepare a loan package that will be needed by most lenders. (Investors will need a business plan instead of a loan package; this was discussed in Chapter 1.)

Choosing a Bank

Choosing a bank is one of your most important business decisions. A business-oriented bank will provide needed services quickly and never be more than a phone call away. The bank should also stay in the background until needed and not get in the way. Within the industry, banks may specialize in retail (consumer-oriented) banking, commercial lending, real estate, and other areas, so first look for a bank that specializes in working with small businesses. You will know this quickly if a bank officer is assigned as your personal representative and asks detailed questions about the business, so that the appropriate bank products may be discussed. Listen carefully because not all banks offer all products to all businesses.

Factors to Consider When Choosing a Bank

Most small business owners just look at the fees structure when considering a bank, but this should not make a difference. Instead, weigh the following factors when deciding which bank will best meet your needs:

☐ **Convenience.** This is actually a huge factor because time is so valuable. The bank that is within walking distance trumps a similar bank located across town. Beyond location, consider related factors such as branch offices, parking, ATMs, on-line access (more on this), and hours. A bank may overcome the convenience factor by offering courier services, where they pick up deposits or deliver important documents. Couriers usually are banned from carrying cash, so this may limit their usefulness to retail businesses or those needing cash to pay expenses. It is worth repeating that time is valuable. Do you want to spend extra time driving across town to save on fees, or generating extra revenues?

☐ **Relationships.** This intangible factor can mean a lot. Sometimes, small business owners and bankers feel good about each other, and sometimes they don't. Banks won't bend rules just because everyone likes each other, but the relationship can make a difference in marginal situations. Further, it is good to deepen relationships among others at the bank because employee turnover is always a possibility.

☐ **Fees.** Ask up front about the fees related to the most-needed services, and don't worry about the rest. Further, don't become obsessed with fees, because the bank is merely charging for services which it is actually providing. If the profitability of your business is significantly affected by bank fees, this is not a good sign. Business-oriented banks can normally perform an analysis and recommend a particular group of products and services along with an estimate of fees, after receiving copies of three or more recent bank statements. Of course, as average balances at just about any bank increase, the fees and overall deal get better.

☐ **Line of Credit (LOC) Needed?** Many small businesses need cash from time to time, and most business-oriented banks offer this in the form of a revolving line of credit. It is relatively easy to get this approved when a new relationship is started with a bank, because you are providing them with much of the needed information anyway—and because they want the business. There is some truth to the old saying, "Banks only lend money when you don't need it," so why not apply for a revolving line of credit when the banking relationship commences? See more on LOCs in a later discussion.

☐ **On-line Services.** Most banks allow small business owners to see account details through the Internet without any special software or connections. Just about any Internet browsing program (such as Microsoft Internet Explorer) should work. The following are some special features to ask about, beyond access to the checking account:

- Can you see details of money market and loan accounts?

- Can you execute on-line transfers between accounts (for example, pay down the LOC)?

- Can you request stop payments or wire-transfers on-line?

- Are there levels to the security? (For example, you, the owner, may transfer funds, but bookkeepers may only see and download account ledgers.)

- Finally, for on-line banking, make sure the address bar is an "https" and not "http" (https://www.nicebank.com is a secure connection, whereas http://www.nicebank.com is not encrypted and may be seen more easily by hackers).

The Four Cs of Credit

Banks are in operation to make profits through loans. Fees pay for a portion of the expenses, but without interest income from loans, banks could not survive. Therefore, banks want to lend money—if the deal makes sense. This section provides an understanding of how banks and other lenders evaluate deals. The lending business has been around for a long time now, and there is a right way and lots of wrong ways to evaluate loan proposals. Lenders usually evaluate each new lending opportunity against "The Four Cs of Credit":

Capacity. This sometimes just comes down to another "C" letter—Cash. Does your business have the capacity, or cash, to pay down a new loan? For a profitable and established business that needs a little extra funding to pay for a piece of equipment that generates even more business, this will be easy—especially if cash flow from the existing business covers the new loan payments. If the capacity to make the new loan payments comes from revenues generated from the new piece of equipment, this is somewhat trickier: What if plans do not develop as expected? And if a new small business needs a loan to finance entry into a business, the only lender likely to approve this deal would be the Mafia. Banks will conduct a detailed analysis of the financial information provided to determine capacity to repay the loan, so take this seriously.

Credit. Some businesses have lots of cash and can easily pay their bills—but they don't. They find that profitability increases if they do not disburse cash to others. Other small businesses find a way to pay everyone, even in lean times. Lenders will check both personal and business credit to see if you actually pay your bills. Credit is especially important in line-of-credit or unsecured lending situations, where there is little or no collateral available to the lender.

Collateral. Collateral means business or personal assets that are offered to the lender as security for the loan. Banks and other lenders sleep better at night when they know that just in case there is a problem in repaying the loan, they can grab other assets, sell them, and recover unpaid loan balances. Many lenders specialize in this area, known as asset-based lending or collateralized loans (to be discussed). Other lenders will attach available collateral to strengthen line-of-credit or other lending arrangements. For more information, see the discussion on Business Equipment (Collateralized) Loans.

Character. When all else checks out, lenders will take a look at the character of the persons involved in the loan. This includes factors such as family situation, education, judgments and lawsuits, tax problems, and comments gained from reference checks with vendors and customers. Sorry if this seems politically incorrect, but banks know that character does affect the probability of loan repayment.

Finally, before approaching a bank for a loan, consider that the deal must make sense—bankers make deals based upon actual results and history, not on hope. Related to this, all lenders will be looking at the owner's investment in the small business in relation to the loan. There is no fixed rule, but if the balance sheet shows total equity of $20,000, don't bother applying for a $200,000 loan.

Joe's Management Declines a Customer Loan Request After Meeting in a Strip Bar

Many years ago, my cohort Tony and I traveled through many Appalachian states to offer asset-based loans to small businesses in the mining and construction businesses.

Most were diligent, hardworking industry veterans desiring to grow equity in their small businesses and feed their families.

One day, we were at lunch in a small diner in eastern Kentucky with papers spread over the table, when Arnie introduced himself to us.

"It looks like you boys are in the strip mining business just like me," he said. We talked for a few minutes and he wanted to continue the conversation at the Pink Greyhound, which he said was nearby. We had other plans, but agreed to talk on the phone about a new deal.

Over the next few days, Arnie explained that he needed a large amount of financing for some heavy equipment—just the kind of deal we were looking for. He sent us a loan package and the deal was moving along.

Our management wanted to approve the new loan request, but only after meeting Arnie, because he had requested a large amount of financing and this was our first loan to him.

Arnie insisted that we all meet at the Pink Greyhound. We drove from Pittsburgh with a senior loan officer and were chagrined to see that the restaurant featured "Showgirl Dancers" at lunchtime. This was not the style of our conservative management.

During lunch, we talked to Arnie about mining equipment and the market for coal at local power plants, but he seemed more interested in relaxing and chatting with the servers—who were not fully dressed. He lectured us on the nutritional value of the grapefruit juice and vodka he was enjoying. He invited us to do the same, but we declined.

Our senior manager cut the lunch short and remarked that he had not brought the loan documents after all. He excused himself and said he would need further approval from the home office.

Apparently, Arnie didn't pass the "Character" test with our senior loan officer, who later told us that Arnie didn't seem very concerned about operating his small business and paying bills. He questioned Arnie's commitment if things turned difficult. The deal was declined. We were instructed to inform Arnie about this on the telephone and avoid any future meetings at the Pink Greyhound.

Small Business Financing Sources

Most small businesses need access to outside funding, whether to set up and begin operations, to help complete a big job, or perhaps to buy extra equipment and grow.

Because all means of acquiring capital require large amounts of time and effort that cannot readily be delegated to others, it is important to know all the options and decide on just one or two. Some options are mutually exclusive. For example, once a small business has entered into an agreement to borrow funds on a bank line of credit—which requires a first lien on all business assets—an SBA loan probably cannot be considered.

The many financing options covered in this chapter describe the principal ways small businesses gain access to capital.

Most of theses methods involve debt financing in one form or another, but gaining capital through the sale of a portion of the stock (or equity) in a small business is also described (Venture Capital and Angel Investing). Remember that debt financing allows small business owners to walk away from the relationship when the funds are paid back, but equity-related capital involves giving up a portion of the ownership and control of the company, and investors may or may not agree to sell back their interest.

Note also that your small business is, after all, a business, and is therefore not protected by the large body of laws and regulations sheltering consumers. The law considers businesses to be more sophisticated than consumers, better able to protect themselves, and able to pay for legal and attorney fees. Besides, businesses can't vote. It is entirely possible to enter into a bad agreement at a very high price with a disreputable financing firm, and when the worst happens, there may be no way out of the deal except to take it on the chin.

Bank Lines of Credit Lines and Revolving Loans

Perhaps the most common bank lending product for small businesses is the revolving loan account, or bank lines of credit (LOCs). Basically, this arrangement works like a credit card, or as overdraft protection on a checking account. The big differences are that bank LOC rates are much lower than credit card rates (but higher than collateralized loans), and the normal monthly payment is "interest only."

Bank credit lines are similar to credit cards, where funds may be drawn by writing an LOC check to a vendor or by depositing an LOC check in the business checking account. Most banks will require a personal guarantee from the small business owners. LOCs are ideal for providing the short-term financing that may be needed to pay expenses on a big job before collecting from customers, or to cover expenses for seasonal businesses during slow times. If additional equipment, furniture, computers, or other assets are needed, a secured loan or equipment lease may be the better alternative.

Most profitable businesses more than three years old can easily get approved for $100,000 in LOC financing. Applications for more than this amount will meet much greater scrutiny.

The fee for all of this is normally 1 percent of the approved balance, plus maybe $500 in processing fees (which may be waived for new accounts and for good negotiators). For a $100,000 LOC, expect to pay about $1,500 in up-front fees.

Small businesses use many sources to obtain credit:

Personal credit card	46 percent
Business credit card	34 percent
Line of credit	28 percent
Vehicle loan	21 percent
Owner loan	14 percent
Mortgage loan	13 percent
Equipment lease	11 percent
Equipment loan	10 percent
Other	10 percent

Source: "The Great Money Hunt," *Wall Street Journal*, 29 November 2004, Section R, sourced from Small Business Administration, Office of Advocacy.

Trade Credit

Trade credit is a financing arrangement whereby a small business orders and receives raw materials, inventory, parts, and supplies from vendors and pays later, such as on net 10-, net 15-, or net 30-day terms.

Trade credit is a great way to extend finances, further establish a good reputation, and makes life easier because paying by cash is no longer needed.

Most vendors will want to see the purchase history of your small business before even considering trade credit, so don't be offended when you learn that the relationship with a new vendor will begin on a cash-only basis. After a few checks are in the bank and everyone knows each other a little better, it may be time to ask about trade credit.

Some types of vendors operate almost completely on trade credit; others can't make this work because their margins are too low. Before approaching a vendor, make sure trade credit is commonly offered to customers in that industry.

To gain approval, most vendors will ask for a bank reference and three trade references. They will then get a report and see additional information from Dunn and Bradstreet (http://www.dnb.com/us/). Rather than fill out the vendor's application, many small businesses respond to this request with a professionally prepared Bank and Credit Reference Summary, where all the information is presented neatly on a single page document. (For a sample see www.TheSmallBusinessOwnersManual.com.) This looks better than filling in a form by hand, and is a lot faster. In either case, the small business must provide complete contact information on each reference, including the account number, the nature of the relationship ("purchase spare parts for machines"), and the fax number (because many companies require a formal, signed, written request to provide a credit reference).

If your small business is just getting started, ask the new vendor to look at the personal credit of the principals, and also explain that for now, all that is needed is a small credit line that will be used heavily (read: "We will buy a lot") and paid diligently to establish good business credit. Of course, this will most likely be approved after speaking with a well-placed sales rep or someone higher up in the company rather than a clerk in the credit department.

Personal Credit Lines and Credit Cards

Personal credit lines and credit cards are used more frequently among small businesses these days and have gained acceptance among vendors as a preferred payment method for items such as inventory, parts, and certain services. Small businesses often prefer losing the 2 percent or 3 percent from their invoice amounts and seeing the remaining funds hit their bank account within a day or two, rather than run the risk of getting paid on standard net 30-day invoicing terms. In a way, this is an alternate form of accounts receivable factoring, as discussed shortly. An increasing number of small businesses will not extend trade credit to customers, but will accept credit cards.

Small business owners should be prepared to use their personal credit cards and credit lines as a short-term financing method under the following conditions:

- Credit cards often carry interest rates as high as 18 percent. Carrying balances past 30 days can affect your personal credit even if paid in a timely manner. The small business must reimburse you or pay off each credit card in full before interest charges kick in (usually 30 days after the statement arrives).

- The accounting must be correct; if it isn't, there is a chance the IRS will demand that your small business incur payroll taxes on credit card reimbursements to owners and employees, even though the payments are not compensation but rather expense reimbursement. This is often accomplished through an "Officer Loan Account."

- If the business cannot afford to pay off personal credit accounts in full at the end of the month, this is a danger signal. Financing the day-to-day operating expenses of a small business with personal credit can be tricky and may lead to big-time credit trouble.

An additional advantage to using credit cards, however, is the benefit of the warranty on any products and services purchased. Many credit cards allow purchasers to return products or receive refunds for services, beyond what the vendor offers. Unsatisfactory business purchases may be returned with the help of the credit card dispute process. In contrast, purchases paid for in cash or on vendor accounts offer less protection.

If a card or credit line is used frequently, it may be a good security measure to call customer service every few months and request that the current account be closed and reopened under a new account number. Further, use cards with low credit lines so that credit card thieves will not get far when messing with your accounts.

More information on the credit card payments system and accepting credit cards for payments is found in Chapter 13.

Asset-Based Lending and Business Equipment (Collateralized) Loans

Asset-based lending is a great alternative for small businesses in need of capital equipment. Lenders need collateral for the loan, so the purchased equipment and perhaps other business and personal assets are used as security for this purpose. The small business signs a number of documents, including a:

- **Conditional Sales Contract.** The sale is conditional on making all the loan payments, and title to the equipment does not transfer to the borrower until the loan is repaid.

- **Security Agreement.** Assets are pledged to the lender. This document also details what happens in case of default, and the borrower agrees that the lender may seize the assets if default occurs. Other important borrower requirements, such as maintenance and insurance, are also detailed.

- **UCC1 Financing Statement.** This is a government form where the pledged assets are recorded in the office of the secretary of state, so that others may see this publicly available information. The UCC1 perfects the lender's security interest in the named collateral and establishes priority in case of default or bankruptcy.

Ironically, asset-based lenders prefer "low-tech" equipment rather than computers or high-technology assets, since the value of the equipment declines much more slowly. Desktop computer systems, for example, often decline in value 5 percent per month, whereas boring old backhoes may not decline in value at all.

For most collateralized loans, the value of the equipment remains above the unpaid loan balance for the duration of the loan. As a result, these deals are a bit safer than others, and so the interest rate is less than for unsecured financing. Further, collateralized loans have frequently allowed small businesses to build equity slowly and steadily. At first, the payments may seem burdensome, but as the loan is finally paid off, owners find they are sitting on assets of significant value (such as construction equipment, machine tools, and printing equipment).

You may apply for a collateralized or asset-based loan by preparing the loan package (discussed shortly). There is no need to add an extra section analyzing the collateral because the lenders do it themselves. Note that when the UCC1 is filed, elements of the lending arrangement may be seen by anyone searching UCC records. Further, it is illegal to use the same assets as collateral in more than one loan unless properly disclosed to, and approved by, all secured parties. The reason these lending instruments are referred to as "asset-based" or "collateralized" loans is because if the borrower defaults, the lender may gain legal permission to enter the premises physically, remove the assets, sell them, and keep the proceeds.

In some situations, the collateral is the basis of the loan, and if lenders see a strong ratio of collateral to the loan balance, the loan may be approved even if the small business is relatively new. In other cases, lenders will ask for a lien on all unencumbered business assets, even if they really consider the arrangement to be "unsecured" (such as bank lines of credit). Lenders often ask for this just to make the deal a little stronger. Think about your potential needs first, however, because pledging all business assets to one lender means that nothing is then available to other lenders.

Asset-based lenders are not difficult to find. Ask an equipment vendor for a referral, because these lenders often work with equipment sellers to refer business. Many equipment vendors offer programs to finance the purchase of their own equipment (which are often sold back to asset-based lenders as soon as the equipment is shipped, since equipment vendors usually want to stay out of the lending business).

Some firms specialize in a form of asset-based lending for inventory, sometimes known as floor-financing. This is more complex, because the lender must keep track of the large amounts of inventory coming in and out of the retail location, making both interest rates and fees higher.

Equipment Leasing

Many small businesses are strapped for cash and need equipment to expand, but they have difficulty with the financing. Other companies need tax advantages, and still others want the flexibility to change. In these cases, equipment leasing may be the best alternative, rather than purchase. Equipment leasing differs from purchasing in many respects, as described in this section.

In a lease, the small business ("lessee") usually instructs the leasing company ("lessor") to purchase a shopping list of equipment, parts, supplies, and perhaps even pay for delivery, installation, associated software, and maintenance (the "equipment") from one or more vendors. The lessor then owns and retains title to the equipment; however, the equipment is delivered and used by the lessee during the term of the lease. At the end of the lease, everything must be returned to the lessor. The lease documents describe how certain rights and responsibilities are conveyed to the lessee, with others retained by the lessor. Benefits to the lessee usually include the ability to use, maintain, and perhaps upgrade the equipment, and claim the entire lease payment (net of sales and use taxes) as a tax deduction. The lessee's responsibilities may vary, and this is a point of concern when assessing the lease documents, but normally the lessee must insure and maintain the equipment in good working order, keep the equipment in a specified geographical area, and at the end of the lease term, de-install, pack, and return the equipment to a location specified by the lessor.

Further, the lessee may or may not have the right to purchase the equipment at the end of the lease. In a "True Lease" the lessee may purchase the equipment only at Fair Market Value (FMV), which is not known and cannot be specified when the lease documents are signed. But lessees often want additional assurances, such as "FMV not to exceed $10,000." Adding this language may be dangerous, however, because the IRS could then rule that the lease is not really a lease but a purchase, and the lessee must restate the transaction as such. The actual rules are quite complex, but basically, if the lessee pays for more than 90 percent of the net present value of an asset, the "lease" may be ruled as a purchase, regardless of the intent of the parties to the transaction. Unpleasant surprises such as this are complicated and costly, because back taxes, penalties, and interest may perhaps be charged by the IRS. The lessee wants assurances that the lessor will not take advantage of the situation and overstated FMV, and the lessor may claim that IRS regulations and Financial Accounting Standards Board (FASB) guidelines do not allow this type of assurance.

Lessees (again, that's you, the small business owner) often feel better if the FMV is better defined. The default language in many leases will say something such as:

> Lessee may purchase the equipment from lessor, at fair market value, as determined by lessor.

What if the lessor has an inflated opinion of FMV? For thinly traded machines, for example, the lessee may see listings for $5,000, but the lessor may say, "We have it on our books for $50,000, and we cannot sell it for less."

In that case, a clever option is to return the lessor's equipment and then purchase and reinstall a similar model. Of course, small businesses do not like the disruption associated with repairing equipment to "good working order," packing it, returning it to the lessor, and at the same time purchasing, shipping, and reinstalling a similar machine. Lessors know this, and at times take advantage of the situation. Further, some lessors are quite difficult about equipment return and lease termination procedures. For example, some leases provide that the lease term will automatically renew for one-year periods at the end of the term unless the lessor is properly notified not less than 30, but not more than 90, days before the end of the lease. Other lessors may demand that lesees return the exact equipment on the original equipment schedule, right down to the serial number of a small, obscure component. If the small business has upgraded the equipment, the lessor may not accept the return at the end of the lease term. In that case, the lessee should have negotiated "like-kind or better" language into the return provisions of the lease.

Equipment leasing was the rage until the 1986 Tax Reform Act, in which certain special tax benefits were revoked. Despite all this, equipment leasing remains a popular financing alternative and accounts for about one-third of all equipment acquisitions by small businesses. Here are the most common reasons to lease rather than purchase equipment:

☐ You can't afford to pay cash or make monthly financing payments. Lease payments are usually lower than financing payments for a similar lease term. As an example, for equipment that cost $100,000, a small business would pay $2,125 per month under a 60-month Conditional Sales Contract arrangement; after the last payment, title to the equipment automatically reverts to the small business. For a 60-month lease, the monthly payment should, at maximum, be the Lease Rate Factor, or LRF, of .01979 x $100,000, or $1,979 per month. If the equipment has a very long expected life and retains its value well after 60 months, the payment might be dramatically lower. If the equipment had an FMV at this point of, say, $50,000, then the LRF could be around .01467, and the resulting monthly payment would be $1467.

☐ You need equipment for only a portion of its expected productive life. Small businesses often need equipment right away, with the expectation that they will grow and need larger or better models long before the equipment is obsolete. In that case, equipment leasing may be a great alternative. But watch out for technology-related items, such as computers. Small businesses may prefer to trade up three-year-old PCs for newer models, but so does everyone else! Lessors cannot miraculously sell old equipment for high prices, offer low lease payments, and provide the flexibility to trade up for better models. When computers or other rapidly changing equipment is needed, leasing rarely makes sense, and it is better to purchase and then to scrap these items when the time comes to change.

☐ You need additional up-front tax effects. Leases are treated differently than purchases for accounting and tax purposes. Here is a summary:

Acquisition Method	Purchase for Cash	Finance	Lease
Depreciation Deduction?	Yes	Yes	No
Interest Expense Deduction?	n/a	Yes	No
Lease Payment Deduction?	n/a	n/a	Yes
Show Asset On Balance Sheet?	Yes	Yes	No
Show Debt on Balance Sheet?	n/a	Yes	No

Note that at the beginning of a lease, the expenses for financing (vs. leasing) seem highest, because the combined effects of depreciation and interest expense exceed the lease payment deduction. This will dampen the spirits of bankers and tax authorities, because net income is dragged down. On the other hand, profitable small businesses like this, because taxes are deferred (that is, taxes are pushed into later years and don't have to be paid now). Later in the lease, the effects are reversed, and the fixed lease payment exceeds the diminishing depreciation and interest expense effects from financing the purchase. The crossover point and overall effects are determined by the term of the transactions, the FMV of the equipment, and interest rates.

Finally, note that we discussed how asset-based loans allow small businesses to build equity in their businesses slowly and steadily. This is not the case, however, with equipment leasing, where the small business owner has no interest in the asset at the end of the lease term.

A few final notes about equipment leasing:

- Lease payments are normally scheduled "in advance," like office rent, rather than "in arrears," like equipment loans or automobile payments.

- Many items appearing on a lease cannot actually be leased at all! The documents may say "Equipment Lease" in a hundred places, but the IRS may demand that the transaction be treated as a purchase. For example, installation fees and shipping cannot be leased—the customer is really paying for this over a period of time. Although software has appeared on leases for many years, look closely at the software vendor's agreement—the vendor is not selling the software but licensing it to your small business. Neither the lessee nor the lessor can "own" a licensed product. It appears on the lease, however, to make the overall acquisition more palatable.

- Finally, what is the difference between renting and leasing? Renting usually is done for short periods of time, such as renting a front-loader for two weeks on a particular job. Leasing is for the longer term, such as leasing a machine for a year or more for use over many jobs. This can be confusing because leases often refer to rental payments, rental term, etc.

AR Factoring—Ouch!

Small businesses offering trade credit to their clients often experience liquidity issues even when the business is profitable. In some cases, selling your accounts receivable, or AR factoring, may be the right tool. Although invoices may turn into cash within hours, AR factoring is expensive, and it is often difficult to get out of it.

Here is how it normally works. A cash-hungry small business realizes that it has a continuing stream of invoices from commercial clients. The invoices are assigned or factored to an AR factoring company. The factor then examines the invoices to make sure they are acceptable (more on this shortly) and wires 70 percent to 95 percent of the amount due to the small business. Later, the client pays the invoice by sending a check to the address shown on the invoice—which is not the small business address but the AR factor's location—so the factor receives payment directly from the customer.

Before all this begins, however, the small business owner must sign lots of documents with the AR factor, for example, assigning to them the right to deposit customer checks into their account. The factor must also be given the right to place a lien on all of the accounts receivable—and maybe other assets—of the small business. Most factors also want an all-or-nothing deal. That is, all invoices must be assigned to the factor after the paperwork is finished; and "cherry picking" (holding on to the biggest and best invoices) is not allowed. The AR factoring company, however, is allowed to cherry pick. They do this by examining all invoices before funding to make sure that each is:

- Payable to your small business from U.S.-based commercial clients.
- Within the minimum and maximum amounts allowed in the agreement.
- Not aged more than 30 days.
- Not from known deadbeat customers.
- Other restrictions.

It is unlikely the factor will release this lien until all amounts due to them have been repaid. Many small businesses find it difficult to stash enough money in the bank to walk away from the factor and then survive for 30 or more days until customer payments commence again. This becomes even more difficult for fast-growing small businesses, because the amount of operating capital needed to bridge the 30 days or so from invoice until payment keeps growing.

When other small business financing instruments such as loans and credit are limited, some small business owners will turn to AR financing. But is this right for your business?

Here are some pros, cons, and misconceptions about AR financing.

Reasons to Consider AR Factoring

☐ Outsource the Accounts Receivable Department. Most AR factors have very capable staffs. They will make sure that your small business does not extend credit to known deadbeats. Once the business starts flowing, they will do the bookkeeping and follow-up to get invoices paid on time. This may give your business a more professional edge. But why care about prompt payment if the invoice is now the problem of the AR factor? Because most factors will kick back deadbeat invoices (aged 90 days or more) to clients, take back the advanced funds, and then it's your problem once again. Even if invoices are paid but beyond established terms, the factor will charge a lot for fees and interest.

☐ Fast Cash. Many small businesses find themselves profitable but strangled for cash and unable to pay bills, expand, or take on bigger jobs, often because too much capital is locked up in receivables. In that case, AR factoring may be the solution.

☐ Easy Entry. AR factoring will not require the extensive loan package described above. The time from the first phone call until cash arrives can be just a few days.

☐ Nothing Personal. Many Small business owners know their customers personally, and it doesn't help the relationship when one friend calls another to say, "Hey, pay me the money!" It's also a bit awkward to follow up this demand with "Hey, what happened to that deal we were talking about last week—are you going to award us the new business?" Speaking with friends and not-so-friendly customers will now be the work of the AR factor.

☐ Lean on the Strength of the Customers' Credit. The AR factor is looking at the credit of customers with invoices up for collection, and not the small business. They are therefore not especially concerned if your firm pays bills a little slowly.

☐ Better Credit. Since your small business will have more cash, paying bills should be easier, thus improving the firm's credit rating and making room for even more business credit.

☐ Grow Fast. AR factoring may provide the working capital you need to grow, which might otherwise be unavailable.

Reasons to Avoid AR Factoring

☐ AR Factoring is Expensive. There are many discounts, fees, and charges associated with this form of financing, and many surprise and confuse small business owners. When the dust settles, get ready to pay an interest rate of 25 percent to 40 percent per year.

☐ Breaking Up Is Hard. Once AR factoring is in place, it's difficult to break away, as described earlier in this section.

☐ Clients May Be Surprised. Some clients may consider this to be a sign of financial weakness—especially if AR factoring is not common in your industry.

What types of small businesses may gain the most from AR financing? Consider this especially if your firm is growing quickly, is unable to get needed funds from cheaper sources, or is in bankruptcy or in difficult financial times.

AR factoring is especially popular in parts of the apparel industry, manufacturing, trucking, temp agencies, employee leasing, the recruiting industries, and others.

Finally, we have already noted that consumer protection laws do not apply to small businesses, so don't look for help in getting out of a bad deal. Note that not even banking regulations apply to AR factoring companies, and so small businesses have even less protection if problems occur.

AR Crunching and AP Stretching

Small businesses should always pay bills on time to build good credit—and because it's the right thing to do. But if things are getting tight, stretching the payables and crunching receivables may be an alternative to consider.

This is not complicated, and there are only two things to do. First, call customers with outstanding invoices and say:

> I am just calling to make sure you received our latest invoice. Please be sure to pay this on time because we have had some problems with other customers and we must now assess late charges on all late payments. I am calling all of our customers to warn everyone about this.

Obviously, this is not the type of call that will make a lot of new friends, so it's better to request that these calls be made by an accounting, clerical, or even a receptionist-type employee. This is especially true if new business may be expected from these same customers. Most companies believe it is good business practice to separate the sales and accounting functions as much as possible, and this situation helps explain why. It is a little awkward for a small business owner to call a client and ask for payment on a late invoice, and then call back an hour later asking for a new order.

Many small businesses also offer special discounts to customers who pay early, such as:

> I can reduce the invoice by 5 percent if we can pick up the check later today.

This all depends on how badly the money is needed.

The second part of this strategy is easy, because it actually requires no action at all. Payments made to vendors must be held for an extra week, month, or perhaps even more until the finances even out and some big payments are collected from customers.

"Crunching and stretching" is a short-term strategy designed to get through difficult times and is not a long-term strategy, because discounting invoices due from customers may eventually become very expensive. In addition, it is not acceptable to pay other vendors on a consistently late basis.

SBA Loans

The U.S. Small Business Administration (SBA) was formed in 1953 from the vestiges of a 1932 federal government program aimed at helping businesses recover from the Great Depression. The SBA is charged with the mission to "promote and assist small businesses by providing financing assistance through loan guarantees, management counseling and training, and assistance in obtaining government procurement contracts." The SBA now manages over 200,000 loans to small businesses, totaling $45 billion. Beyond lending to small businesses, the

SBA is also involved in providing disaster loans and conducting minority outreach programs. Our concern here is whether SBA loans make sense to you.

Small businesses do not communicate directly with the SBA but deal with various SBA-approved banks (Certified Lenders and Preferred Lenders) that discuss borrower needs, take the application, and work to gain approval. If the loan is approved, the deal is made directly between the borrower and the SBA-approved bank, and the SBA guarantees to the bank that a portion of the loan will be repaid (usually 50 percent or 75 percent). The SBA repays the bank only in the event of default.

SBA loans can be used to:

- Construct, expand, or modernize commercial buildings, or purchase existing facilities for use by the borrower (and not for investment, rental, or speculative purposes)

- Purchase machinery, equipment, inventory, furniture and fixtures, or leasehold improvements

- Finance increased receivables and working capital

The SBA and its banking affiliates are not chumps, and this is not a source of easy government money. SBA loans may vary from $250,000 to $2,000,000, and a full-blown loan package such as the one described in this chapter will be needed. The application will be studied to make sure that a loan to your small business make sense and that the loan can be repaid from existing—not projected—cash flows. (Note that this precludes the argument, "Well, I don't have enough money now, but if you make the loan, I will be able to repay from the new revenues.") Further, the SBA normally takes all or some business assets as collateral, and usually requires a personal guarantee. If repayment terms are not met, the SBA and its banking partners repay the bank, but it will also seize and sell all pledged business and personal assets to recover as much as possible. During the approval process, loan committees will look to see if the principals are of good character with strong management skills, consider the net worth of the small business against the loan amount, and make sure other financial ratios are consistent with industry averages.

Not surprisingly, Small Business Administration loans are only for small businesses, and the SBA defines "small" as:

- A business that is independently owned and operated, and is not dominant in its field.

- Manufacturing: generally up to 500 employees.

- Wholesale: maximum of 100 employees.

- Services: varies by industry from $2.5 million to $20 million in annual revenues.

- Construction: $7 million to $17 million in annual receipts.

- Agriculture: from $500,000 to $9 million in annual receipts.

Following are details on the two main SBA lending programs and the small business investment company equity investment program.

Section 7(a) Loan

The 7(a) program is the largest SBA arrangement, where over 70,000 loans totaling over $12 billion are funded each year. The average loan size is about $150,000, with a $2 million maximum. Section 7(a) lenders are flexible about how the funds can be used and will consider purchases of equipment, buildings, real estate, furniture and fixtures, inventory, or working capital if the deal appears to be strong. Among the factors they consider are existing cash flow, collateral, management talent, and owners' equity (15 percent to 35 percent of the total loan amount). Variations of the 7(a) program allow special deals for exporters, pollution control programs, credit lines for contractors, bridge financing to cover seasonal cash-flow needs, and ESOPs (Employee Stock Ownership Plans).

Interest rates are normally prime plus 2.25 percent to 4.75 percent, in addition to many fees, including a one-time "guarantee fee" of as much as 2.25 percent and an "annual service fee" of up to 0.50 percent. These fees are somewhat negotiable but may significantly increase the real cost of the loan.

504 Loan

The 504 program funds about 30 percent of the amount of the Section 7(a) program, because it is intended for narrower purposes: 504 loans are directed toward small businesses that may increase or retain jobs or otherwise meet public policy goals. Loans may range from $200,000 to $10 million. About 8,000 504 loans are funded per year (in contrast to 70,000-plus Section 7(a) loans). Funds are typically used to provide long-term financing for the construction or renovation of buildings, equipment, real estate, leasehold improvements, parking lots, and landscaping. 504 loans may be more difficult to obtain because small businesses must go through the normal loan approval process but also jump through a complex set of political hoops.

Small businesses usually invest 10 percent of their own funds into a project, a commercial lender provides 50 percent, and a Certified Development Company (CDC) puts up the remaining 40 percent. CDCs are non-profit organizations that put the project together for the other parties. A list of CDCs is available at www.sbc.gov. Note that the 10 percent small business contribution is less than required in other programs.

As for rates and fees, commercial lenders are able to provide funds at normal commercial rates because the deal is safer, and because of their first lien on collateral. Similarly, the CDC charges 0.50 percent to 0.75 percent below commercial rates because the SBA guarantees this amount. However, the SBA charges 3 percent of the guaranteed amount as a one-time fee, thus significantly increasing the real cost of funds.

In summary, if a small business is having trouble gaining financing from traditional lenders who want a longer history and more assets, the SBA process may also prove to be time-consuming, onerous, and in the end, not fruitful. The SBA is not a likely financing source for new businesses, but may work especially well for established firms seeking expansion capital or equipment. Remember, too, that you must be willing to put all unencumbered assets—business and personal—on the line as collateral. For those who can jump through all these hoops, the benefits of working within the SBA program include longer terms (up to seven years for working capital, 10 to 15 years for equipment, and up to 25 years for real estate), good interest rates, flexible repayment options, and acceptable fees and costs.

SBA Small Business Investment Companies ("SBIC") Program

Since 1958, small businesses considering venture capital financing have been able to look for the right "match-up" through the U.S. Small Business Administration (SBIC) Program. SBIC calls itself "the nation's largest fund of funds" because it does not provide financing directly but instead sets up venture capital investors with small businesses. SBIC investors provide 8 percent of all venture financing amounts and over 60 percent of all seed (start-up) financings according to the U.S. Small Business Administration.

Venture capital investors are not meek and will consider needs that would petrify most lenders, including seed financing, start-up capital, early stage investments, expansion financing, later-stage financing, and even management of leveraged buyouts and other forms of acquisition financing.

Funds from SBICs may come in a variety of forms, including equity, long-term loans, or more exotic financial instruments. SBICs often also provide management expertise in special areas.

Similar to conventional SBA loans, SBIC investments are not from the SBA but from privately owned investment firms that are in business to make serious money by investing in winners. SBICs do not distribute government largess, and this is not the place for businesses with anything less than great expectations. Outback Steakhouse, Intel, Apple, FedEx, AOL, and Compaq are all a part of the SBA's SBIC legacy.

The SBA Website (http://www.sba.gov/INV/) allows small businesses to search directories and find the SBICs most likely to consider particular opportunities. Different investors prefer different types of deals depending upon industry, type of financing needed, and geographical location, so a short list must be culled from the various directories.

Small businesses may contact investors directly, and later send a professionally prepared business plan and make personal presentations. Expect to spend a large amount of time over a number of months to do all this.

SBIC financing may be provided only to eligible firms, generally, small businesses with a net worth of $18 million or less and an average after-tax net income of $6 million or less in the last two years.

The following two sections of this chapter offer additional information on this subject.

Venture Capital (VC)

Here is the lowdown on venture capital: It seems glamorous, but it's not easy, cheap, or pleasant. With that positive introduction out of the way, let's see exactly what venture capital is.

Venture capitalists are institutional risk takers and may be groups of wealthy individuals, government-assisted sources, or major financial institutions. Most specialize in one or a few closely related industries, so it's important to target the right ones.

Venture capitalists are active equity investors in small businesses. Their capital is invested in very specific types of investment opportunities for shares of stock—meaning partial ownership—and not as a loan. Capital invested in a business certainly improves the chances of additional debt financing because equity increases and the assets of the company are not offered directly as collateral. Still, giving up ownership and control often is not easy. Unlike conventional equity investors, venture capitalists seek to be actively involved in the management of their various investments. These firms have special expertise in many areas and will normally require one or more seats on the board of directors.

VC financiers are looking for small businesses with explosive growth potential and the ability to generate compounded investment returns of 25 percent to 40 percent. This usually requires a compelling new product or service in a bleeding-edge type of business area, including many high-technology business niches. To get such financing, you must first write a very formal, M.B.A.-style business plan, requiring immense amounts of time and effort, and present this numerous times to some very serious people.

Even with this, less than 1 percent of venture capital candidates ever get the funding they desire. For those that do, about 80 percent fail to deliver the required returns. In that case, most VC agreements allow the investors to fire the small business owner and take control of the company. This happens in the majority of cases. The converse is not true: If the small business wants out of the deal with the VC investor, it normally can't be done without buying back the VC's stock shares for a huge return. If your small business needs funding this badly, the Mafia may be a more appealing source of funds.

Angels: Hitting Up Rich People Works

Perhaps the most common form of outside small business investment comes from "angel" investors. Angels are basically any people with money to invest or loan, including business colleagues, friends-of-friends-of-friends, professional investors, or the proverbial rich uncle. These are often semiretired businesspeople with special interests and talents—or best yet, perhaps other small business owners just like yourself.

Groups of angels often work together to examine, invest, and manage new investment opportunities. Here, the "archangel" often directs the relationship with your small business and communicates back to the investor-angels.

Although the relationship here may be less formal, assume that whoever your angels are, they seek high returns from working with hot new business concepts and capable management. In many cases, the angels want to participate in the day-to-day operations of the small business by consulting, teaching, mentoring, and inspiring the company in areas of special expertise. This could be of great benefit.

Angels should at first be approached as venture capital investors: Be prepared to deliver a formal business plan and a ready-for-prime-time presentation on why your small business is a great money-making opportunity. Also, suggest an investment vehicle such as stock ownership with a cash-out plan, or a high-interest loan convertible to stock. It doesn't look professional to say, "We'll consider any idea that is fair."

In many cases, prudent small business owners will demand that before discussing anything, the not-yet verified angel must agree not to divulge, disclose, sell, or commercially benefit from the business concept, except through your small business. In not so nice words, don't discuss anything before gaining assurances that your idea will not be stolen. (A non-disclosure agreement dealing with this subject may be downloaded from www.TheSmallBusinessOwnersManual.com.)

Finding and romancing an angel is an art; the relationship is by definition special and apart from that with more formal venture capitalists, SBICs, and others. The best way to find an angel is to work your social and business circles, pound the telephones, and employ conventional networking techniques.

Angels are normally hard-nosed investors with plenty of options, so the deal must make sense; but personal factors come into play if the business plan and personal chemistry are especially attractive. Here, these investors may be the best financing alternative by providing great energy under attractive financing terms.

Home Equity Loans

Most small business owners cringe at the idea of putting their home on the line for the business, but the pros and cons of this financing alternative should at least be considered. The business actually has little to do with the financing, and the small business owner simply applies for a home-equity loan (usually referred to as a Home Equity Line of Credit, or HELOC) just like any other homeowner. When the loan is approved, funds may be transferred from the HELOC to the small business, usually by writing checks. Then, funds are disbursed from the business to vendors. In an accounting sense, the transfer of funds to the small business is considered a loan from the small business owner. The journals of many firms refer to this as an "officer loan" account, and this should appear in both the business (balance sheet) and personal financial statements when assembling a loan package. Be sure to keep the IRS at bay by writing a promissory note between yourself and the business to document the loan, interest rate, and repayment terms. (A sample loan agreement may be downloaded at www.TheSmallBusinessOwnersManual.com.)

Here are some other points to consider regarding the use of HELOC funds:

- Since HELOCs are associated with your home, the interest charges are tax-deductible to the small business owner personally.

- HELOC loan interest rates are very low compared with just about any other form of financing.

- HELOC credit lines may end up as significantly greater than what your business could otherwise receive, depending upon the value of the home and the first mortgage amount. For early-stage small businesses, this may be the only way to borrow cash.

- If worse comes to worse and your business tanks, your home is indeed on the line and there is a real possibility that hungry creditors may eventually seize and sell it.

Business Credit Cards?

Small business owners will often receive mail solicitations offering something such as the following:

> Mr. Jones, as a business owner, we are authorized to offer you this opportunity to apply for our no-annual-fee Business Platinum Card.

or

> You have been chosen to receive this offer for a KapitalBank Business Card, including a credit line of up to $100,000 and a variable rate as low as 7.9 percent.

Sometimes, the advertisement will include a credit card with your company name imprinted on it.

Look carefully and read the fine print. In most cases, the business has not been preapproved for anything, but the small business owner is merely applying for a credit card like any other chump. This can be seen in the signature area of the application, where there is usually language that reads something like:

> On behalf of the Company and myself, I have read the Important Disclosures and Offer Terms...and I agree on behalf of the Company and myself that the Company and I will be bound as specified therein. You are authorized to check the Company's (and my) credit record...

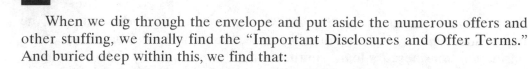

When we dig through the envelope and put aside the numerous offers and other stuffing, we finally find the "Important Disclosures and Offer Terms." And buried deep within this, we find that:

> ...the Company and the Authorizing Signatory (that's you!) will be liable for all transactions made with all cards and checks on the account, and anyone issued a card on the account as an Authorized User will also be liable for all transactions made with their card. I agree that all cards and checks will be used solely for business or commercial purposes and not for personal, family or household purposes.

Note that the business *and* the small business owner here are personally liable for any and all charges. Also, personal credit records will reflect the fact that you have applied for this card and show whether it was approved or not, and unlike regular credit cards, it cannot be used for non-business purposes. This is probably not a very good deal, and if credit of this sort is needed, just use personal credit cards—they are much less restrictive.

Should You Offer a Personal Guarantee?

Small business owners are often confronted with the question of whether to offer a personal guarantee on obligations of their business.

A personal guarantee (PG) allows financing partners to place a lien on personal assets, and if your small business cannot pay the bills, the lender may seize and liquidate items such as automobiles, pleasure craft, furniture, jewelry, antiques, investments, and anything else that will sell in a public auction, including your home. The first liquidation proceeds are used to pay the lenders' balances, including interest, late charges, collection expenses, and expensive attorneys. Any remaining amounts would be returned to you. Lenders must follow certain rules to attempt to obtain a reasonable value for your personal assets, but no minimum amounts are assured. If grandmother's '65 Mustang sells for $1, there is little you can do.

In some agreements, an "event of default" (allowing the lender to move on the personal guarantee and personal assets) is bankruptcy; in other cases, "default" may mean that you simply do not pay amounts that are due.

Of the financing alternatives discussed in this chapter, most may ask for a PG in one form or another.

Small business owners usually loathe this suggestion because many are born risk-takers but still balk at putting their home and personal assets on the line. Further, many formed their small businesses as corporations with limited liability in mind, and a PG seems to defeat this purpose. And indeed it does.

The reality is, however, that access to large amounts of outside financing will improve when a personal guarantee is available to lenders. For new businesses especially, the PG will make or break a deal. Collateral-based lenders, for example, may not see enough assets in a small business borrower until the PG is added. Also, lenders know it is easy enough for borrowers to walk away from certain small businesses, but the loss of a home ups the stakes.

In good times, a personal guarantee may seem like a low-risk proposition and the new funding may be enough to propel your small business into much greater profitability—allowing you to pay off the lender and live happily ever after. But if things get difficult before the loan is paid off, a PG offered to a lender may result in lost sleep at night, and a lost home.

The Loan Package

Many of the financing arrangements described in this chapter require large amounts of documents and supporting information from the borrower. There are two ways to do this: Give each item to the lender in piecemeal fashion as additional information is requested, or prepare a professional-looking loan package. A loan package is a lot of work to prepare, but in the end it saves time and will impress lenders. Once this is prepared for one lender, the exact same package may be given to others for competitive quotes.

Here are the contents you should assemble for a professional-looking loan package. In fact, this may even be used as the loan package table of contents.

Contents of a Loan Package

- Requested Financing
- Background of Company
- Loan Application (signed)
- Marketing Materials and Partial Customer List (past and present)
- Company Management and Staffing
- Year-to-Date Financial Statements
- Accounts Receivable Aging Schedule
- Accounts Payable Aging Schedule
- Business Income Tax Returns (from the last three years)
- Personal Income Tax Returns (from the last three years)
- Personal Financial Statement of Owners
- Business Bank Statements (from the last three months)
- Personal Bank Statements (from the last three months)
- Projected Financial Results (for the next one to three years)
- Certificate of Secretary and Articles of Incorporation (or related documents from non-corporate entities)

If your small business has developed the business plan described earlier in this book, then many of these tasks have been completed. If that is the case, the business plan may be slightly modified and inserted in place of various sections, including Requested Financing, Background of Company, Marketing Materials, Company Management and Staffing, and Financials.

Requested Financing

The requested financing section leads off most loan packages and is one of the few sections actually created from scratch by the small business owner. This should be easy: Write a few sentences about why your small business is seeking additional financing.

The reason for funding could be anything from the need to pay bills on projects in advance of customer payments, to purchases of additional equipment. Be sure that the requested financing is consistent with the operations of your current business. For example, the bank will look favorably upon a pizza shop's plans to purchase larger ovens, but may not be wild about plans to expand into the garage next door and purchase automotive diagnostic equipment. Keep it simple, as in the following example:

> Aaardvark provides computer programming services to local companies and has worked with many of its clients for almost a decade. Aaardvard charges its clients on a per-hour basis and in turn pays its contactors on a per-hour basis. Our clients manage the projects and our contractors, and so Aaardvark simply bills by the hour and we do not commit to specific deliverables. And when projects are finished, Aaardvark has no continuing financial, contracting, or employment commitment to contractors.

> Our main asset is receivables from well-known companies that have established a strong payments record.

> Aaardvark's rapid growth in recent times may be impeded without receivables financing, a large line of credit, or both.

> The Company is submitting this loan package to several lenders. Criteria for selecting a new financing partner will be (in this order): (1) How can Aaardvark obtain the maximum amount of financing? (2) How can Aaardvard minimize bank fees and interest charges? and (3) What is the most convent banking alternative?

> Aaardvark and its owner desire a long-term and mutually profitable relationship for both business and personal banking activities and look forward to working with you as we grow.

Background of Company

The business description should be very simple—just a few lines. Or print out a few pages from your Website. This gives the bank a flavor of the business and its special place in the market. Emphasize stability and controlled growth in an established business segment, if possible. The following example may be helpful:

> Aaardvark was formed in 1996 and is now experiencing accelerated growth, largely as a result of its entry into a rapidly growing area of the computer services industry: TDX Programming.
>
> The typical customer may be a large local company or a Fortune 1000 firm (see attached customer list).
>
> In 1996, several Aaardvark clients approached us about the shortage of TDX professionals available to support the $1 million to $25 million investments in their TDX mission-critical systems (example: U.S. Treasury IRS). These clients asked us to provide them with TDX programmers.
>
> Aaardvark ventured into this very rapidly growing business area, which we call "Aaardvark PS," or "Aaardvark Professional Services."
>
> The nature of this business is that Aaardvark enters into contracts with TDX contractors and normally pays them two times each month, net 10 days from receipt of invoice. But we can only invoice our larger corporate clients once per month on net 30 terms. And Aaardvark cannot invoice its customers until time and expense information is received from our contractors. The business is quite profitable, but sometimes almost 60 days have passed since the time work was performed and when we are paid. During this time, we have paid our contractors four times. Thus, cash is needed to finance the difference between our accounts payable and accounts receivable cycles.
>
> Aaardvark operates in a well-known and established business segment. Since the 1960s many other firms have offered contract computer programmers and some have grown to be large publicly traded firms. But few understand Aaardvark's special niche in TDX programming ,and this is where we excel.
>
> Aaardvark booked profits in all years except 2000 and 2001, when the business downturn caused a decline in TDX-related revenues.
>
> Aaardvark PS revenues began increasing in September 2001 and continue to grow. Aaardvark revenues have increased at a 15-percent rate in the several years since 2001, and future growth is expected at the same rate for the foreseeable future.
>
> Aaardvark PS growth in TDX will continue to be driven by business use of the Internet, e-commerce, and business-to-business ("B2B") systems, which are solid and rapidly growing areas of our economy.

Loan Application, Signed

The bank or lender will provide a loan application, which must be signed and returned. Without a signature, the bank cannot begin work on your loan request.

Marketing Materials

Banks feel most comfortable working with established businesses, and this can be accomplished by providing marketing materials such as brochures, mailers, or even flyers or copies of newspaper and magazine ads. Consider also printing a few pages from your Website. You may also want to provide a list of major customers, if this is relevant.

Make sure all the materials are reduced or folded to standard 8.5" × 11" size so that they may be spiral-bound with the rest of the package; they should not stick out. Undersized materials such as post-card mailers may be copied onto 8.5" × 11" paper.

Company Management and Staffing

Many small business owners do not put much effort into this section, assuming that the numbers provided elsewhere speak for themselves. But take this seriously, because bankers are looking to ensure that you and other management are capable of handling the small business—and the lender's funds! Many bankers say that it is infinitely better to work with good management in a lackluster business than the other way around. Provide a resume for all top management, highlighting longevity and success in the business and the ability of others to step in, should the current regime become disabled.

Year-to-Date Financial Statements

Bankers live to review financial statements, so this part of the loan package is critical. More often than not, the deal turns on these numbers. Having said this, there is little that can be done beyond neatly copying all of the required statements, because the past cannot be changed.

In the loan package, include the income statement (also known as profit and loss, or P and L), balance sheet, and statement of cash flows for the last three full years. These are the three most important and most commonly used financial statements. In some cases, signed business tax returns may be substituted for CPA-prepared financial statements. Most lenders will not accept internally prepared statements for credibility reasons, except for year-to-date results.

CPAs can normally prepare these statements very quickly with the help of accounting software, especially if the tax returns are finished. A signed "CPA-reviewed" letter must be returned with the statements, basically stating that a CPA prepared the statements but did not audit the underlying information. The bank is comforted to know that a CPA is familiar with your business.

CPA-reviewed statements are far less expensive than audited tax returns, which require a close examination of records to test the accuracy of the numbers.

Note that banks love to see slow, steady growth of maybe 5 percent to 15 percent per year. If results fluctuate a lot and if they trend down in the last year or two, this will not help, and a written explanation may be a good idea. If the business has not been around for three years, ask the lender if the application can be considered at all.

Accounts Receivable Aging

This is a list of all current customers, showing the amounts owed by each and the age of the receivable. Banks like to see a lot of customers, all of whom pay within 30 days. Lenders are uncomfortable when a small business relies upon just one or two clients, especially when invoices are not paid on time. The AR aging schedule is a standard report that can be run off on any computer-based business accounting program. Only one schedule is needed, printed within 30 days of the time of the loan application.

Accounts Payable Aging

The AP aging schedule is a list of all bills and payments due within 30 days. Bankers like to see that all bills are paid on time; they will be understandably upset if your small business does not pay amounts due. Similar to the AR aging schedule, the AP report is easily produced from any computer-based accounting program and should be printed within 30 days of the loan application.

Interim Financial Statements

If the accounting year-end is more than three months after the date of the last business tax returns, year-to-date interim financial statements (income statement, balance sheet, and cash flow) will be needed. Internally prepared statements are normally acceptable here, which means they can be produced from any business accounting program. It's still a good idea to have your CPA look them over to make sure there are no glaring problems. Most CPAs know what banks are looking for and can advise on how to "window dress" for the best possible outcome. (For example, pay down accounts payable to reduce current liabilities, which increases the working capital ratio.) Make sure that the numbers all work together. For example, if the balance sheet shows total accounts payable of $20,000, then the AP aging schedule should show the same amount. Finally, sign each page before copying.

Business Income Tax Returns

This is an easy one. Just copy the business tax returns for the last full three years. Make sure the IRS forms have been signed.

Personal Income Tax Returns

Include the personal tax returns (IRS Form 1040) of all owners/partners for the last three years. These are important, because the bank wants to see if your personal financial situation is acceptable, and to learn the strength of personal guarantees.

Personal Financial Statement of Owners

Lenders will provide a form that can be completed, copied into the loan package, and even accepted by other lenders. This statement is similar to a personal balance sheet, and basically requires a list of all personal assets and debts. The difference is equity, and a big number here makes lenders happy. Assets such as real estate and investments in mutual funds are easily understood; banks do not seriously consider assets such as art, coin collections, or furniture. Again, the bank will verify some of the information presented here to learn the strength of personal guarantees. Allow time to gather credible information on all important assets, because this may be the most tedious part of the application. The bank may also want copies of statements supporting amounts invested in securities and retirement accounts.

Business Bank Statements

For important business checking accounts, copy the last three months for insertion into the loan package. Banks want to see average balances, how many checks are written each month, and the number of deposits, credit card debits and credits, fees, and other transactions. They also want to see that the bank statements support the financial statements. So if the P and L shows $50,000 in sales per month, deposits into the business checking account should be about the same. If the balance sheet shows bank deposits of $100,000, the bank statements must support this amount.

Personal Bank Statements

Again, just copy the last three months of your main personal checking account for insertion into the loan package. Some lenders will look here to trace transactions between the small business owner and the business. These should tie in with the personal financial statement and business financial statements. If your personal financial statement lists $10,000 in checking account balances, this should be about the average balance in your personal checking account statements.

Corporate Documents

In this section, include documents such as the Certificate of Secretary and Articles of Incorporation. These documents were produced when the business was incorporated. For DBAs, partnerships, and other entities, similar documents will be requested. Bank underwriters need to see when and where the business was incorporated (or registered to do business), and they need to see the names of officers and directors and verify that they are authorized to negotiate and execute loan agreements.

Banks will also ask for a declaration from the board of directors attesting that an officer (likely, you) is charged with entering into a lending agreement. For most small businesses, this amounts to a short letter written by the chairman of the board of directors (you), stating that a meeting was held and naming the president (you) as the officer authorized to negotiate the deal. The letter would be signed by—you. (A sample authorization letter from the board of directors is available at www.TheSmallBusinessOwnersManual.com.)

Projected Financial Results (For the Next One to Three Years)

Some banks will ask for one to three years of projections, or estimates, of future business. This is easy to do with spreadsheets, and a sample financial model may be downloaded from www.TheSmallBusinessOwnersManual.com. If the business is losing money, rosy projections won't help, because most banks make their decisions based upon your history.

Summary

Once everything is assembled, make the package look good by going to a local copy shop and having it spiral-bound using a plastic see-though front cover, where the front page is a nice letter explaining the request, or the table of contents.

Once the loan package is prepared, why not go just a bit further and apply to several banks? This simply requires asking the copy shop to make five or 10 copies rather than one. Pick up everything the next day. Then call competitive lenders and give the same package to everyone.

Alternatively, in situations where the need is not critical, it may be a better idea to apply to just one lender at a time and learn their reaction. Then adjust the package accordingly, and submit it to competitive lenders. For example, a loan underwriter may ask why revenues have decreased. A convincing written explanation of this may then be included in later versions of the loan package.

Providing the bank with all the information they require is a lot of work. There is no way around this. But preparing a professional looking loan package is a lot easier and more professional than waiting for the lender to ask and then dropping off another box full of papers. Lenders will appreciate your professionalism in providing a comprehensive and easy-to-read loan package, and this may well result in a better deal.

Outside consultants may be valuable in helping assemble a loan package for your small business. Look for someone who is familiar with financial statements, spreadsheets, and legal documents, and who understands how various lenders think. For more help on this, see www.TheSmallBusinessOwnersManual.com.

Chapter 12

Offering Credit to Customers

I Mean, Why?

In some industries, offering credit to customers may separate one small business from less sophisticated and more fragile competitors; in other industries, a firm just won't sell anything if customers must pay in cash. Offering credit has its risks, so we review in this chapter how to evaluate credit decisions, how to set up the credit approval process, and what to do if they don't pay.

To answer the question, "Should I offer credit to my customers?" look at competitors: If this is an industry norm, your small business must follow suit. If other companies do not offer credit, maybe this says something, too: Maybe it's been tried and found to be a bad idea.

Offering credit is a great way to make it easy for others to buy from your small business, but it's expensive, too. Here are some considerations:

- The small business must set up a credit approval process. After this is established, new customers must apply for credit, which normally takes a few days and costs time and money.

- If standard credit terms are net-30, then the seller must somehow carry 30 days of sales out of available funds or by borrowing. This also means lost interest income on the free 30-day loans now offered to customers.

- An accounts receivable system must also be set up to make sure invoices are quickly sent to customers and to follow up and make sure they are paid.

- Some customers will not pay, so the seller is stuck with the lost receivable and maybe legal and collections costs.

Some small businesses mitigate the financing problem by working with AR factoring companies (see Chapter 11), or by taking a credit card as a backup in case the customer does not pay. AR factoring companies are very expensive, and when the dust settles, an effective interest rate of 25 percent to 40 percent can be expected. Dishonest customers who don't pay invoices know how to handle credit card companies, too: They have nothing to lose by disputing charges for the feeblest of reasons, and there is a good chance that the seller will lose and suffer a charge-back (see Chapter 13).

The Credit Approval Process

With this cheerful news out of the way, let's focus on setting up the credit approval process. First, the customer must complete an application in which they state the business name, and, most important, the type of ownership. If a company is a sole proprietorship, the business and the owner are on the hook to you; if the business is a corporation, there is no personal recourse if the new customer declares bankruptcy. In the case of partnerships, the business and all general partners are liable.

All of this is nice to know, but it gives no special rights in case of problems. The seller's position is therefore strengthened if the application is beefed up and some legal language is added through which the new customer agrees to certain items such as:

- Payments are due in full within 30 days of the date of this invoice.

- The small business may invoice for late charges at the highest rate permissible by law or 18 percent, whichever is less.

- Applicant states under penalty of perjury that he or she is an authorized officer of the company (and then signs the application, including date and title).

- Other standard but important legal mumbo-jumbo: "This Agreement shall be considered as executed in CITY, STATE and shall be construed for all purposes in accordance with the substantive laws thereof. The local, state and federal courts of STATE shall have exclusive jurisdiction over any and all disputes relating to this Agreement, other than the granting of equitable relief to enforce the Agreement. If any provision of this Agreement is declared void or unenforceable, such provision shall be severed from this Agreement, which shall otherwise remain in full force and effect. In the event any suit or other action is commenced to construe or enforce any provision of this Agreement, the prevailing party, in addition to all other amounts such party shall be entitled to receive from the other party, shall be paid by said party reasonable attorney's fees, collections expenses, and court costs. This Agreement constitutes the entire Agreement between the parties with respect to the subject matters addressed herein. The Agreement may not be amended or modified except in writing and signed by both parties." (Regarding CITY and STATE above, this usually refers to the location of the small business; however, it is best to consult an attorney.)

This language may be added to the application, which then also becomes an agreement if signed by both parties. Many small businesses will want more substantive language than this to cover other matters, and in that case, a separate and formal legal agreement is needed. (Ask a local attorney, or see www.TheSmallBusinessOwnersManual.com.)

Note, however, that most business credit is unsecured. This means that the receivable is backed only by the credit of the customer, and in case of bankruptcy, your small business stands in line with other unsecured creditors. After all major assets are sold and all secured creditors are satisfied and paid in full, the remainder is divided up and distributed evenly to unsecured creditors. Usually, this takes six to 18 months, and there is little left after attorneys' fees. Unsecured creditors are often happy to receive 10 cents on the dollar against the original outstanding balances.

As noted in Chapter 11, credit managers often weigh the "4 C's of Credit" when evaluating a new applicant.

With this in mind, set up a credit approval process for new customers. Ask new customers to sign an application similar to the one described, and then contact the applicant's bank and at least three credit references for credit and payment information. When considering sole proprietorships, a credit and criminal background check on the owner is of immense help (although be sure to get the credit applicant's permission to do this; see Chapter 6), and for customers who are just starting out in business, don't be afraid to ask for a personal guarantee.

Many credit managers rely upon Dunn and Bradstreet (www.dnb.com/us/) to provide a great deal of useful information on the creditworthiness of potential new business customers. Reports include credit information, a credit rating, financial statements, background and historical data, information regarding outstanding liens and judgments, and verification that a company is registered to do business and in good standing in a particular state (if a firm does not pay taxes or incurs other government-related problems, it may lose its "good standing" status). D&B often provides critical information that is otherwise unavailable, but in other cases may have little information on small businesses that choose not to cooperate.

Business Credit USA (www.businesscreditusa.com) offers similar business credit information on over 14 million U.S. and Canadian small businesses.

In some cases, it may be possible to pass the fees for credit and criminal background checks or credit reports on to customers. This depends upon industry norms.

Finally, in situations where the numbers are bigger, it may be acceptable to ask new applicants for financial statements, tax returns, and interim financial statements. Again, this mostly depends upon the particular situation.

When in doubt, many small businesses approve new customers for small amounts of credit and then increase this later if additional credit will result in significant new business, if payments are received in a timely manner, and if the overall business relationship has been good.

A sample credit application, and credit and criminal background check release forms in Microsoft Word format are available at www.TheSmallBusinessOwnersManual.com. Also, get a DUNS number, consider listing your small business with Dunn and Bradstreet, and learn more at www.dnb.com/us/.

What If They Don't Pay?

Some customers just will not pay. In some cases, dishonest new customers will understand that only a small balance is owing and it is not economical for a small business to pursue this through the legal system. In other cases, valued and established longtime customers will run into troubled waters and just be unable to pay.

When customers won't pay, legal action may eventually be considered, but other remedies must be exhausted before the courts will consider the matter.

First, note that small business collections issues are generally not governed by the FTC Fair Credit Reporting Act (which is mostly concerned with consumers), so just about anything goes.

If invoices are not paid on time, most small businesses proceed with a polite but cordial phone call to the accounting department of the customer, and verify that all invoices were received. For example, sometimes invoices are sent to the wrong location. Then, explain that payment is delinquent and ask why, under the assumption that the problem is a mere misunderstanding or bureaucratic snafu. Also, ask about the payment process at this company, including the following questions:

- Where do invoices go after receipt?
- Is the customer mailing payments to the correct address?
- Are you in their system as an approved vendor?
- Which persons must approve the invoices?
- Are invoices stacking up on the desk of a manager who travels frequently?
- When are checks cut, signed, and mailed?
- On what exact date will your check be printed (and available for pick up)?

Ask these questions in a collegial manner to prevent the client from getting defensive. Explain that there is no need to bother the wrong people over these issues; your job is to make sure payments are received in a timely manner, and understanding the customer's processes is helpful to all.

It is often not a good idea for the small business owner to be involved at this point. It's a little difficult to place a collections call at one point in the day and then call for additional business later. Also, the customer may want to settle any outstanding amounts with an accounting person quickly, in the hopes that you, the small business owner, are unaware that a delinquency issue is at hand. Face-saving measures such as this can often allow a small problem to remain just a small problem.

Sometimes, invoices may arrive at the correct address, be routed to the right manager, and just sit until someone calls looking for payment. Perhaps all that is needed is to find and call the manager to get things moving.

Find out if the customer has a problem with the goods or services provided. Don't provide them with an excuse to withhold payment by asking if they are satisfied with everything, but listen to make sure that there is not a problem. If it is an issue, ask for partial payment until disputed amounts are resolved. Throughout the conversation, politely emphasize that your small business is not in a position to lend money, that cash is short all over, and that you expect timely payment of invoices from all customers. Many customers will pay slowly if it appears that no one is concerned, but most are thinking about their reputation and will pay quickly if politely reminded. Sometimes, a few calls in the beginning can set the relationship on a positive course for a long time to come.

Regardless of what is promised (for example, "The check is in the mail"), make sure that invoices and monthly statements (including late charges) continue to be mailed in a timely manner. Also, keep careful notes on "who says what" during collections calls. At the 60- and 90-day delinquency dates, send letters to the company, expressing concern that payments are overdue. This better sets the stage for legal action in the future (sample collections letters are at www.TheSmallBusinessOwnersManual.com).

Many small businesses assume that dealing with large customers is a panacea for late-payment issues, but the opposite is often true. Large customers, including some of the most well-known household names, methodically pay their bills 15, 30, or even 60 days late. These customers can hide behind the excuse, "It's just our bureaucracy." Many also reject late charges (which are actually hard to enforce). Many large companies feel that this is part of the price for the privilege of doing business with them, and will quickly suggest that small businesses that don't like this can go elsewhere. Even in this case, polite but diligent collections efforts can make a difference.

Sometimes, a customer has more bills than cash, so some vendors will get paid and others will not. If you sense that this is indeed the situation, it may be appropriate to inform the customer that future business will be cut off if payment is not made; in other cases, this will not be effective. At this point, there is little downside to making lots of telephone calls, so keep the pressure on. The squeaky wheel often does get the grease.

Some customers always seem to use the wrong address, or their checks are always lost in the mail, despite the fact that the post office delivers more than 99 percent of other mail correctly. Get results now by saying, "Someone will be

Joe Is Dazzled by a Dot-Com Deadbeat

In the days of the dot-com boom, it seemed that nothing could go wrong when dealing with the multitudes of high-tech start-up firms, no matter how far-fetched their business plans.

Our small business was happy to be nearing the close of a big deal with one such company, when a number of seemingly small contractual issues arose at the last minute.

Soon, I was on the telephone with the legal counsel of the glorious dot-com, and we agreed on several points. Finally, he said he could not agree to paying 18 percent on delinquent invoices. "We just don't pay late charges," he said.

I laughed and replied, "Well, I'm not very comfortable with this then, because it seems as if you're telling me up front that you intend to be a payment problem." We were under pressure to get moving, so the deal was signed—without a penalty for late charges.

Sure enough, our new client simply did not pay invoices. Why should they? We were basically offering them a free loan, which helped their desperate cash flow. I soon became concerned as our receivables zoomed north of $100,000.

Legal action was premature, so we decided to cut off services to the client. I was a bit worried that we were being too harsh, but then I was informed that they had beaten us to the punch by unilaterally canceling our agreement, even though this was an egregious breach of the contract.

I immediately called my attorney and told him to do something. "I can't really do anything yet," he said. "They are less than 90-days delinquent. This is going to look premature."

"I don't care," I said. "Just do something. Start writing them mean letters and make idle threats or something. This company is going broke, and we've got to be ahead of everyone else."

I was especially concerned about getting the money in quickly, because any payments made by firms within 90 days of filing for bankruptcy may be called back by the bankruptcy court. In bankruptcy, we were likely to receive only a few pennies on the dollar because a dot-com would have few assets that could be sold and distributed to creditors.

The attorney began to write a series of mean letters and make tough phone calls with lots of idle threats about suing for breach of contract, and suggesting that the world would know that this mighty dot-com could not pay its bills. We apparently hit home when the firm became upset that it's sterling reputation would be damaged. They quickly agreed to pay us all amounts due if we agreed to keep quiet, and a check was express-mailed the next day. It was deposited within hours.

I watched the calendar, concerned that the dot-com would declare bankruptcy within 90 days and the funds would be called back. The dot-com's stock had sunk from $135.50 to less than $1 as it barely struggled past the 90-day mark, still in business. I breathed a sigh of relief, but wondered if the large amounts of time and legal expense had been worth the effort. Maybe I should have relaxed and tried to go with the flow. We would have been paid anyway, I figured.

But only 20 days later we learned the news—our arrogant dot-com client had declared bankruptcy that morning. The huge amount of effort put into collections had paid off. We later learned that we were one of the few, and last, companies to be paid outside of the bankruptcy process.

driving near your office tomorrow. Do you mind if we just stop in and pick up a replacement check?" If this is not possible, say, "We'll be around there the next day, too," and "The day after that is fine too." They will get the message, and you will get the check.

At some point, however, customers run out of excuses, and the realization comes that this is going to be a problem. As the receivable grows, it is often necessary to cut off these customers to minimize possible losses. It is also necessary to increase collections efforts.

Remember that there is little regulation regarding business-to-business collections efforts (unlike the many laws that protect consumers). Don't let up on the calls. One common technique is to increase the number of calls gradually until customers are embarrassed and annoyed into paying. Some businesses do not like their employees and others to be concerned that financial problems may be developing, and these customers will pay just to stop the receptionist from taking yet another message that "Jim from ABC Photography called again about the outstanding invoice." Obviously, a message in this case may be more effective than voice mail. A related technique is to fax the invoice continually with a polite payment reminder message to the main fax number (not the accounting department) of the slow-paying customer.

Get an Attorney and Go Legal

The next step is to begin the legal process by asking your attorney to send a demand letter to the customer. In this communication, the customer is ordered to pay or legal action is threatened. A demand letter is a standard document that requires little customization and can be prepared quickly. This will not cost very much and frequently results in immediate satisfaction. (A sample demand letter may be seen at www.TheSmallBusinessOwnersManual.com.)

If the demand letter goes unanswered, ask your attorney to call the customer and see what's going on. Customers will often level with an attorney and explain the real problem. The attorney can then advise you as to what's really happening and attempt to settle the matter quickly. If an agreement is reached, be ready to sign a release letter, where partial payment is accepted in full and complete settlement of the matter.

Finally, legal action may be considered. If the problem involves less than $3,000 or so and your attorney says that winning in court is possible but you are still responsible for legal and collections expenses, the best move is probably to cut off the customer and write off the account. Legal expenses will likely mean a net loss even with a win in court. For larger amounts, the legal system may be a feasible option, especially if the customer has signed an agreement where, in a dispute, the loser pays for legal expenses. Remember though, winning in court is merely one step in collecting, since many cash-strapped clients will not pay even as demanded by a court judgment.

Figure out what to do by asking the attorney:

- What is the buyer's defense? Is the buyer's defense real or frivolous?
- What is the timetable for a court date?
- What is the timetable including appeals?
- If a judgment is awarded, could this include legal and collections expenses?

Assuming the deadbeat customer will not pay even after a judgment, what will the attorney charge for postjudgment actions, such as a hearing to determine creditor assets? How long will it take to identify and seize assets? Are the assets worth the effort?

With this information, the small business is in an informed position to decide whether to pursue legal channels to collect monies owed.

Small Claims Court

Another option that often makes sense is using a small claims court. Check the Website of your local city or county government to see how "small claims" is defined in the area. If a small claim is, for example, a maximum of $5,000 and amounts due are for a smaller amount, then so far, so good. Next, consider whether the deadbeat customer is local or not. If the deadbeat is located far away, there is a good chance that no one representing the defense will appear in court and you may hope for a default judgment. Remember, though, that a default judgment may have little meaning to someone in another state, and it will not be easy to collect.

Next, fill out the paperwork and enter the small claim into the court system. At this point, a legal argument is not needed, and simply writing one or two lines such as "Defendant purchased goods from plaintiff and failed to pay despite continued written and telephone collections efforts" is good enough to get the case registered with a court date.

Once the case is registered, the defendant must be served with court papers describing the problem and notifying the deadbeat of the date, time, and place of the small claims hearing. These papers must be delivered in a timely manner to the right defendant, which is called "service." The small claims court office will likely offer service by a sheriff or professional process server for a small fee. Carefully enter the address and the right contact person at the deadbeat's business. Owners and officers are always safe bets, or an attorney may advise on the proper persons to be served. Delays in service may result in delays or reregistering of the small claims case.

When the court date arrives, you are an attorney-for-a-day. Prepare your case, but expect to speak no more than five minutes. Also be prepared for the judge to allow only one minute. Judges often step in and begin asking questions of both parties. Judges do not like speeches about how the other party is a jerk, because being a jerk is not against the law. Stick to points of law, and speak in a collegial manner, even when it's time to ask questions of the deadbeat customer. Remember that in our court system, the defendant is innocent until proven guilty, so you must prove that goods or services were provided but not paid for. Take originals and at least three copies of all relevant documents, such as invoices, proof of delivery, canceled checks, etc. Defendants often win merely by confusing the issue, such as claiming that goods and services were not properly received, or that payment was applied to the wrong invoices. Another common technique is for the defendant to say that not one but several invoices are unpaid, and the matter is therefore out of the authority of the small claims court system. Judges do not like to sift through all of this and will often wave off the matter—meaning that you lose.

Once a judgment is gained, many customers still will not pay. In that case, your attorney will advise on how to proceed, including a "hearing on assets," where the customer must disclose all assets—including equipment, bank accounts, and receivables—that could be available to liquidate and pay the delinquent invoices. Then, your small business may seize these assets to liquidate and settle against amounts due. Again, however, legal expenses should be paramount in the decision to sue, and asset seizures often are not economical. And opther liens may get in the way.

Dunn and Bradstreet and other agencies will see and record this judgment eventually, which smears the credit record of the deadbeat customer. Once a judgment is issued, the customer may no longer claim to others that this is merely a payment dispute. Pressures of this sort also encourages the deadbeat client to pay.

Assigning Bad Debts to Collections Agencies

A related alternative is to assign uncollectible invoices to a collections firm. The collections company will ask a small business to enter into an assignment agreement, where uncollectible invoices are assigned to professional collectors, who then write a series of letters and make telephone calls to deadbeat customers. The agreement calls for the collections firm to keep 35 percent to 50 percent of the invoice(s) amount—when they get paid. Invoices that remain unpaid revert back to the issuing small business after a fixed period of time, usually 90 to 180 days. Unfortunately, most collections firms will not initiate legal action against a customer unless the small business pays the additional fees. Savvy deadbeats know that there are no real adverse consequences to ignoring pressure from collections companies, except for the embarrassment factor and perhaps negative credit ratings.

Most collections companies do not really want to buy a single invoice, but look for a continuing relationship with small businesses where delinquent invoices are turned over methodically to the collectors every month.

Additional information on credit and collections, including a directory of firms that may be able to help your small business, is available through the Association of Credit and Collection Specialists, http://www.acainternational.org.

Offering credit to customers may be an essential tool in growing the revenues of a small business, but there are many potential pitfalls. Proceed with caution in setting up and administering credit approval, invoicing, and collections activities.

Chapter 13

Accepting Credit Cards

Your small business is considering accepting credit and debit cards as a new form of payment. It seems like a good idea because so many customers, even businesses, prefer to pay by credit card these days. Many firms like credit or debit cards because customers who pay by plastic tend to purchase a bit more, sales on the Internet or via telephone are now possible, there is no risk of bounced checks, and your small business enjoys enhanced credibility. All of this is correct, but it's a bit complicated, and there are costs and risks to accepting credit cards. In this chapter we review issues thoroughly.

The chapter deals with credit cards and is especially oriented to on-line payments. Most of the information is the same for standard retail credit card purchases, debit cards, and some of the newer forms of payment, such as PayPal.

Definitions

Here are some important definitions that will be needed in this chapter and in conversations with credit card service providers:

☐ **Acquiring Bank** (also known as "Merchant Bank" or "Sponsoring Bank")— open merchant accounts for businesses accepting credit cards. The bank, in effect, is sponsoring the small business, or "merchant," so that they may accept credit cards. These banks must be members of the Visa/MasterCard Network. Small businesses must select a merchant bank, gateway, and processor as vendors in order to accept credit card payments.

☐ **Address Verification Service (AVS)**—an Internet-based system for verifying the addresses of cardholders, in order to minimize risks and deter fraud. This service is especially important in Internet/mail-order/telephone-order transactions.

☐ **Approval.** After a transaction is authorized (to be discussed), an approval request is put through the system. Upon approval, an approval code is issued, and the funds for this sale begin moving towards the merchant account (checking account) of the small business.

☐ **Authorization.** An authorization must be obtained for every sale and is the first part of the credit card payment process where the cardholder account is checked to make sure funds are available to cover the amount of the transaction. At this time, funds for the sale are reserved from the cardholder's credit line, but the funds are not transferred to the small business's merchant account until the transaction is approved.

☐ **Authorization Response.** When a merchant requests authorization of a transaction, the issuing bank responds with "approved," "declined," or "call center" (call the credit card center for approval pending receipt of satisfactory additional information).

☐ **Authorization Code.** When the authorization response is "approved," merchants receive an authorization code from the issuing bank. This code is important and must be kept as proof of the issuing bank's approval.

☐ **Bank Card**—a credit card issued by a bank sponsored through Visa or MasterCard, but not cards issued directly through the issuer, such as American Express, Discover, Diners Club, JCB, and others.

☐ **Batch.** Merchants normally generate a number of credit card payments each day, from many different cardholders and issuing banks. These are processed, consolidated, and deposited in one batch to the merchant's bank account.

☐ **Card Not Present** (also known as "Mail-Order/Telephone-Order" or "MOTO")—an important concept for small businesses engaged in credit card sales. Here the buyer, and the credit card, are not physically present. This arises with e-commerce, mail-order, and telephone-call transactions. "Card not present" sales do not require standard credit card processing equipment such as card-swiping devices and terminals, but there is an increased risk of fraud, so a higher discount rate is customarily charged.

☐ **Cardholder.** Cardholders are your customers. They are approved for credit and issued credit cards from issuing banks.

☐ **Chargeback.** A chargeback occurs when a cardholder disputes a transaction (for example, dissatisfaction, product never delivered) after the amount has been settled. The money is then yanked from your merchant account and not returned unless the resolution process sides with the small business. Even though cardholders are urged to communicate with merchants to resolve problems before disputing a transaction with their issuing bank, many do not, and this can soil the reputation of merchants. Chargebacks are bad for small businesses in many ways, which are detailed in this chapter.

☐ **Credit Card Merchant**—organizations that sell goods and services and accept payment through credit cards. Credit card merchants (small businesses) work with their sponsoring banks to open merchant accounts.

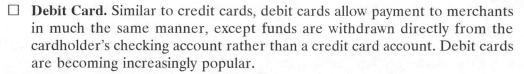

☐ **Debit Card.** Similar to credit cards, debit cards allow payment to merchants in much the same manner, except funds are withdrawn directly from the cardholder's checking account rather than a credit card account. Debit cards are becoming increasingly popular.

☐ **Discount Rate**—the percentage taken off the sales amount by the merchant bank, and retained and distributed among the various parties in the credit card processing network. A typical discount rate is perhaps 2.5 percent.

☐ **Dispute.** Customers purchasing goods and services from a small business may be unhappy with the results, and the first step in the complaint and chargeback process is when the cardholder files a dispute with the issuing bank. Issuing banks are required to investigate every dispute, no matter how frivolous. A typical dispute is, "I want my money back because the product does not really have certain features promised to me by the merchant."

☐ **Gateway.** Small businesses accepting credit card payments in "card not present" situations talk to the credit card processing system only through their gateway. The gateway to most small businesses involves logging on to a special Website to see credit card transactions. The gateway is effectively an on-line credit card terminal, and allows merchants to authorize, settle, and manage electronic transactions via standard servers and personal computers. Small businesses must select a merchant bank, gateway, and processor as vendors in order to accept credit card payments.

☐ **Independent Sales Organization (ISO).** These organizations are ubiquitous in the credit card processing industry, and act as sales agents for banks, processors, and related vendors. ISOs usually perform no services after the credit card processing arrangements are completed. There is a good chance your small business will deal with an ISO, which will recommend a solution that may include anything from POS terminals to PC-based credit card processing software, and e-commerce systems to secure payment gateways.

☐ **Issuing Bank.** These banks accept credit card applications from cardholders, process and approve or decline the applications, and then issue credit cards to future customers, the cardholders. The issuing bank is effectively approving cardholders for a loan, up to the amount of the credit limit. If the cardholder buys something from a small business and does not pay and does not dispute the transaction, the issuing bank is on the hook for the unpaid balance.

☐ **Merchant** (see Credit Card Merchant).

☐ **Merchant Account.** Credit card merchants (small businesses like you) open merchant accounts (normally a checking account) with their sponsoring bank. Credit card payments are deposited into this merchant account from issuing banks, as directed by processors, usually through the Visa/MasterCard network.

☐ **Merchant Bank** (See Acquiring Bank).

☐ **Merchant Identification Number (MID).** This important account number is used as the merchant's identity for transactions processed through the credit card payments system. To log in to accounts, or when problems occur, the first request is often, "Please enter your MID number."

☐ **Mail Order/Telephone Order (MOTO)** (See "Card Not Present").

☐ **Processors**—companies that communicate among merchants, issuing banks, and merchant banks to authorize credit card transactions, and then direct the banks to credit and debit the various accounts. Small businesses must select three vendors in order to accept credit card payments: a merchant bank, a gateway, and a processor.

☐ **Net Settlement Amount**—the amount of a sale, less credit card fees (discount amount).

☐ **Non-Real Time Processing**—the traditional, now old-fashioned way of accepting credit card payments. Here, merchants capture credit card information by swiping or imprinting, and although cardholders usually leave with their purchases, authorizations and approvals are not obtained until they are submitted at a later time. The problem here is that there is little hope of stopping credit card thieves, and the merchant gets stuck with the losses. `

☐ **Processor.** Behind gateways or credit card terminals are processors, which route authorization requests between the merchant and Visa/MasterCard. After the authorization is received, the processor directs funds to be sent from the issuing bank to the merchant bank. Small businesses may select merchant banks and many third-party firms as processors. Small businesses must often select a merchant bank, gateway, and processor as vendors in order to accept credit card payments.

☐ **Real-Time Processing.** In this modern method of working with credit cards, cardholders or merchants enter identification information; authorizations and approvals are then obtained on the spot. The transaction does not move forward until everyone knows the cardholder is approved, which is accomplished in a matter of seconds. Real-time processing slows down (but hardly stops) credit card thieves. A secure payment gateway is an essential component of real-time processing.

☐ **Reserve Account.** The bane of new and fast-growing small businesses, reserve accounts are sales proceeds that are held back by the merchant bank. Reserves are used to help banks mitigate against fraud and credit risks (for example, bankruptcy). If a small business, for example, accepts large amounts of sales deposits and then disappears without shipping the products to cardholders, the merchant bank is on the hook. Normally, merchants perform well, and after a time, the risk is reevaluated. If the merchant has a satisfactory level of chargebacks and a good record for covering returns, the reserve account may be released. Reserve accounts are often set at around 20 percent of expected monthly processing volumes.

- **Sales Draft** (Ticket). This is the small slip of paper that is signed by the cardholder when making the purchase (or more frequently now, captured electronically). The sales draft is a legally binding obligation on the cardholder to pay the issuing bank.

- **Secure Payment Gateway.** As the Internet increasingly becomes the hunting grounds for snoopers and scammers, secure communications are essential. Secure payment gateways, using secure socket layer (SSL) technology allows gateways, cardholders, merchants, processors, and others to encrypt and safely communicate sensitive and confidential data over the Web. (See also "SSL Certificate.")

- **Secure Payment Software/Software Module/Payment Module.** These are software modules that allow Web-based merchants, electronic shipping carts, and other applications to execute credit card authorizations and approvals via encrypted communications. A secure host system is offered to customers by the gateway provider to conduct secure business on the Internet (see also "Real Time Authorization"). Merchants may then also connect to the secure payment gateway host and see their own account information, use a "virtual terminal" to execute transactions for retail or call-in customers, control administrative tasks, and generate reports.

- **Settlement.** This is the process whereby the merchant submits a daily batch of all transactions from all cardholders and issuing banks to the credit card payments network for processing and then payment. For bank cards, the issuing bank pays the merchant (less discount and other fees) with funds from Visa/MasterCard. For non-bank cards (Discover, American Express, Diners Club, etc.) the issuing bank pays the merchant bank directly (again, less fees), and the cardholder is then billed. The large number of transactions is then consolidated into just a few large bank deposits, with detailed reports available as needed. (See also "Bank Cards").

- **Sponsoring Bank** (see "Acquiring Bank").

- **SSL Certificate**—a small electronic file that uniquely identifies individuals and servers on the Internet. SSL certificates allow the Web browser to authenticate an Internet site before entering confidential information such as user names and passwords. Typically, digital SSL certificates are issued by "certification authorities," who are trusted and independent third parties, such as VeriSign (www.Verisign.com) that ensure validity. When on SSL pages, browsers normally see a padlock on the status bar at the bottom right of their browser windows. Double-clicking on this padlock icon then returns additional information. In the world of small businesses, SSL is relevant because customers must know they are entering credit card information to a valid e-commerce system, and not to a scam site that is pretending to be legitimate. In addition, e-store administrators must know that they are logging into a real credit card gateway and not to a site set up by scammers that merely looks familiar.

How Does the Credit Card Transaction Processing System Work?

With all these definitions in mind, it will be much easier to describe what happens when everything is set up and customers begin buying with credit cards.

When a cardholder makes a purchase, the transaction is first sent through the gateway to the processor as an authorization request. The processor then taps the Visa/MasterCard network, which—within seconds—asks the issuing bank if the account is valid and if there is sufficient credit available. A hold is also placed on the cardholder's account, and the transaction amount is subtracted from the credit limit pending approval or rejection—so no one can get at these funds except you.

After authorization, the issuing bank tells the processor and Visa/MasterCard network that the transaction is approved, and the processor then directs that funds be transferred from the issuing bank to your merchant bank account. The funds appear as a deposit one to three days after the transaction is completed.

At this time, your small business is committing to many parties—the merchant bank, processor, Visa/MasterCard, the issuing bank, and the cardholder—that it will make good on the products or services being purchased. This promise must be honored. If not, the funds will be snapped from the merchant account and your company is one step closer to being bounced from the credit card payment acceptance system. Note that the merchant often is also accepting responsibility for the transaction if it is fraudulent. If the real cardholder later reports that the card had been stolen at the time the purchase was made, your small business may be on the hook for the problem. All of this is important because, as can be seen, even though the transaction is "approved," many strings are attached; and if just about anything happens, the "approval" evaporates. We will discuss this further.

Fees are also deducted from the transaction amount before the net settlement amount is deposited.

Now let's talk about trust.

What's All This About "Trust"?

The entire credit card payments system is built upon trust. Understanding this will help the small business owner make better decisions about managing this important revenue source.

To begin, when the merchant submits a deposit transaction, the system trusts that your small business will deliver the goods and services promised to the cardholder. No one asks if the cardholder did indeed receive what was purchased. Everyone trusts the merchant and expects an acceptable level of performance.

The merchant (small business) also works on trust, since merchants must ship, deliver, or release the goods or services before payment is actually received. After an authorization and approval are obtained, the merchant trusts that the funds will be properly deposited into the proper merchant account. But there are strings attached to this promise of payment, because long after the deposit has landed in the account (up to 180 days in some situations), the cardholder may claim that the products or services did not meet expectations, or were not provided at all. Further, although the merchant trusts the credit card system to deposit funds after approvals and authorizations are provided, the small business is still at risk if the card was stolen. In these cases, the funds will be pulled from the merchant checking account weeks or months later, without notice.

The merchant and the entire credit card payments system are also trusting the cardholder, because it is easy to claim that the goods arrived but were damaged. Or, if the shipment is sent to the customer's business address rather than the home address (used for credit card billing purposes), the customer may claim that the shipment was never actually received, but was stolen. In most cases, the customer will win these types of disputes. While few take advantage of this trust for dishonest purposes, credit card scamming is a big and growing business, and in many cases, just one credit card rip-off can easily wipe out an entire day of profits. Small business owners must understand and work the system to minimize fraud. We'll talk more about this later.

Chargebacks and the Credit Card Dispute Process

When problems occur (real, imagined, dumb, or fraudulent), the cardholder is encouraged first to contact the merchant and work things out. Take this seriously, because at this point, the situation may be controlled; later, your small business is at the mercy of others. Many cardholders simply skip this step and go directly to disputing the transaction with their issuing bank.

The disputed transaction is then formalized by the issuing bank into a dispute or retrieval request, which is sent to the processor and then to the merchant. Before receipt of the retrieval request, the funds are withdrawn from the merchant account and are held pending resolution of the problem. Now you are at the mercy of others.

The small business must then respond to the dispute by proving that the products or services were properly provided. This is often accomplished with shipping documents, where the cardholder has hopefully signed for the package, or with other documents supporting the merchant's side of the case. For example, if a small business sells a copier to a customer, proof of delivery by UPS or another shipping firm must be provided to help resolve the dispute. If the customer claims that the machine only produces 10 copies per minute instead of the expected 20, the merchant needs to provide sales literature from the manufacturer verifying that it produces 10 copies per minute. Here, the matter is rather straightforward, but things can get complicated if the cardholder then says, "I don't care what the brochure says, the salesperson told me 20 copies per minute." That is why it's important to meet customer expectations and to disclose everything before the credit card transaction goes through.

If disputes are resolved in favor of the cardholder, this normally results in a chargeback to the merchant. Chargebacks are bad for several reasons.

First, the small business probably expended the same amount of time, effort, and money to fulfill a chargeback transaction as a normal one. Now more resources are expended to undo the transaction and perhaps test or inspect and put the item back into stock. That's a lot of work to end up with nothing.

Second, part of the collateral damage of chargebacks is the creation of unhappy customers. Again, why go to all this effort if your small business ends up with no sale and displeased customers?

Third, if too many chargebacks occur, your merchant bank will begin rethinking its trust in you. Most banks will allow a certain amount of chargebacks, understanding that sometimes good companies make mistakes, that some customers are fickle, and that misunderstandings occur. After this level, however, the bank will begin suspecting that maybe the merchant is not quite right. At that point, the merchant bank may ask to audit records, and perhaps demand a reserve account or shut down the account entirely. When this occurs, the termination is entered into a database accessible to all merchant banks worldwide, and it is unlikely that any other merchant bank will then sponsor the maligned merchant; accepting credit cards will be a thing of the past.

Avoiding Chargebacks and Fraud

A small business must do everything possible to keep fraud and credit card chargebacks to a minimum. Here are some guidelines to help you.

Verify That the Credit Card Belongs to the Cardholder

This sounds simple, but it is an effective first line of defense against credit card scammers. In retail situations, ask for a second form of identification, and then see if the names and signatures from the ID, credit card, and sales slip all match. Note that if a small business does not properly verify the information, an "approval" then disappears if the customer reports that a card was stolen, even months after the transaction occurs.

In card-not-present situations, make sure your e-commerce system requires that customers enter one or more telephone numbers, and in suspicious situations call under the guise of telling the customer his order is about to be shipped, but see if everything adds up. Scammers will often insist on expedited delivery but will not give out much additional information, so watch out for this. At all times, pretend that this is your own money and not that of the big anonymous credit card system—because it is.

Joe Nabs New York Scammers; Police Are Not Excited

A Los Angeles-based e-commerce and telephone call-center operation were shipping printers all over the U.S. out of a warehouse in Memphis. Business was brisk, and no one noticed when an order was phoned in for delivery of a high-end color printer to Queens in New York.

Just before shipment, however, the customer (we'll call him Charlie) called and said he would be out of town. Charlie asked if we could instead ship to his neighbor. We agreed. Big mistake. But the shipment went out.

Three months later, we received a retrieval request. A cardholder with a Chicago billing address had filed a dispute with her issuing bank and was upset that her card had been used for this purchase. She claimed the card was stolen and that she knew nothing of this transaction.

I was befuddled. I said, "But how could she wait this long to report a stolen card?" And, "But we had an approval." Too bad, said the processor, you did not ship to the billing address.

We called the cardholder and were convinced she was not one of the scammers, although she could not explain why she had waited so long to report the problem. Oddly, the scammer made only two purchases on this stolen card.

Next, one of my fast-talking telephone reps called the bad guys in their Queens apartment. It was a tense moment on a dark and dreary night:

"Hi, this is Bob from PrinterCom Marketing. Is Charlie there?"

"No, he's not here right now."

"Well, we're doing a marketing survey and we want to know if that PC 4992 color printer he received from us a few months ago is working okay."

"Yep, it's working fine," said Charlie's roommate.

"Do you think he is satisfied with his purchase?"

"Sure, he seems to like it."

"And can you answer one more question, please. Look at the printer and tell me the serial number."

That was the big moment. But as we waited, the bad guy's roommate read the correct serial number of the stolen printer.

Now, the problem is what to do next. The credit card people were not interested in the story, because we had not filed a police report, and even then it seemed the chances of any action were slim. "We're just too busy these days," they said.

The Los Angeles police told us the matter was not in their jurisdiction and suggested we call New York.

We had a lot of trouble actually speaking with anyone relevant at NYPD, but finally a detective said something such as, "Well, let's see, you're in Los Angeles, the printer was shipped from Memphis on a stolen credit card from Chicago to a New York address. I can take a report, but I doubt if we can do anything about this." The problem was very complicated for such a small amount of money, and the NYPD had bigger things to do.

We protested and argued "but we know exactly who did it, and the stolen equipment is in their apartment. All you have to do is go there and verify. No investigation is required." We also argued that this could be a major operation where the bad guys are ripping off many people in small transactions every day.

"But we'll have to get a search warrant," said the detective.

We knew it was a lost cause and so we completed the police report, informed the credit card company, and moved on. We lost the money, endured a chargeback, and are still waiting for action by an NYPD SWAT team.

Address Verification System (AVS)

Most processors these days offer an AVS, or address verification system, where card-not-present merchants may verify that the customer shipping address is the same as the billing address. When the addresses are not the same, look further to see if this could be a fraudulent transaction.

Working the AVS is more than just a nice thing to do. An AVS address match is required in many situations, or the merchant automatically loses the dispute if the card is later reported as stolen. The chargeback hits your merchant account, and there is no argument with any of the parties involved in the credit card payments system. You lose. Case closed.

Merchants who ship to businesses are often in a pickle here, because many employees or small business owners use their personal credit cards and request that shipments be sent to their office. In those cases, the cardholder may be called to check whether the person answering is a scammer or a real customer; or you might suggest that the cardholder call the credit card issuer and add the business address as an alternative "ship-to address." If the shipment is sent to the business address, however, a dishonest customer can claim it was stolen by the person who signed for it, and the merchant will lose that dispute, too. And no, there will be no investigation of the person who signed.

Finally, note that AVS only works in the U.S. and not with international shipments.

Fraud Detection Systems

Many credit card processors and gateways now offer sophisticated tools to help vendors detect fraud. These systems collect past data and from this suggest factors that result in increased fraud. For example, fraud occurs more often at night, in certain locations, for certain products, and for certain dollar amounts. These Internet-based systems allow on-line merchants to check each transaction against the different parameters as determined by the merchant. For example, purchases for business products occurring in the day for under $50 are shown as green lights, whereas fashionable and expensive consumer products ordered at night in New York City, where no phone number is provided, may be flagged in red.

Since merchants are ultimately responsible for fraud, these systems are of great utility. If properly worked, Web-based fraud detection services will generate large amounts of savings by avoiding scam transactions.

Get Signed Delivery Receipts

Another best practice for reducing chargebacks is to ship with carriers that provide a signed delivery receipt, or proof of delivery. UPS, FedEx, the U.S. Postal Service, and other major package and express shipping firms all offer this alternative. Even with this, it may be necessary to insist on a signature by the actual cardholder, since package receipt by roommates, friends, guys next door, and others will not impress the issuing bank investigating the dispute, and it is not practical to call around to see if someone received but forgot to give the package to the customer—especially if the customer is a scammer.

Keep the signed receipts for at least a year in case a retrieval request still comes up, or in case the merchant bank requests an audit. And for card-present situations, keep a signed copy of the sales draft for three years.

Ship First, Then Deposit

The credit card agreement requires that the sale be fulfilled before the cardholder's account is charged. In many cases, this makes little difference, because credit card processing and shipping take place on the same day. If items are back ordered and the waiting customer becomes unhappy, the sale may be disputed and the investigation may reveal that a violation of the credit card agreement occurs when the merchant deposits the sales proceeds before fulfillment. This is also true of custom-built products.

Many small businesses engaging in e-commerce are in a dilemma these days, because many sellers don't ship from inventory but merely place drop-ship orders with distributors. If the distributor does not ship on time, the small business is exposed to a chargeback if a dispute occurs.

Be Careful About International Shipments

Many people from other countries love Americans, partly because it's so easy to get away with credit card scams. In fact, credit card scamming is a major industry in some countries, and the small business is usually on the hook when problems occur.

Call to ask for a list of problem shipping locations. Certain countries are black-listed, and shipments to them are not covered by fraud protection policies. Even if everything seems to check out, if the card is later reported as stolen, the small business automatically loses the dispute and gets a chargeback.

Finally, for all international shipments, get insurance, tracking, and a signed delivery receipt. In many countries, including Europe, employees of the shipping companies and postal services supplement their incomes by stealing attractive-looking packages.

A final suggestion: Ship in plain, boring-looking boxes with a minimal amount of printed information. Boxes with advertisements such as "Your Beautiful Jewelry From Needless-Markup in America Has Arrived!" will probably never arrive.

Don't Expect Help From the Authorities

Police have little interest in credit card fraud. Even other parties in the credit card payments system take the attitude that if your small business is dumb enough to be tricked, then learn a lesson.

Joe Outsmarts Another Credit Card Scammer

This credit card scamming attempt was so obvious I won't even try to pretend we didn't catch it immediately.

One morning, an accounting person came to me and said, "You've got to look at a special sale we had last night and decide whether we'll approve it."

The customer had purchased not one, but five digital cameras in the middle of the night. The cameras were one of our most expensive models. Lots of accessories were also ordered. Money seemed like no object to this buyer. There was no phone number. The address sounded like a post office box in a grimy area of New York City.

For just a moment I was puzzled, when the accounting person said, "Not sure Joe? Did you see the e-mail address?"

I quickly looked at the screen again and in an instant announced to all, "Okay, this one is a definite reject!"

The customer wanted us to ship next-day express (yet another red flag) and send the tracking number to imascammin@aol.com (the real e-mail address is very close to this, but cannot be printed since it contains additional profanity).

Inform Cardholders of Returns, Exchange, and Warranty Policies

Many customers these days assume that anything can be returned at any time for any reason, and problems occur if they don't get their way. One way to avoid this is to inform buyers constantly of your policies as they purchase on the Internet, telephone your call-center, or browse through the printed catalog. This is especially true of small businesses that are attempting to be the low-price leader, but must sacrifice on customer service for this model to work. Cardholders may still complain and file disputes, but fewer will be decided in favor of the unhappy customer.

Avoid a Confusing Seller Name

Some small businesses advertise and promote under one name, but use a different name for credit card billing purposes. Many e-commerce companies, for example, operate many different e-stores but use just one credit card processing account. When the cardholder purchases a gift from FrenchBabyClothes.com but sees a charge from LKL Enterprises a month later on their credit card statement, confusion may result, and the transaction will be disputed. Resolving this is normally easy, but the extra time and alarm will be appreciated by no one.

Keep Information Confidential

A final best practice in reducing chargebacks is to keep all information associated with credit card vendors, and customers, confidential. Your small business is responsible for the safety of terminal equipment, merchant IDs, passwords, and access to the gateway. Keep equipment in a safe place and turned off when not in use, and make sure employees have access to cardholder information on a "need to know" basis only. After the transaction is completed, take measures to make sure that sensitive cardholder information is not available at all. For example, lock and encrypt spreadsheets and blank-out database fields displaying this information.

Of course, your small business is backing up data every night (Chapter 14), so make sure the data is encrypted during backup and stored in a safe place off the premises. Also, use the features available in modern operating systems such as Windows 2000 Server or Windows XP to limit access to certain folders on the Local Area Network, and tell employees they may use only their assigned PC.

This may seem like a lot of work, but if an employee steals such information and sells it to a credit card scammer, the results would be catastrophic and your small business might lose its right to accept credit cards. Also, credit card auditors often look into this area when examining the operations of merchants.

IP Address Tracing

Make sure the e-commerce system in use records the cardholder's IP address (Chapter 14). This can sometimes be used to trace the transaction down to a particular place, date, and time. More important, however, announce this on your Website to scare away the bad guys. Unfortunately, IP address tracing is mostly a scare tactic, because law enforcement authorities will not be enthusiastic about pursuing this matter, regardless of the evidence provided.

Fraud Warnings

Place scary statements throughout the e-store saying that in order to keep prices low, attempts at fraud are tracked and pursued to the maximum extent allowed by law. Upon reading this, some of the bad guys will drift off to other places.

Remaining a Merchant in Good Standing

The survival of many small businesses depends upon the credit card processing and payments system. But this is a bit complex and requires the constant attention of the small business owner. Allocate some time and be sure to do the following:

- Read the agreements from the merchant bank and processor very carefully. They are not all the same, and include important additional details on your responsibilities.

- Protect the security of customers by limiting access to the on-line system and printed records on a "need to know" basis only. Watch for common employee-related problems such as skimming, where dishonest employees use their own card readers, or even just a pencil and paper, to write down customer credit card information. This information is typically sold to other bad people for credit card and identity theft. Your small business may be fined or terminated if this problem occurs.

- Only charge for goods and services clearly purchased by the customer—be careful about taking liberties and increasing charges or adding fees.

- The merchant bank may audit vendor records, so keep everything organized and up-to-date.

- Review credit card transactions on a daily basis to make sure all transactions are processed properly. This prevents common problems such as shipping and not collecting the payment, or collecting the payment and not shipping. Make sure the totals in your system match the amounts processed, and later trace the daily batch amounts to actual deposits into the bank account. Things can happen. Further, these problems are time-consuming and tedious to deal with if handled immediately, but accounting problems only get worse when accountants must go back and fix old problems at a later time.

Selecting Credit Card Vendors

Small businesses need to choose a merchant bank, gateway, and processor before accepting credit card payments. The best place to begin is to ask the bank now hosting your checking account if it offers credit card merchant banking services; it will also recommend related providers such as the gateway. Of course, ask other local banks or get recommendations from business colleagues with experience in this area. Credit card services vendors are easy to find, and a personal reference from a friend or business colleague is comforting but hardly necessary.

Beyond this, if your small business is setting up an on-line store, ask the software or services provider which gateways are compatible with their system; not all processors work with all e-stores. That is good in a way, because these vendors have presumably qualified the integrity of the credit card services providers.

To find even more vendors, just search for "Credit Card Processor" through a favorite search engine, and literally millions of links will be returned.

Be careful, however, since exaggeration and hyperbole are a fact of life in the credit card processing industry, especially among the many ISOs. Watch out for this and the many creative garbage-fees that may turn a good deal into an expensive one. These may include:

- Account Setup Fees
- Annual Fees
- Bank Card Setup Fees
- Bank Setup fees
- Cancellation Fees
- Chargeback Fees
- Customer Service Fees
- Daily Batch Fees
- Daily Closeout Fees
- Gateway Access Fees
- Minimum Monthly Service Charge Fee
- Network Access Fees
- NSF (Non-Sufficient Funds) Fees
- Over Limit Fees
- Pass Through Fees
- Retrieval Fees
- Software Licensing Fees
- Statement Fees
- Technical Support Fees
- Termination Fees
- Voice Authorization Fees
- Voice Address Verification System Fees
- Website Access Fees

Just about every service will demand some of these charges, but compare closely to separate the good deals from the bad. Most small businesses simply consider the discount rate, but sometimes the real money is in the fees.

Credit cards are a powerful and increasingly significant form of revenues collection by many small businesses, but knowledge and vigilance are required to set up and successfully manage the many relationships necessary to fully exploit the advantages of this complex and important payments system.

Chapter 14

Everything You Need to Know About Computers in Just a Few Pages

We begin by asking readers to translate the following VBA code into Java Script:

```
Sub VariableN1Dim ()
Dim IX as Integer
Range ("N1:L12").Select
ActiveCell.Offset (0,3).Select
For IX = 1 To 3
Range (("N1"), Range("N1").End(x1Down)).EntireRow.Copy
Next I
End Sub
```

Just kidding.

Keeping Computers in Perspective

This is not a technical discussion. The purpose of this chapter is to equip small business owners with the information that is necessary to purchase and operate the machines needed to manage the business. There is a lot to know, but you don't need to know it all. This chapter is called "Everything You *Need* to Know About Computers in Just a Few Pages," because small business owners don't need to know everything. The focus here is on getting by with the least possible involvement with computers and other technology and keeping the focus on the business itself. Our concern is with what to buy, security (much on this), and how to manage a small IT infrastructure.

Computers are ubiquitous, and it is not easy to keep up with the latest hardware, software, Internet services, and concepts. In fact, it can easily become a major distraction for the small business owner when time is better spent doing other things. Over the years, I have come to recognize two approaches to technology and computers by small business owners: There are the "techno" types," who consider themselves to be amateur gurus, and the "Jed Clampett" types, who look at a keyboard with disinterest. I have not formally studied this area but would wager that the Jed Clampett types are the most successful over time. The reason is that computers are an immensely powerful tool in business, but they can also absorb huge amounts of time (studying, purchasing, installing, configuring, updating, fixing, maintaining, learning, tweaking, and just fooling around with all of the various products and services). This chapter reviews what every small business owner absolutely must know about information technology to get by in the world today and run a business—and nothing more. The author has the license to say these things after having invested over 15 years of his career in various ends of the IT industry. If you already know a lot about IT, skip this chapter. On the other hand, many small business owners will find this chapter a useful guide.

Joe Meets the Jed Clampett of Computers

I recently had a meeting with the founder and president of a very successful cosmetics-industry small business. I will call him "Jed."

Jed started the business 20 years ago and now employs over 50 people on two continents. We talked about various aspects of the business. As a computer buff, I couldn't wait to get to the question: "So what type of Customer Relationship Management system is used here Mr. Clampett?"

"I'm not sure," he responded uncomfortably, "but my sales and marketing VP tells me it's one of the best."

"Okay. Well what is your accounting software?"

"Umm. I know we upgraded to something really good a while back and it's working great now."

I thought, "Wow, he doesn't know!"

I ventured one more question: "I can probably guess the software being used here if you tell me what kind of hardware you're running. So what is the biggest machine here? A UNIX server, or maybe an AS/400?"

Jed came clean. "I don't know that kind of stuff," he said. "I just hire good people to figure that out for me and I buy what they want. Then I get back to work and close some more business."

You can't argue with success.

Definitions

There are terabytes of IT words these days, and they keep changing. But to get through this chapter, we'll need to know just a few:

☐ **Browser.** A computer application that displays Web pages on computer workstations. Microsoft Internet Explorer and Mozilla Firefox are the most popular browsers in use today.

☐ **Cookies.** Small files placed on the computers of Internet users allowing Websites to remember the user and personalize the experience. Cookies may also be used for nefarious purposes and often are unknowingly saved on computers when Internet browsers visit certain sites.

☐ **Domain Naming System (DNS)**—Internet databases which translate domain names and IP addresses back and forth. See chapter 5 for more information.

☐ **Firewall.** A protective barrier (hardware or software) between the Internet and the computers and network within a small business.

☐ **https.** A Website that encrypts transmitted data and starts with "https", rather than the normal "http". These sites are especially safe and secure from snoopers. Example: A credit card holder enters the account number and receives back a page of recent transactions. In more technical terms, https uses SSL, or the secure socket layers protocol, where a frequently changing private key encrypts data that is undecipherable except at the sending and receiving locations.

☐ **Gigabyte (GB).** Computer storage is often measure in bytes. One byte is simply one character of data. For example, the number "7" is one byte, and "77" is 2 bytes. A Gigabyte is 1,073,741,824 bytes (2 raised to the 30th power, or 2^{30}). One GB is equal to 1,024 MB (Megabytes). A new computer workstation should have at least 40 GB of hard disk space, and 512 MB (or 0.5 GB) of memory. As a very rough rule of thumb, a typical employee may need about 5 GB to 10 GB of storage for workstation system files, applications, and data.

☐ **Internet Protocol (IP) Address.** Information is transferred throughout the Internet in packets, enveloped by IP addresses. IP addresses take the form of four digits of up to three characters in length, such as 111.222.333.444 or 987.65.43.2.

☐ **IMAP.** See Post Office Protocol

☐ **Local Area Network (LAN).** See Network.

☐ **Network** (or LAN, Local Area Network). In this context, a network is a group of client computers (also known as workstations or PCs) connected via Ethernet cable or wireless devices within a small business environment. Servers and peripheral devices such as printers are also part of the network. The LAN is within a closed environment and does not include the Internet.

☐ **Peer-to-peer network.** A group of networked computers where any machine can be, at the same time, both a client and/or a server. Although all machines are clients, no machine is a dedicated server. All machines have the ability to access files on all other machines. In simpler terms, a group of workstations simply connected together via Ethernet or wireless devices is a peer-to-peer network. Microsoft's Windows for Workgroups and Artisoft's LANtastic are the best known peer-to-peer products.

☐ **Phishing.** An Internet user receives fake e-mails (usually warning employees of fake problems) linking to fraudulent Websites. The e-mail queries are intended to fool recipients into divulging personal financial data such as account sign-in names, passwords, credit card numbers, Social Security numbers, etc. Phishers then log in to the stolen accounts and transfer funds, make purchases, steal identities, and further enrich themselves through illegal or criminal activities.

☐ **Post Office Protocol (POP3).** A protocol for retrieving e-mails, stored on a central repository (or server). Programs such as Microsoft Outlook and Microsoft Outlook Express are based on POP3. SMTP (Simple Mail Transport Protocol) is used to route e-mail among servers. POP3 remains the most popular e-mail protocol, but some users now opt for the newer IMAP4 (Internet Message Access Protocol).

☐ **Scum ware, spy ware, trash ware, trojans, mal ware, ad ware, browser hijackers, tracking components, pop-ups, data-miners, etc.** Different forms of badly or maliciously designed software, that fall short of being viruses, but generally reduce the performance and productivity of computers. For the most part, these small programs send information to advertisers who then send back advertisements as pop-up ads and in other forms. The programs use the disk and processing resources of small business workstations and may seriously distract employees when the advertisements become overbearing. Often, clicking on an ad to "remove" the program only makes matters worse. Scum ware and others are often buried in free downloads of other programs and work in the background without a user's knowledge.

☐ **Servers.** Computers in a client/server architecture that supply files or services (either to the Internet or to LAN users), and also perform administrative and support functions such as nightly backups, antivirus administration, software installs, updates (pushed to other computers), and more. Servers are often kept in secure environments and are more robust than workstations.

☐ **Virus(Computer Virus).** Unlike the scum ware and related trash previously described, viruses are designed to cause harm to computers. These are small programs that infiltrate systems through e-mail, floppy disks, CDs, network connections to other machines, and other means. There are thousands of known computer viruses, and dozens more are found each month. A computer virus can quickly and silently destroy important information on a computer, or render it useless.

☐ **Workstations** (also called "Clients" or "PCs"). Connect to servers and other workstations and peripherals to request files, services, printing, and other functions. The client may request file transfer, remote log-ins, printing, or other available services. Workstations are the machines that do the actual production work, such as word processing, spreadsheets, accounting, e-mail, Internet browsing, etc.

A great source for quickly looking up other IT terms is www.webopedia.com.

What Kind of Computers Are Really Needed?

What to Buy

There is a lot to know about buying computers for a small business; and prices, configurations, and options are always changing. It is true that this market changes so quickly that even the experts have trouble keeping up. What is the small business owner to do when it's time to buy new machines?

Actually, the answer is simple: Go into a favorite PC store and buy whatever is in the middle of the product lineup. Virtually every machine has several times the power that will ever be needed to run most business applications (such as word processing, accounting, and spreadsheets), and all have the capability of connecting to the Internet. Rather than becoming concerned with processor speeds, processor cache, memory-read rates in nanoseconds, disk-spin rates and the rest of the technobabble, just get a quick understanding of prices and then pick something in the middle.

Computers are much more standardized these days, and the chances of buying the wrong machine are about the same as buying a color television that doesn't work in a particular home; it's pretty unlikely. Pricing everywhere is very competitive, which works to the advantage of the small business owner. Fortunately, "You get what you pay for." If one machine is a bit more expensive than another, there is a reason. Chances are, it is a reason that is not relevant to small business computing needs.

Is there a chance of spending a few dollars extra on unneeded capabilities? The answer is yes, it's a virtual certainty. But these machines are so productive, it won't matter; so don't belabor the issue.

New PCs are a great way to improve employee morale. Everyone loves to work on a hot, new machine, so be sure to take this into account. Also, employees appreciate working on the latest hardware and software to keep their skills keen and current.

Finally, note that it is consumers—not small businesses—that need the extra horsepower, bells, and whistles on computers. Extra capabilities are needed to run many modern PC-based video games, and the home PC is increasingly melding into the heart of the home-entertainment center. Most businesses need only be concerned about running stodgy old office and accounting programs and connecting to the Internet—none of which require special capacities. Don't feel bad for not buying the most glitzy machines in the shop, because high-end configurations are just not needed.

Where to Buy

Now that you know what to buy, where is the best place to shop? Many small businesses simply purchase on the Internet, through well-known sites such as Dell.com, Gateway.com, Hewlett-Packard (hp.com) and many others, including eBay. Most buyers browse online and then call to order, which is a great alternative. The main advantage of buying from big-name companies is that products are well-engineered and reliable, and warranties include one- to three-years' parts and labor, 24-hour toll-free help lines, and Internet-based support. Remember, though, that warranty support covers broken parts and technical mismatches, not questions such as "How do I set up my email?" Finally, note that while shipping fees are often charged, there is a good chance that sales tax will not be incurred (especially from smaller vendors), because out-of-state buyers are supposed to report the purchase to local authorities and instead pay a use tax.

Another alternative is a local retailer. Here also, prices are very competitive (markups are usually 5 percent to 15 percent), immediate delivery with no shipping charges are the norm, but sales taxes are charged in most states. It's possible to get to know the retailer a bit and gain the benefits of a relationship. Most retailers will stand by their products to keep the business, but of course PC stores come and go. Don't expect huge discounts from a local dealer, because there is little margin to play with. Also, local retailers can normally send or refer technical experts to visit your site and fix problems, for a price. But of course, all small businesses should have this type of technical expertise on-call anyway (see Chapter 8).

Finally, there are the big-box stores such as Best Buy and Circuit City. Here, prices are also competitive. The selection may be a bit larger, but the level of help and expertise is a little less.

Is there a chance that a machine purchased at FreddieTheGeekPCs.com cannot be supported by a local fix-it contractor? The answer is no. All machines these days are made of standard components and everything is easily available everywhere.

In conclusion, prices are competitive just about everywhere, the purchase decision may come down largely to time and convenience, and it's hard to make a mistake in deciding where to buy.

"Must Have" Business Computer Programs
Operating System

The operating system is the overall unifier of the components of any computer, from hardware to software and everything in between. For all practical purposes, a small business should choose only one operating system; it's just way too much work to learn and support more than this.

Many operating systems are available for different types and sizes of machines. These include Microsoft Windows XP (and predecessors such as Windows 2000 and Windows 98), Linux, Apple MAC OS, UNIX (in several versions), and others.

The criteria for purchasing an operating system are:

- Can I run all of the hardware and software needed on this OS?
- Is it easy to find outside support?
- What is the price?

Does this question require a lot of analysis? The answer is no. Just go with Microsoft's latest operating system for business machines, currently XP Pro. It is true that Microsoft and Windows have experienced their share of controversy over the years, but this is inherent in any product that controls the market. Ironically, the reason to go with Microsoft is that it does indeed control the market. The system has its share of flaws, but every major business software vendor writes its programs first for Microsoft, and if this is a success, then the program may be rewritten for the other operating systems. For small business owners, this translates into lots and lots of software to do just about anything, and battalions of capable support people available at reasonable prices for installations, support, fixes, and maintenance.

A possible exception is firms in the advertising or creative areas, where perhaps the industry norm is Apple-based systems. If most of the programs used in your industry are Apple-based, and if employees are more comfortable with Apple, then this must be considered against Windows.

A Small Step Forward, Every Day

It is important for small business owners to understand how to use an operating system and the business applications programs described here. Although the theme of this chapter is "Everything You Need to Know" rather than "Everything There Is to Know," the programs described here are so commonplace that small business owners risk being out of touch if not familiar with the operating system, word processing, e-mail, Internet browsing, and perhaps other applications, such as spreadsheets.

Here is a great tip: There is too much to learn all at once, so every day, learn one new feature of one program, no matter how small. For example, learn how to center text in the word processing program. The next day, learn how to use the spell-check feature.

Also, keep a mental list of other concepts to learn later. Learn the feature either from the Help sections or by asking someone. For a list of features and interesting things to know, press the F1 key and print some pages from the Help section to read in the evening.

Small business owners may become immensely productive through this small investment of time in their IT systems.

Business Programs

Almost all business machines should be capable of running programs for the following functions: word processing, electronic spreadsheets, e-mail, viewing pictures, and a browser to see pages from the Internet.

Word Processing, Spreadsheets, and More: Microsoft Office

There are many products on the market, but once again, most Small businesses should simply go with the Microsoft offerings. These include Microsoft Word for word processing, Excel for electronic spreadsheets, Picture Manager (previously known as Photo Editor) for viewing pictures, Outlook or Outlook Express for e-mail, and Internet Explorer for browsing the Internet.

Microsoft groups these products together, and the packaged price is far less than buying each component separately. The suite of products is called Microsoft Office, which comes in different versions and price points depending upon the products included. All the products work together, so there is no concern about transferring information between them. Moreover, a large majority of vendors, customers, and others use these same products, so your small business will be on an equal footing with the rest of the world and there will be no need to translate documents as they are sent or received.

To learn more about the latest product groupings and prices, see www.microsoftoffice.com. Microsoft does not sell directly to small businesses. Instead, buy these products from a computer vendor (hopefully installed upon purchase), from most big-box electronics stores, or just shop on-line.

For Internet browsing, there is no need to purchase anything, because Microsoft includes Internet Explorer in the operating system (to be discussed shortly).

Some hold that Microsoft's products are not the best, but they are used by far more clients than all other competitors combined. Further, few users ever need or learn the advanced features anyway. These are older, mature products now. It's been a long time since anyone came out with an exciting new word processing or similar feature, and these products will work just fine for just about any small business. They are also reasonably easy to learn, and acceptably priced. It's easy to find all types of support, including books in just about any store, help from www.microsoft.com, or the services of local contractors who can install, train, and maintain these applications.

E-mail

E-mail is an essential form of communication, and every small business owner should use it. Those who do not are increasingly marginalized from the mainstream of any business.

There are two basic forms of e-mail: POP3 (or alternatively SMTP) and Web-based. In POP3 (Post Office Protocol, Version 3), e-mail is delivered to a workstation for viewing; Web-based e-mail remains on another server but is viewed from the local workstation using a browser such as Internet Explorer.

The most ubiquitous POP3 e-mail program is Microsoft Outlook, or its little brother, Outlook Express (next paragraph). Outlook is normally sold together with other products, such as Microsoft Word, as previously described. It is a solid, proven program, and most small business owners should go with this offering because it is well-integrated with other Microsoft products and other third-party software; it is cheap and painless to learn; and support is easy to find. There are other great e-mail programs, but Outlook is a good default if there are no other preferences.

Outlook Express is a free e-mail program included with Microsoft Internet Explorer (also free). It works just fine but has fewer features than Outlook. Outlook Express does not include a fully integrated calendar, a tasks or notes folder, or spam filters. These features are not important to most users, and so Outlook Express is a good choice. Big brother Outlook is used in most small business situations because it is packaged in the Microsoft Office suite of products, and because Outlook Express cannot retrieve e-mail from a Microsoft exchange server (used in more formal small business settings for e-mail and collaborative work).

Web-based e-mail does not require a special program but is simply viewed through an Internet browser. Free e-mail accounts are available from many sources, including Yahoo (www.yahoo.com), MSN (www.MSN.com), and Netscape (www.netscape.com). A good Web-based e-mail alternative will offer free storage of 250MB or more (useful for temporary storage of files), a service that scans e-mails for viruses (but don't rely solely upon this for protection), filters to stop spam, and an address book. Another important advantage of Web-based e-mail is that new and old messages may be viewed anytime, anywhere, as long as the user has Internet access. POP3 e-mail is installed and delivered to a particular machine, and some serious reconfiguring is required to receive e-mail elsewhere. E-mail already received and sitting on one workstation cannot be viewed at all from other machines.

At many small businesses, POP3 e-mail can also be viewed through an Internet browser, but technical expertise is required to make this available.

Many people have two or more e-mail accounts for different purposes, both POP3 and Web-based. Users may then send e-mail to themselves (handy when traveling, for work performed at home, and for other reasons).

Internet Browser

For most people, the browser is just the big blue "e" that is clicked to go on the Internet. This is Microsoft Internet Explorer (www.microsoft.com/windows/ie), which has ruled the browser world since it dethroned Netscape Navigator in the 1990s.

IE does the job just fine, but as a result of its near universal acceptance, Explorer has been heavily targeted by hackers and virus writers. Some have been critical of the security flaws in IE and its many updates and patches, so about 10 million users have switched to Mozilla Firefox. Firefox (information at www.mozilla.org ; download at www.download.com) claims that its product works faster, and with greater safety, than IE. In fact, both products work fine, except that Explorer users must be much more conscientious about security. And both are free.

Internet browsers allow users to decide upon certain security, privacy, and content settings. Ask someone who knows about this somewhat complex area to set these options in the best way for your situation. Also, learn about deleting cookies and unneeded files to make sure time spent on the Internet is a productive experience.

Antivirus

The breach of computer security is a growing threat and poses real risks to small business owners. It's only a matter of time before any small business is threatened by outside attacks that either render machines unusable or steal confidential company or customer data.

Many books are available on how to protect business networks from outside attack. These are written for computer security experts, and as a small business grows, the time will come when this talent is needed. For now, much of this can be condensed into a few simple procedures. Protecting your investment in IT equipment is actually not difficult, and requires just a little understanding of the different types of threats and how to manage them.

Computer viruses are small programs that cause intentional harm to computers. Most arrive these days via e-mail, but viruses can enter machines from other points, such as floppy disk drives, zip drives, CDs brought in by employees, and other means.

Fortunately, viruses are easy to stop if the right measures are taken. Two types of measure are required: antivirus (AV) software protection and informed employees.

For antivirus protection, use offerings from either Symantec (www.symantec.com, formerly known as Norton Antivirus) or McAfee (www.mcafee.com). Both are solid products with a large user base, so it will be easy to find support.

Every workstation and server in a small business must be protected, first by installing the AV program and then by telling the machines to continually check with the vendor to see if there are new antivirus definitions.

What's the difference between the antivirus program and the antivirus definitions? Look at it this way. Doctors (the program) examine patients (computers) for problems, but then the doctor needs the latest medicines (the antivirus definitions) to treat the latest infections. The best doctor in the world cannot help much without knowing about the latest infectious diseases and the medicines for treatment. It's the latest viruses that pose the greatest problems.

Both the Symantec and McAfee products can be configured to call-home to their respective antivirus definitions servers weekly, or even daily, to see if there is anything new to worry about. This is normally scheduled to take place at night, when the machines are not busy.

A small business is still exposed, however, if a new virus outbreak occurs just after the latest antivirus definitions file is downloaded. Then, if someone opens an infected file attached to an e-mail (or on a floppy drive, etc.), the virus executes and does its dirty work on that machine. It can also jump around and infect every other machine on the Local Area Network.

The damage can usually be undone by following the instructions downloaded from the AV vendor, but this often requires considerable time from a computer pro, and downtime as employees sit idle, waiting for everything to be fixed.

PCs are also exposed to computer viruses when a malicious or well-meaning but dumb employee screws with the AV program. The program may be de-installed or configured in a bad way, such that the machine becomes easy prey to any virus, new or old.

This exposure may be resolved by using a slightly different model, where all workstations are "locked-down" and managed by a server. Employees then cannot de-install or reconfigure the AV program; only the administrator has the right to do this. Symantec calls their version of this product "Symantec Antivirus Corporate Edition" or "Small Business Edition" and McAfee's is "McAfee VirusScan ASaP".

If a small business has more than three or four workstations in a peer-to-peer architecture, it's time to get a server and upgrade to the more secure versions of these AV products.

Programs to Stop Scum Ware, Spy Ware, Trash Ware, Trojans, Mal Ware, Ad Ware, Browser Hijackers, Tracking Components, Pop-Ups, Data-Miners, Etc.

As noted in the definitions section at the beginning of this chapter, these maliciously designed programs can bring a computer to its knees and stop all productive work, as employees are overwhelmed with advertisements. Anyone browsing the Internet without protection from scum ware and others will quickly be bombarded with ads and unable to continue working.

Without permission or knowledge, these recklessly designed and distributed nuisances track Internet surfing habits, use computing assets to send this data to others, watch shopping habits, force Internet browser to use advertisers' sites as their home page, and change important system files. There are obvious and frightening privacy and security implications to all of this.

Joe Succumbs to Ad-Bombardment During Big Sales Presentation

I recently met with the owners of a small business to give a sales pitch on a concept developed for a Website and e-store. The client was a bit naïve about computers but told me in advance I would get to use their newest workstation.

I arrived and after some small talk, it was time for the big show. Of course, I had prepared everything in advance, and my materials were located on various Internet-based servers.

The first task was to open a browser window and go to the first Internet site of my presentation. I never got that far. The workstation was new, but the Internet browser had very lax security settings. One of the employees had already done a bit of Internet product-pricing and marketing research for a competitive analysis. To scum purveyors on the Internet, this looked like plain-old shopping.

I connected to the Internet, opened the first browser window, but could get no further. As I began typing the address of my first Internet site, a blizzard of pop-up ads appeared. I tried to close a few, but they were popping open far faster than I could close them. I soon gave up and shut down the machine.

When I restarted, the first job was not my sales presentation but configuring the machine so that it could properly work on the Internet. I had to take several measures to get around the problems temporarily,

because the solution to these disturbances were actually on the Internet.

After an hour or so, I had set up an antivirus program, scanned the machine, and fixed an infection. Then I installed a program to protect the machine from scum ware and its evil cousins, and scanned the machine and deleted dozens of data-mining cookies and related trash. Along the way, I increased the security settings in the browser and deleted a few malicious processes that ran silently in the background.

No doubt about it, I was a hero. The machine had been useless, but I had brought it back to health. It could now roam the Internet, hold its own, and defend itself from all the bad things out there.

The only problem is that the patience of my hot prospects had worn thin. They had a limited clock for things-computer anyway, and were getting hungry. "Let's just talk it over at lunch," they said.

I was unenthusiastic about skipping my big presentation, but hunger ruled. We discussed the idea for a few minutes at lunch, but without the visual impact of the Internet. Because one of their few Internet experiences was my hijacked presentation, where advertisements derailed everything, the initial excitement faded away and the deal was put on the back-burner, unlikely to come to life again anytime soon.

All workstations should therefore have protection from this blight, through programs such as ZoneAlarm Pro (from Encore Software, and available at www.download.com), or Lavasoft Ad-aware Professional SE (available at www.lavasoft.com and also at www.download.com). The programs run in a similar manner to the antivirus programs previously described, where the latest definitions must be downloaded periodically. Then a scan is performed and the trash may be removed.

Pop-up ads are a related nuisance, and Internet users are bombarded with advertising windows that open on the computer screen faster than they may be closed. The ZoneAlarm program already described contains a pop-up blocker to resolve this problem. Another simple alternative is available for free from Google in a small program that may be downloaded and installed from http://toolbar.google.com. Or just go to Google.com and search for "google pop up stopper." Finally, Earthlink offers a free combination pop-up stopper and anti-Phishing toolbar, as described in the "No Phishing" section. This is available at www.earthlink.net/earthlinktoolbar/download/.

Contact Manager

A contact manager is a database dedicated to keeping track of all persons, businesses, and communications of importance to a small business. Contact managers may sound unnecessary to entrepreneurs used to manual systems, but these powerful tools are easy to learn and can offer a critical competitive edge.

Two contact managers dominate the market for small businesses: ACT by Best Software, and Goldmine from Frontrange Solutions. Both are capable products and have similar features.

At the simplest level, a contact manager keeps tracks of names, addresses, and telephone numbers. Other fields in the database may be filled in such that users can ask questions such as, "I met this customer from Florida a few years ago and forget the company name but remember that they sold truck parts. What is the name, company, address, telephone number, and Website of the person I met, and what communications did we exchange?"

These applications can keep records of all telephone, fax, mail, e-mail, and advertising communications, and can sort names to build mailing lists, print customized letters and mailing labels, and send faxes and e-mails directly to selected groups.

New contacts may be entered or changed at any time, and lists may be purchased from outside sources such as InfoUSA (see also Chapter 4) and merged with existing records. This is a great way to quickly build an effective sales prospect list.

Many small businesses use these products to manage salespeople and marketing campaigns. The typical setup involves a contacts database that can be shared by everyone simultaneously. Sales reps may be assigned accounts, and managers can easily monitor all sales activities, including call notes and correspondence.

Setting this up may be a bit complicated, so small business owners may delegate the task to a knowledgeable pro. But learning to use the program after setup is easy and intuitive.

Protecting and Maintaining IT Investments
Rules for Employees

All employees should be informed about the dangers of using computers and the Internet, and follow certain rules regarding use of IT equipment. If just one person screws up one time, all the machines at a small business can be put out of action for days until a computer maintenance pro is paid a lot of money.

These guidelines could be incorporated into the employee handbook (Chapter 6) but must be distributed and continually promoted so that all are aware:

- Employees may not add or install any programs, Internet services, or even update programs without permission in advance. Programs and updates may contain embedded viruses, or inadvertently cause problems with other hardware or software. Scum ware often describes itself as a "critical update" to benevolent programs.

- Everyone should check twice a day to make sure the antivirus protection on workstations is indeed working. Ditto for the anti-scum-ware program and antiphishing programs. (More on this later.)

- E-mails often arrive with files attached. Employees should immediately delete and never open files from unknown sources (because much is scum-ware-laden spam). But there is no danger in simply viewing e-mail messages.

- Extreme caution should be used when opening files even from known persons, because many viruses burrow into a friend's machine, and in seconds then send themselves to everyone in the friend's address book. (See "Joe Gets a Virus From a Nice Friend.")

- Do an anti-scum-ware scan and then reboot at the end of each business day, so the machine is fresh the next morning.

- Watch the Web-browser toolbar to see known Phishing fraud websites. Be alert for new ones.

Rules for Small Business Owners

- Have a network administrator and troubleshooter who is always available by cell phone, and who can be at the site within a few business hours. Pay this person to take an inventory of your systems so that the original layout is known when trouble occurs.

- Back up every machine every day. (More on this later.)

- Maintain all IT investments with the "If it ain't broke, don't fix it" strategy (except for security-related items).

- Install the following security tools on every computer: antivirus, anti-scum-ware, and antiphishing (as described previously).

- Check on-line accounts regularly and look for unexplained activity.

- Consider changing account numbers, or opening and closing new accounts, when employees leave or if the information is otherwise compromised.

- Change passwords every 30 days, but don't be predictable about the exact time or the new passwords.

- Make sure that Internet browsers and Internet firewalls are always up-to-date with the latest security patches.

- Educate employees about the dangers of using the Internet.

Joe Gets a Virus From a Nice Friend

A very knowledgeable and savvy computer pro was helping me with a project, and one morning he sent me an e-mail with a small file attached. The short note said to open the file.

This was unexpected and looked a bit suspicious, but hey, this guy was a pro and knew much more than me. There was no way he would send me a virus.

I clicked on the program and saw dozens of lines of strange computer code flash on the screen. I knew it was a virus, but before I could react, the program completed and the computer seemed normal again. After a few minutes, though, I knew something was terribly wrong. I could not browse the Internet because strange sites kept popping up, the e-mail program was disabled, and other programs crashed. Then the computer froze.

A coworker ran in a few seconds later and said he had the same problem. I acted surprised. I was embarrassed to tell him that it was because I had uncorked a virus, and it jumped around our network and infected all of the other machines. The normal procedure when this occurs is to panic, and then research the problem at the Internet site of the antivirus program vendor. But this was not possible, because the virus blocked their site.

We fixed the problem over the next eight hours by begging a neighbor to allow us to research the problem on one of his workstations. With this, we disconnected the cables going to each of our machines, executed a tedious checklist of complex tasks, and then put our network back together. An entire day of work was lost by eight people.

My friend was not at fault, because he did not know that the virus had infected his machine and had sent itself out to every person in his address book. I was embarrassed to tell him, because he assumed that I would not fall victim to such a well-known way of getting infected.

Death to Phish

Phishing is a very rapidly growing scam these days, and employees should be on the alert for e-mails from even the most trusted sources. Phishing occurs when an inattentive, busy, or just dumb employee responds to a message such as the following, and your account and money are now under the exclusive control of someone really bad.

Joe No Fool With Phishing

The following is an e-mail Phishing scam. I didn't respond, but make sure no one at your small business gets fooled by something like this:

Dear Big Fee Bank Customer,

We recently reviewed your account and suspect that it may have been accessed by an unauthorized third party. Protecting the security of your account and of the small business bank network is our primary concern.

Therefore, as a preventive measure, we have temporarily limited access to sensitive account features. To restore your account access, please take the following steps to ensure that your account has not been compromised:

1. Log in to your big fee Internet banking account. In case you are not enrolled in Internet banking, you will have to fill in all the required information, including your name and account number.

2. Review your recent account history for any unauthorized withdrawals or deposits, and check your account profile to make sure changes have not been made. If any unauthorized activity has taken place on your account, report this to the big fee banking staff immediately.

To get started, please click the following link: www.BigFee.com (Fake link to small business bank but really goes to Phishers). We apologize for any inconvenience this may cause, and appreciate your assistance in helping us maintain the integrity of the entire big fee banking system.

Sincerely,
The Big Fee Banking Team

Phishing is now the rage among Internet scammers, and large Internet merchants, including well-known banks, merchants, major on-line retailers, credit card vendors, and other household names, are incensed that their good names and logos are being used on a wholesale basis to trick customers into revealing sensitive account information and becoming the victims of identity theft and fraud. Phishing scams typically convince an astonishing 5 percent of recipients into responding. This could be you or anemployee.

One of the most frustrating dimensions of Phishing is that you, the legitimate owner of the account, must then convince the bank, credit card service, or vendor that you are the real owner, since the Phisher now has exclusive access to the account.

The best way to stop Phishing is never to click links in e-mails. Instead, open a new browser window and type in the correct address yourself.

The risks of Phishing can be further reduced by installing a Web-browser toolbar on every workstation to warn against known Phishing fraud websites. A good one is the Earthlink ScamBlocker (part of their browser and pop-up stopper toolbar) available for free at www.earthlink.net/earthlinktoolbar/download. Small business owners and all e-mail users must still remain vigilant to Phishing schemes.

Data Backups

More and more small business owners recognize that their most valuable asset is information; and most information is stored on workstations and servers and is not backed up until a disaster occurs. This is like the proverbial closing of the barn door after the horse runs away.

Think of the many different ways your small business may experience losing important data, such as the accounting system. These may include:

- Fire
- Earthquake, flood, hurricane
- Theft (and resale of your data and equipment)
- Virus attack, hackers
- Power surge
- Accidental overwrite
- Deleted files by employee sabotage, or even by well-meaning employees
- Disk crash

It is only a matter of time before a small business falls victim to one of these threats, so if you run a serious business, data backup should be of paramount concern.

One of your most important tasks is to decide which data to back up, and how frequently. Remember that the newest data is always the most important. The best answer is to schedule a backup of all data every night, or at least back up files that have changed recently. This is increasingly possible and affordable with modern backup systems for small businesses. To accomplish this, additional hardware, software, and media may be needed.

A backup device (such as a tape drive) should be installed on a server, but it can run on workstations. This chapter assumes that backups will be run from a server. Backup software allows data to be collected from all machines on a network. During the collection process, data may be checked for viruses, verified for integrity, encrypted, and compressed to save space.

Many businesses forget to backup laptops, even though laptops are especially vulnerable to theft and accidents; so include laptop backups in your plans.

Hardware and Media

Tape backups have always been my favorite. Data written to tape has been around since the 1950s, and for decades was the only feasible backup device. Tape is easy to use, has a huge capacity (up to 160 GB per 8mm tape), and can be quickly removed and stored off the premises. Here is a comparison of various devices:

> **Backing Up the Small Business Owners Manual**
>
> This book was produced on a PC probably much like yours. The writing took about 600 hours over about six months, in sessions of about three hours each.
>
> The author did not want to lose work due to the computer problems described above or for any reason, so the following measures were taken:
>
> 1. Enter text.
> 2. Text immediately backed up on mirrored SCSI (business grade) disk drives.
> 3. Tape backup every night on 20 rotating tapes. Remove tape and store off-site the next day.
> 4. All files synchronized between home and office machines every two days.
> 5. All files compressed, encrypted, and sent to an online backup service provider every week.
>
> Note that all of these measures were automated except Step 1.
>
> Indeed, a disk crash wiped out the entire book a month before the first draft was finished, but everything was easily restored. Only an area-wide meteor hit could destroy all of the copies.

- **Tape.** Tapes are cheap, durable, and can be removed from the premises and stored in a safe location. Industrial strength backup software is available from many vendors, allowing different jobs to be saved and scheduled for quiet times of the day. Tapes may also be encrypted and checked for viruses. But tape write and recovery times are relatively slow—and tapes hate magnets. Magnets may silently corrupt data, and this can remain unknown until restoration time. Capacity: up to 160GB (170,000 MB) per 8MM tape (there are several other formats; all are fine).

- **Zip-Drives.** Tens of millions of zip-drives have been sold to both consumer and small business users since the zip was introduced in 1995. They are popular because the capacity is six times greater than that of a floppy. It is also faster and the media is durable, easy to store, and can be password-protected. Different jobs can be saved and scheduled through backup software. Capacity: 0.7 GB or 750 MB.

- **CD ROMs.** A popular alternative among small businesses, but maybe not the greatest idea because the process is manual (cannot be scheduled automatically), write times are lengthy, the CD media is cheap but a bit delicate, and multiple CDs must be used for all but the smallest jobs. As business grows, a large off-premises storage location and good organization will be needed (try finding one lost document among 1,000 CDs with cryptic labels). Security may also be a problem because just about any thief will have a computer capable of reading a CD. Capacity: 0.61 GB or 650 MB capacity.

- **DVDs.** This alternative is much the same as CDs except that DVDs have a much larger capacity. DVDs are now sold in five different formats that are not cross-compatible, and this can be a headache. DVDs are also much more expensive than CDs. Capacity: 4.7 GB or 5,000 MB.

- **Removable Hard Disk.** Hard Drives were once delicate; but rugged, portable disks are now available in huge capacities. The drives are not expensive, and prices are always headed south, so these devices may someday replace tape, especially since write and recovery speeds are much faster. Professional backup software may be used to set up and run jobs, with features including data encryption, virus checks, and password protection. But removable hard drives are tempting to steal, and data may easily be seen by anyone with a PC, a little knowledge, and a few minutes. Capacity: Up to 60 GB or 64,000MB.

Prices cannot be discussed here because they change often, and because they vary, depending upon the device age and capacity. For example, an older Exabyte tape drive may be found on eBay for $25, but a newer model may sell for $1,000.

A good range of backup devices, including current pricing, can be seen at www.iomega.com. See www.exabyte.com for tape backup alternatives.

Two backup devices should be purchased at the same time, in case one later fails. Otherwise, it may take significant time to find, purchase, and receive a compatible piece of hardware.

Backup Software

Backup software is not essential in the beginning, but as the business becomes more formidable, it will be important to use professional products so that the backup process can be scheduled and automated. In this way, important files will not be forgotten, and the backups run automatically at night when you're home sleeping.

Operating systems from Microsoft normally include backup capabilities, but they're not very good, and few stick with the Microsoft option for long. Veritas Backup Exec is a great product used by many small businesses. BEX is normally installed on a server, and runs every night when the machines are quiet by methodically moving around to each machine and pulling files through the server and onto tape.

Backups are "differential," "incremental," or "full." Differential and incremental backups include only the files changed or created since the last full backup, so they are smaller and take less time. Full backups include all files, but several tapes over several nights may be needed. Note that during the backup process, a virus check is normally performed, and files are encrypted in case a tape is stolen.

The next morning, tapes are removed and then stored off the premises in case of disaster.

The objective for most small business owners is to purchase a server with the backup devices already installed, or add to an existing machine. A computer pro should set up the hardware and software, because this is a complex one-time operation. Then, explain your operation and let the computer maven set up automated backup jobs. When everything is ready to go, get a short presentation on how to use the software, insert and remove media, and how to recover files. This part is not difficult.

On-Line Backup Services

A different approach to backups is to use Internet-based solutions, where backup jobs run from local machines at night (as previously described), but files are sent to a remote server. The information is then held at an off-site location until needed, and can then be downloaded and restored to the original machine or a new one.

The advantages here are that no additional hardware, media, or off-site storage locations are needed. Small business owners also do not need to worry about loading and unloading tapes or disks every day, and there is much less maintenance. Security is tight also because data may be encrypted, and most locations claim that access to the secure locked server rooms with airconditioning and high-quality electrical power is tightly controlled.

Pricing may be an issue, however, especially as more and more data accumulate over time. The average monthly bill may vary from $35 to $350 per month, averaging about $50. This depends upon the number of machines backed up, and the quantity of data. You may also need to pay more for a faster Internet uplink connection.

Additional information and alternatives may be found by searching for "Online Backup Service" on a favorite search engine, or by visiting www.TheSmallBusinessOwnersManual.com.

Data Recovery

Many small businesses methodically back up their machines on a regular basis, but when disaster strikes, they are chagrined to find that data recovery is not possible, usually due to minor misunderstandings.

For this reason, it is important to do test backups, and then recover files to make sure that everything is working as expected.

Also, make sure employees know that backups are taking place at night, and encourage them to ask for needed files that have somehow disappeared.

One area we have not reviewed here is building a Website and e-store; this is discussed completely in Chapter 5.

This chapter tells you, the small business owner, what you *need* to know about computers and computing to run your small business. There will always be an endless array of distracting new products, services, and software streaming onto the market, but entrepreneurs need to keep everything in perspective and focus on running the business with computers rather than letting computers run the business.

Afterword

In the first few sentences of this book we heard that "success is 90 percent perspiration and 10 percent inspiration." Nowadays, this expression may be adjusted to "success is 90 percent information and 10 percent perspiration." Hopefully, you opened this book with a lot of information about your particular area of business expertise, and now close it with a lot more about all of the different hats you must wear as a small business owner—from insurance pro to recruiting expert.

But now it's time for just a few words on the inspiration and perspiration parts.

For decades, there has been an endless stream of books on how to cut through it all and just get rich, usually by working for yourself as a small business owner. There are two variations of this book: one type encourages hard work; the other provides a strategy where hard work is minimized by working smarter or tougher so that others do the hard work. I have read my share of the latter (often wondering how they puffed up an idea that can explained in 25 pages into a 200-page book), and while some of the information is useful, there is no getting around the hard work.

Even more amusing are the dozens of "get rich" infomercials on late-night television. I often watch them for a few minutes after working late into the night, before going to bed. I learn new ways to spend a few hundred dollars, skim through some manuals and tapes, and get into a small business that will quickly yield the easy lifestyle we all want—a huge beachfront house with yachts and parties and family all around. In this scenario, I would make a few phone calls every morning in my Hawaiian shirt and then have lunch by the pool before a game of golf. None of the people in these infomercials seem all that smart, yet they are wealthy and don't work very hard.

Don't expect it to be that way. The world is too competitive these days, and small business owners must work hard, fast, and smart to keep ahead. There is no letting up and there is no finish line where it's time to relax and count the money. Just when revenues begin coming in from a new product, it's time to beef up the accounting system. Then it's off to shop for a new warehouse or decide how to finance a new piece of equipment. After that, deal with computer problems and meet with unhappy customers. All the while, the small business owner must plan for the next product.

Everything is moving ahead at a faster and faster pace, so small business owners must work hard just to keep up with the latest news and information.

As things get even busier, it's time to find even more time in the day to recruit, hire, and train new employees. The business is growing, and there is no

---

Small Business COO Works a Little Too Hard

A small business owner had grown his firm to dizzying heights over a 20-year period, but was tired and recognized that it was time to bring in professional management. Like many entrepreneurs, he had taken the business as far as he could and was not experienced in dealing with big numbers. We all gave him credit for understanding it was time to step back.

The new Chief Operating Officer (COO) was a hard worker. I mean really hard. I mean really really hard. He regularly chewed out the professional staff for not working until 10 p.m. He scowled when others went to lunch while he ate a microwaved potato at his desk. He didn't walk around the office, he stormed. No one dared talk to him or even make eye contact.

Once he corned me in a busy hallway and asked me a number from a financial statement that I had calculated a month ago.

"I don't remember," I said. "I'll look it up and tell you."

That wasn't good enough. The new COO was livid that I didn't remember and told me so in front of everyone.

But he was producing big and fast-growing numbers, and it's hard to argue with success.

The one day he finally went too far. He threw a tantrum when the board of directors would not immediately agree to his plans to buy another company. He screamed at the popular but ageing company founder and demanded a huge bonus for his hard work over the last two years.

Despite all his impressive numbers, management decided they could no longer live with this megalomaniac; however, they needed a good reason to terminate his agreement. The legal counsel was instructed to hire a private detective to follow him around and report things of interest. Finally, a board meeting was held where the COO was told that he no longer possessed sound mental reasoning skills and, for this reason, he was terminated (with a nice buyout bonus).

His hard work had yielded a huge increase in the company's value, but at a price too high for all involved.

time to relax. Grow or die. There is always something important to do. This will never change. But rather than buy all those books and tapes, perhaps all you need to do is keep these last few pointers in mind.

You must integrate your work into your family, spiritual, and personal interests. Hard work is critical because others are affected by the success or failure of your small business, but cutting out your personal side will likely lead to a shorter life without much meaning.

Work really hard all the time. If at first you don't succeed, try again. Persistence pays. (Maybe you've heard this before?)

Find happiness in what you have right now. Everyone is disappointed that things aren't happening faster, and there will always be stress. But at least you are working for your own dreams and well-being and not someone else's. You won't have it all by the end of the day or even for many years to come. But all of this perspiration is an investment in your own destiny.

Well, it's late and I'm tired and I want to finish this and watch television for a few minutes before going to bed. A new infomercial just started and it seems there's this new opportunity to make a lot of money without working very hard by owning my own small business.

Meet me at www.tsbom.com

I want to hear your stories and feedback on this book, and so do other small business colleagues. All of this can be seen at www.TheSmallBusinessOwnersManual.com. Also, don't forget that buyers of this book also have "all you can eat" download access to the growing number of legal documents, letters, spreadsheets, links, and information of special interest to small business owners available at this site. Visit regularly because more information and features are frequently added, and we want you to be part of the community!

Index

About the Author

AN EAST COAST NATIVE, JOE KENNEDY received a B.S. in finance and an M.B.A. in marketing from the Pennsylvania State University. He has worked with some of the world's largest firms—including McDonnell Douglas (Boeing) and Chase Manhattan Bank—and some of the smallest. Not content merely to give seminars or write about small businesses, Joe has worked as an officer, director, vendor, client, and adviser with dozens of small companies, including several of his own, all over the U.S. While most of his experience is in the information technology and finance areas, he has worked with firms in many different industries, from aerospace to strip mining. Joe now specializes in consulting services to small businesses through www.TSBOM.com. A California resident since 1981, he has two children and is married to the prettiest girl in France.